THE NAMDHARI SIKHS

The Namdhari Sikhs

Their Changing Social and Cultural Landscape

JOGINDER SINGH

MANOHAR
2013

First published, 2013

ISBN 978-81-7304-996-5

Published by
Ajay Kumar Jain *for*
Manohar Publishers & Distributors
4753/23 Ansari Road, Daryaganj
New Delhi 110 002

Typeset at
Digigrafics
New Delhi 110 049

Printed at
Salasar Imaging Systems
Delhi 110 035

For
my late brother
AVTAR SINGH PHULL

Contents

Acknowledgements

With deep gratitude I remember His Late Holiness Satguru Jagjit Singh who blessed me to inititate and complete this project on *Demographic, Occupational, Social and Cultural Changes among the Contemporary Namdhari Sikhs of the Punjab* in 2008. I also express my heart-felt gratitude to Satguru Uday Singh who appreciated and encouraged me for conceptualizing and completing the present research pursuit. Late Satguru's confidants, personal attendents and administrative personnel helped me and my team to collect data of 1,545 Namdhari families of 18 districts of Punjab. Several *subas*, hundreds of local leaders/heads of Namdhari families cooperated with patience to answer my fundamental and secondary questions. I owe an enduring gratitude to the Namdhari respondents who extended a warm welcome to my team and endured lengthy meetings. In the entire exercise I am grateful to Sarbshrees H.S. Hanspal, Jagtar Singh, Surinder Singh, Jagir Singh, Ajit Singh, Jagdish Singh Waryam and *subas* of several districts for their logistic support. Suba Balwinder Singh Jhall deserves my special thanks in this regards. I am equally thankful to Namdhari scholars Tara Singh Anjan, Kirpal Singh Kasel, Jaswinder Singh Historian, Suwaran Singh Virk, Harpal Singh and Bibi Surinder Kaur Kharal for their valuable comments, observations and suggestions. I am grateful to Dr. Parminder Singh, Dr. Paramjit Singh Judge and Dr. Jagroop Singh Sekhon with whom I held informal discussions on several historical and sociological terms and concepts which were relevant to this work. They provided analytical insights to comprehend Namdhari community's behaviour patterns in the contemporary socio political milieu of Punjab. My thanks are due to Dr. Amarjit Singh Sidhu, members of Departments of History, Sociology and Guru Nanak Studies who showed a keen interest in my work and furthered it considerably. The preliminary surveys on the Namdhari community by research scholars Amit Syal, Babusha Maingi, Simarjit Kaur and Anuradha Paul went a long way in strengthening my understanding of changes the Namdhari community has undergone over a period of hundred fifty years.

I owe a great deal to Professor A.S. Brar, Vice-Chancellor, Guru Nanak Dev University, for allowing me to conceive and execute sociological projects which ultimately took the shape of this work. He has been quite generous in extending moral and requisite support to the Namdhari Guru Ram Singh Chair for its research work. My thanks are due to Professor Rajinder Kaur Pawar, Dean Academic Affairs, Dr. Sharanjit Singh Dhillon, Professor in-charge Finance and Development and University administrative personnel for helping me to run this Chair. I may be failing in my duty if I don't thank Sant Surinder Singh for getting financial help from the present Punjab Government which has sustained this Chair. I thank Sarb Shree Sukhchain Singh and Sourabh Kumar, Data Entry Operators who produced several computer versions of the manuscript. The non-teaching and library staff of the Department of History and Bhai Gurdas Library, Guru Nanak Dev University provided every help which I asked for. I thank them all. I express my thanks to Manohar Publishers & Distributors for their keen interest in each stage of copy-editing and publication of this work.

In the end I would like to thank my wife Jaspal, son Mandeep Phull and his wife Tania who inspired me to carry on with my research pursuits.

JOGINDER SINGH

Glossary

Adi Granth	:	(the *Guru Granth Sahib*), the sacred scripture of the Sikhs recorded by Bhai Gurdas at the instructions of Guru Arjan Dev in 1603-4.
Ahankar	:	Ego.
Akal Purakh	:	the one beyond Time, God.
Akal Takhat	:	throne (*q.v.*, located immediately adjacent to Harmandir Sahib (*q.v.*, the Golden Temple). One of the five centres of temporal authority in the Panth.
Akhand Path	:	'unbroken reading'; an uninterrupted reading of the entire contents of the *Adi Granth* performed by a relay of readers.
Amrit	:	'nectar of immorality', sweetened initiation water used in *amrit sanskar.*
Anand-riti/karaj	:	a Sikh marriage ceremony.
Ardasan	:	letters of Namdhari Guru Ram Singh.
Arora/Khatri	:	mercantile castes.
Avtarvad	:	a belief in the continuity of incarnation of a deity.
Baba	:	'father', a term of respect applied to holy men.
Bania/Baniya	:	traditional bankers, mercantile caste.
Bani	:	word of God—works of the gurus and other poets included in the Sikh sacred scriptures.
Begar	:	literally means forced labour without payment; in actual practice undefined tasks for land-owners for nominal payment.
Bhagat	:	devotee, one who practices *bhagati* or devotion.
Bhajan	:	a mystic/sacred word.
Bhog	:	performing recitation of *Granth Sahib.*
Brahmin	:	the highest caste, traditionally priests.
Chamar	:	an untouchable caste of leather-tanners and workers.
Chaubis avatar	:	Hindu mythology of incarnation.

Chhemba : a calico-dyer.
Chuhra : the lowest untouchable caste, traditionally sweepers.
Dan : charity.
Darbar : a court of leave, also the executive government of a native state.
Darbaris : courtiers.
Dasam Granth : 'the Book of the Tenth (Guru)'; a collection of writings attributed to Guru Gobind Singh.
Dastar : turban.
Daswand : one-tenth donation of earning.
Dera : camp; seminary; dwelling place of a saint and followers.
Devidavaras : Hindu temples.
Dharamsala : place of worship of Namdhari Sikhs. Also a place of worship for early Sikh Panth (later *gurdwara*).
Diwan : court; minister of state; assembly; assembly hall; congregation; collected verse of a poet.
Ghumar : the potter caste, spread all over the Punjab.
Giani : a reputed Sikh scholar; a Sikh theologian.
Granthi : custodian of a *gurdwara*, the professional reader of *Guru Granth Sahib*; the functionary in charge of a *gurdwara*.
Granth : the '[Sacred] Volume', the *Adi Granth* or *Guru Granth Sahib* (*qq.v.*).
Gurbani : compositions of the gurus.
Gurdwara a Sikh temple.
Gur-mantar : a mystical formula given by a guru to a disciple.
Guru Granth : the *Granth* (*q.v.*) in its role as guru.
Havan-yag : ritual fire ceremony practised by the Namdhari Sikhs (*q.v.*); also called a *hom*.
Holla : religious festival.
Hukmanama : 'letter of command'; document containing a command or a request issued by one of the Namdhari gurus to an individual or a *sangat*; a similar document issued to the Panth by the Akal Takhat.
Jajman : Brahmin's client or patron; the patron of a sepidar.

Jajmani : the system of traditional relationship between the service performing manual workers and artisans, and the landowning cultivators involving mutual obligations of work and remuneration.

Janam Sakhi : hagiographic narrative, especially of the life of Guru Nanak.

Jatha : a group, a band; used particularly for Akali volunteers during their agitations.

Jathedar : the leader of a *jatha;* a leader-organizer of the Shiromani Akali Dal.

Jat : the dominant agricultural caste of Punjab.

Jhiwar : a water-carrier, the water carrier caste

Julaha : a weaver, the weaver caste.

Kakkars : five items (each beginning with 'k') which Sikhs of the Khalsa must wear: *kes*, *kangha*, *kachh*, *kirpan*, and *kara*.

Kalyuga : the fourth and last of the cosmic ages; the age of degeneracy.

Kamboj : a minor agriculturalist/caste.

Kamin : a village servant of low caste.

Kammi or Kamin : village menials.

Karah Prasad : sacramental food dispensed in *gurdwaras/dharamsalas.*

Kharas : bullock-driven mill.

Lambardar : a cultivator who, on his own account or as representative of other members of the village, pays the government dues.

Langar : the kitchen attached to every *gurdwara* which serves food to all, regardless of caste or creed.

Mahant : chief, superior of a monastery or other religious institution, manager and head of a religious centre

Mahasha : literally, great hope, term given to members of Megh caste by the Arya Samaj.

Mala : woollen rosary.

Mantar : a sacred formula or utterance; a prayer.

Maryada : code of conduct.

Mazhabi : literally religious; term given to members of the Chuhra caste who became Sikhs.

Mehra/Kohar/	:	a water-carrier by caste.
Mela	:	especially a religious festival or fair to which people often come from great distances.
Mirasi	:	a village bard, well known for his humour.
Mochi	:	a shoe-maker.
Naam-karan	:	a ritual for giving name to the child.
Nai	:	a barber, also called *hajjam*; he was generally the bearer of formal messages from one village to another.
Nam-simran	:	the devotional practice of meditating on the divine name.
Nam	:	the divine name, a summary term expressing the total being of Akal Purakh.
Nitnam	:	the Sikh daily liturgy.
Panth	:	system of religious beliefs and practices; the form 'Panth' designates the Sikh community.
Pathi	:	a scripture reader.
Patwari	:	the village accountant.
Pir	:	teacher of the Sufi path or a popular miracle saint.
Pothi	:	volume, tome.
Pujari	:	priest.
Ragi	:	a singer, particularly of the verses in the Sikh scriptures.
Rahit-Maryada	:	a code of discipline of the Khalsa/Sikh/ Namdhari Sikh; also a specific text on this subject.
Rahit-Nama	:	a manual of *rahit*, principles.
Rajput	:	the dominant caste of the Punjab hills.
Ramdasia	:	a name given to people of the Chamar caste who become Sikhs.
Ramgarhia	:	a Sikh Tarkhan claiming links with the eighteenth century Sardar Jassa Singh Ramgarhia; elites of Lohars and Tarkhans.
Saini	:	a minor agriculturist/caste.
Sakhi	:	hagiographic narrative.
Sanatan	:	ancient, eternal. Used here to refer to the pluralistic and polycentric mode of Sikh tradition.
Sangat	:	assembly, religious congregation.

Satguru	:	a true lord; term used by the Namdhari Sikhs for their spiritual lord.
Satiyug	:	the Age of Truth, the first and the best of the cosmic eras which follows the *Kaliyuga* in the cosmic cycle.
Sep	:	hereditary relationship between agriculturists and village artisans and other menials under which the latter got a fixed share of crops.
Suba	:	a province or primary division of an empire.
Sunar/Suniara	:	a goldsmith by caste.
Takhat	:	'throne' one of the five major seats of authority among Sikhs. The *takhats* are located at Amritsar, Anandpur, Damdama (all in the Punjab), Patna (in Bihar), and Nander (in Maharashtra).
Tarkhan	:	a carpenter by caste.
Varni	:	a Namdhari ritual.
Zamindar	:	a landlord, proprietor or an occupant of land.
Zat	:	endogamous caste grouping

Introduction

HISTORICAL BACKGROUND

The Namdhari Sikhs are a small religious community in Punjab (India). They are in very few of them in Haryana, Himachal Pradesh, Rajasthan, Delhi, and Uttar Pradesh. Hundreds of their families have emigrated to Thailand, Australia, USA, Canada, and England. Observing distinct codes of religious practices and ethical values; they perform supplication in the name of the twelfth guru on all socio-religious occasions; and also observe eating taboos and a dress code. Their headquarters, the Gurdwara Shri Bhaini Sahib, are in Ludhiana and comprise the palatial residence of *satguru* congregational halls, a community kitchen, a holy tank, an administrative block, residential houses, and sheds for livestock. The Namdhari guru is the spiritual and temporal head of his community, guiding its destiny. The Namdhari Sikhs address him reverentially as *satguru*.

Some 25 *subas* (governors) look after community affairs in Punjab. In terms of representation of the *subas*, the Malwa region (14) of Punjab is ahead of Doaba (6) and Majha (3) regions. However, the representation of *subas* and other local leaders is determined by historical, administrative, and demographic factors. Haryana has six *subas* for the simple reason that in the post-Independence period, Sri Jiwan Nagar in Sirsa district came into being as its headquarters with modern infrastructure. New Delhi has emerged as another important centre and several Namdhari leaders and functionaries belong to Delhi. Representation has also been given to the Namdhari *sangats* (congregations) in Jammu (J&K), Himachal Pradesh, Rajasthan, UP and Madhya Pradesh, where many Namdharis are immigrants from Pakistan. A few *subas* represent these Namdhari Sikhs. Besides, about twelve *subas* represent the diasporic Namdhari Sikhs of Thailand, Australia, the African countries, Canada and England. The Namdhari guru has recognized their contribution (largely financial) and has built-up rapport with the local Namdhari Sikhs of these countries. The majority of these Namdhari Sikhs belong to the Khatri, Arora, and Ramgarhia castes.

The Namdhari guru is assisted by confidants and administrative personnel. Among the prominent administrative personnel of Bhaini Sahib headquarters are Sant Jagtar Singh, Sant Kashmir Singh Bhinder, Sant Daljit Singh Dhaliwal, Sant Gurdial Singh Raisar and Sant Chanan Singh. Sewak Rachhpal Singh and Sewak Harpal Singh are personal attendants of *satguru*. Sant Jagtar Singh, Sant Avtar Singh, Sewak Didar Singh, Sant Harvendra Singh Hanspal, and Sant Surinder Singh Namdhari hold special status in the administrative hierarchy of the Namdhari community. Sant Harvendra Singh Hanspal is president of the Namdhari Darbar. He is also the chief editor of *Satjug*—a weekly Gurmukhi periodical. He is a former member of Rajya Sabha (for two terms) and president of the Punjab Pradesh Congress Committee. Sant Surinder Singh is senior vice-president of Namdhari Darbar, vice-chairman of Namdhari Martyrs Memorial Trust, general attorney of Satguru Jagjit Singh and director of Satguru Partap Singh Apollo Hospital, Ludhiana. Bibi Sukhjit Kaur, Suba Surinder Kaur Kharal (trustee of Kuka Martyrs Memorial Trust and a writer) and Bibi Kulwant Kaur are the prominent Namdhari activists and functionaries of the Vishav Namdhari Vidyak Jatha. Suba Balwinder Singh is the president of this *jatha*. Prominent among scholars and writers are Sant Jagdish Singh, editor, *Waryam*, a monthly Punjabi magazine published from Jalandhar; Tara Singh Anjan, editor, *Satjug*; Jaswinder Singh historian, Kirpal Singh Kasel, S.S. Virk and Sawaran Singh Snehi. They have made an important contributions to the study of Namdhari traditions, institutions, literature (Punjabi), and history.

The local leaders as well as the influential members of the community strive to promote cohesion and harmony and settle civil disputes among the Namdhari families. They also perform social and religious duties assigned to them by the *satguru*, looking after the community's institutions and religious places, organizing religious congregations, and making arrangements to transpot their brethren to Bhaini Sahib on certain occasions.

Satguru Balak Singh and Satguru Ram Singh developed the Namdhari mission on the basis of Sikh scripture and traditions in the nineteenth century. Namdhari Guru Balak Singh (1785-1862) established a centre of propagation at Hazro, district Attock (Pakistan), asked his followers to meditate continuously on the name of God at all the times and perform no ritual other than repeating God's name. He asked his followers to offer *prasad* (sacred food) of rupee one and four *annas* (1/16th of rupee) in the name of God. He instructed his followers to bathe twice a day and to keep a small symbol of the sword in their *pagri* (turban); to earn their livelihoods by their own efforts and hard work and to eat food cooked only by a Namdhari Sikh. They were to be ethical in their day-to-day life and avoid indulgences. Guru Balak Singh prohibited the use of meat, tobacco, and liquor. The founder of the Namdhari mission also started the *anand riti* (a custom of marriage).

Namdhari Guru Ram Singh extended the scope of Namdhari mission in terms of the revival of Khalsa traditions. He was inspired to found an alternative polity, the Sant Khalsa. On 12 April 1857 at Bhaini Sahib he told a congregation that he had formed the Sant Khalsa on behalf of Guru Gobind Singh. It was, according to him, the real Khalsa. He was convinced that his Sant Khalsa was morally superior to its contemporary in the Lahore kingdom. For him the latter was as corrupt and unscrupulous as the British were. Both were responsible for the destruction of the Khalsa raj. After initiating the Sikhs to the Sant Khalsa, he evolved a code of conduct to inculcate a martial spirit. The Sant Khalsa was to observe five *kakkars—kes* (uncut hair), *kangha* (small wooden comb), *kachh* (a pair of breeches), *kara* (iron bangle) and *kirpan* (sword). Since *kirpan* had been disallowed by the government, a heavy *lathi* (wooden stick) was to take its place. The Sant Khalsa was required to lead pure and pious lives attuned to the Name of God and develop regular and disciplined habits. For instance, they were to rise at 3.00 a.m., brush their teeth, bathe, and recite the Name of God, especially the *Chandi di Var*—Guru Gobind Singh's composition.[1] Recitation of *Chandi di Var* was intended to inculcate the martial spirit among the members of the Sant Khalsa so that they could fight against tyranny. The Namdhari Guru laid down a specific mode for reciting it in an assembly which lasted for two to three days.[2] Namdhari Guru Ram Singh also made an arrangement for the training of young Sant Khalsa in the use of *gadka* (a traditional martial art), horse-riding, and weapons. Already distinct in physical appearance, he wished the Sant Khalsa to feel as if they were the chosen ones while others were *mlechh* (unclean).

Guru Ram Singh also evolved the *suba* system, a mode of communication, and a traditional strategy of mobilizing his followers. In each district, there was a representative who coordinated the work of the local functionaries. Next to the latter were *naib subas* (deputy governors), *jathedars* (heads of a group), *granthis* (scripture readers) and the local *sangat*.

Naib Subas and Jathedars were given smaller areas to operate in and were required to organize and supervise the missionary work of their respective places. The local Sangats constituted the base of the Kuka organisation. A Sangat was a society composed of the Kukas (the word Kuka stuck to their names when the Namdhari Sikhs emitted loud shrieks (*kook*) in a state of frenzy) living in a particular village, which had a dharamsala (temple) of its own and a Granthi (scripture-reciter) to look after it and to teach Gurmukhi letters and Gurbani (Sikh scripture) to the members of the Sangat and their children, organised regular congregations and ran a free kitchen to feed the visitors from outside.[3]

The Namdhari guru assigned these *subas* the task of (a) propagating the Namdhari mission, administering *bhajan* (mystic word) and *amrit* (nectar for initiation) and making arrangements for performing *paths* (recitation of scripture); (b) settling local disputes, (c) collecting *daswand* (voluntary donations); (d) ensuring peace in their respective areas; and (e) bringing cases of disobedience to the notice of the *satguru*. Presumably, the *subas* performed these duties to their guru's satisfaction. His charismatic personality attracted thousands of Sikh agriculturists and artisans. 'His fame had spread rapidly and by 1863 he had been able to recruit as many as 40,000 disciples and by 1866, the number of these disciples multiplied to 60,000. His rank and file swelled as a result of the 1857 resurrection.'[4] Even so, only a small section of the old Khalsa, *jagirdars* (holders of land assignments) and *zamindars* (landlords/proprietors) supported his movement.

By 1864, Namdhari guru declared his political mission:

> I, Guru Govind Singh, will be born in a carpenter's shop, and will be called Ram Singh. My house will be between the Jamna and Sutlej rivers. I will declare my religion. I will defeat the Faringhis and put the crown on my own head, and blow the *sankh*. The musicians shall praise me in 1921 (1864). I, the carpenter, will sit on the throne. When I have got one lakh and twenty-five thousand Sikhs with me, I will cut off the heads of the *Fringhis* [*sic*]. I will never be conquered in battle, and will shout 'Akal, Akal'. The Christians will desert their wives and fly [*sic*] from the country when they hear the shout of 1¼ lakhs of Khalsas. A great battle will take place on the banks of the Jamna, and blood will flow like the waters of the Ravi, and no Frunghi [*sic*] be left alive. Insurrections will take place in the country in 1922 (1865). The Khalsa will reign, and Rajah and ryot will live in peace and comfort, and no one shall molest another.
>
> Day by day Ram Singh's rule will be enlarged. God has written this. It is no lie, my brethren. In 1865, the whole country will be ruled by Ram Singh. My followers will worship Wahaguru. God says this will happen.[5]

In fact, the *sakhi* literature resurrected by Sikh veterans and by Namdhari Guru Ram Singh during and after the Uprising of 1857, reflected an old unfulfilled desire of the Khalsa to establish its hegemony over the Gangetic plans.The Namdhari Guru made some efforts to build up political links with the native rulers of neighbouring states. He thought that his followers could be given some military training. He made an attempt to get a Kuka regiment set up in the army of the Maharaja of Kashmir. So some prominent Kukas approached the Maharaja, who promised to do so. For some time, about 200 to 250 persons were enrolled and given training. The Namdhari Guru also sent his confidants to Nepal with gifts for the government of the state. A deputation under Kahn Singh was sent to get help in arms, men, and money. Since the ruler of Nepal did not have good relations with British, the Namdhari Guru thought of taking advantage of that situation. Similarly, centres were established in Gwalior, Peshawar, Kabul, and Bhutan.

Meanwhile, the clash of the Kuka Sikhs with the British government became more or less inevitable after the issue of cow-slaughter arose. The British officials had lifted the ban on cow-slaughter and permitted Muslim butchers to open their slaughter houses. Within a short time, beef and kine-leather were sold in most of the towns of the province. This offended the Hindus and the Sikhs, especially when beef was sold in the streets of the holy city of Amritsar. They protested but officials did not bother to stop the slaughter of acttle. The Kuka Sikhs could no longer restrain their anger as the cow was an object of veneration and protection for them and on the night of 14 June 1871, about eight Namdhari Sikhs attacked some butchers inside a slaughter house in Amritsar. Three butchers were killed on the spot and three were badly wounded. The local police officer arrested and charged twelve Hindu and Sikh inhabitants of the city for these murders. The police tortured them to confess their crime. The accused were committed to the sessions by the deputy commissioner. When the Namdhari Guru came to know that innocent men were going to be punished, he ordered the culprits (Namdhari Sikhs) to present themselves before the magistrate and confess. On their own confession, four Kuka Sikhs were hanged on 15 September 1871 and one more in August 1873.

Murders of butchers by Kuka Sikhs had also taken place at Raikot in Ludhiana district on 15 July 1871. Seven accused, five belonging to Nabha state and two to Patiala state, were arrested with the help of the Maharajas of Patiala and Nabha. They were produced before a magistrate at village Bassian. An effort was made by the police to implicate and involve Namdhari Guru Ram Singh as instigator and abettor. He was summoned before the magistrate at Bassian. He appeared on 5 August 1871. Three conspirators were hanged in Raikot in the presence of a large gathering. The remaining two accused in this case, Giani Rattan Singh and Rattan Singh of Naiwala, were later hanged in Ludhiana outside the jail premises on 26 November 1871.[6]

The climax followed on 13 January 1872. A group of Kuka Sikhs from Bhaini attacked the obscure fort of Malodh in Ludhiana district and tried to force their way into the town of Malerkotla. Kukas planned to overpower Malodh estate and then Malerkotla, and secure arms and horses. Nevertheless, they could not anticipate the resistance from Malodh fort of Badan Singh. In the battle that ensued they suffered losses to the tune of two killed and four wounded but were able to get three swords, a gun, two horses, and a mare. Delay in attacking Malerkotla gave the defenders time to prepare. In the fighting that ensued between the Kukas (125 in number) and state forces there, both suffered several casualties.

These incidences gave a much awaited opportunity to the government to crush the Kuka Sikhs. L. Cowan, officiating deputy commissioner of Ludhiana, arrested 68 Kuka Sikhs including two women and had 66 of them blown off. The blowing of Kuka Sikhs out of guns was not only an arbitrary act against the established legal procedure but also 'repugnant to humanity, and a punishment unfit to be inflicted by civilized men'. The Government of India conceded that it 'cannot admit that any necessity existed in the present case'. Cowan's manner was 'unusual and so barbarous'.[7] All who had been unfortunate enough to witness such an execution knew that a more horrible and revolting spectacle could not be conceived. Cowan was dismissed from service and Forsyth transferred to Oudh as commissioner. Namdhari Guru Ram Singh and a few of his confidants were deported to Burma (Myanmar) in 1872.

Although for some time the deportation created a leadership vacuum, under Hari Singh (1872-1906), Namdhari Guru Ram Singh's brother, the Namdhari resumed their political activities. The Deputy Superintendent Police, J.P. Warburton wrote to Colonel H.N. Millter, IGP, Punjab on 31 August 1878 that he believed that the number of Kukas had increaed and was becoming a source of political danger. In 1881, the abstract of intelligence of Punjab Police noted that a secret meeting was held by 150 Kukas in the *dhak* jungle near village Lalton (not far from Bhaini) on 17 March. The police reached the spot and arrested 39 men who were later released on bail. Suba Kahn Singh and Jaimal Singh were arrested and asked to furnish security of the sum of Rs. 1,000 each for abusing the policemen at Bhaini. On 28 March, Gurdas Singh, Khushal Singh, and Natha Singh were ordered to furnish security of Rs. 1,000 each for one year. In the meantime, a message was spread among the Kukas that as 'Satguru' (Ram Singh) willed, they should assemble at Bhaini Sahib and work out their future plans. However, some of them were arrested at the Sahnewal Railway Station. One of these Kukas was in possession of a 'seditious' letter purportedly written by the Namdhari Guru from abroad in 1877. The letter was brought by Naina Singh of Varyiah and Bhagwan Singh who belonged to Amritsar district. The arrested Kukas were asked to furnish security of Rs. 1,000 each for one year.[8]

That the Namdhari struggle assumed political overtones under Hari Singh's leadership is established by the fact that some of his *subas* and activists continued to spread anti-British propaganda and push for the restoration of the Khalsa raj. Contemporary documents contain comprehensive details about the visits of Baba Gurcharn Singh and Baba Bishan Singh to Russia in the late nineteenth century.[9] Details of Gurcharan Singh's visit are contained in a letter which he carried on behalf of his 'Satguru' (Ram Singh) to the Russian authorities.[10] The letter makes us believe that a massive Kuka following running into 3,15,000 was ready to rebel against the British under the leadership of their Satguru Ram Singh as well as Hari Singh.[11] The letter also mentions prophecies of Ram Singh about a Russian invasion on India.

Concurrent, with the exertions of Kukas for the restoration of the Khalsa raj came the proclamation of ex-Maharaja Dalip Singh as the sovereign of the Sikh 'nation'.[12] In 1886, he sailed for India and the news of his journey generated a great excitement among the Punjabis. The Kukas believed that Ram Singh's spirit had entered Dalip Singh and their deputation reached Bombay to greet him. But the British government foresaw the danger of his arrival in the Punjab and detained Dalip Singh in Aden. Determined in his resolve against the

British, the ex-maharaja reached Russia in 1887.[13] Meanwhile, rumours were spread in the Punjab that Suba Bishan Singh had joined Dalip Singh in Russia and that the maharaja was now arranging assistance for the invasion of the Punjab.[14]

Kuka plans to secure aid from other sources proved futile, however. For instance, the Maharaja of Kashmir, to express his loyalty to the British, dismissed Kuka Sikhs from his army. Similarly, the ruler of Nepal had actually no sympathy with the Kuka cause.[15] Like the Maharaja of Kashmir, he also thought to use Kuka Sikhs as a political lever in dealing with British. The Russians too did not want to annoy the British either by helping the Kuka Sikhs or Dalip Singh. The disillusioned maharaja left Russia for Europe in 1888 and died in exile in Paris on 22 October 1893. With his death, all plans of organizing anti-British forces were given up.[16]

In the post-1857 period, circumstances were much less favourable for anti-British struggle. The *nambardars* (cultivators collecting government dues), *zaildars* (head of circle of villages), *jagirdars*, and leading rulers of native states (largely Sikhs) were favourably treated by the British. They were so content that when ex-Maharaja Dalip Singh proclaimed himself as the sovereign of the Sikh nation in 1887 and asked his fellowmen to rise against the British, they called him a pretender and proclaimed to the contrary that they would die for their Sovereign Empress and would never accept Dalip Singh as their ruler. Earlier, the Sikh aristocracy and the priestly classes demonstrated their loyalty to the British when they prepared a memorandum against the Kukas and submitted it to the Lieutenant Governor in a Darbar at Amritsar on 22 March 1872.[17] In fact, the might of the British raj and its allies (landed gentry and priestly classes) was too powerful to allow the Namdharis to groom and continue anti-British struggle.

When Namdhari Guru Partap Singh assumed spiritual and temporal leadership in 1906, his followers faced serious problems as well as new challenges. First and foremost was the hostility of the British officials. The officials did not allow them to perform *akhand paths* (uninterrupted reading of *Adi-Granth*) or gather in public congregations. In the villages, *ahalkars* (courtiers), *zaildars* and *nambardars* kept a close watch on the movements of the Kuka Sikhs and often harassed and humiliated them. The second major problem was that the Kuka Sikhs had been alienated from the Sikhs of the mainstream and their organizations. The Singh Sabha leaders condemned some of the beliefs and practices of the Kuka Sikhs. Thus the Namdhari leadership felt it important to build rapport with the nationalist forces.

At the same time the general political milieu of Punjab was gradually changing in favour of the Namdhari Sikhs. The Punjabi elite began to perceive a clash of interest between the socio-economic interests of Indians and their alien rulers. Under the impact of the Swadeshi movement in 1906 (promoting the use of Indian made goods instead of British), they came to know that the revenue, excise and taxation, and legal apparatus of the British raj was not oriented towards producing a betterment of the Indian people. Having imbibed the impact of the economic and politico-cultural nationalism of Bal Gangadhar Tilak and Gopal Krishna Gokhale, and articulating the disenchantment of the agriculturists, businessmen, and emerging professional classes, Lala Lajpat Rai, Ajit Singh and Sufi Amba Prasad launched an agitation in 1907. It opposed the proposed agrarian legislation which comprised the Colonization Bill, a Bill raising water rates in Chenab colony and an Amendment Bill pertaining to the Land Alienation Act 1900. Thousands of professionals, students and retired soldiers held rallies in the towns of Lahore, Rawalpindi, and Sialkot, voicing their grievances. Although the 'agrarian' agitation was suppressed it exploded the myth of Punjabi loyalty to the raj and the concept of *mai-bap-sarkar* (benevolent government).

The Ghadar revolutionaries were in fact inspired by the ideology and lifestyle of the Kuka Sikhs. Baba Sohan Singh Bhakna, president of this party, stated that his dislike of the British raj was nurtured by his interaction with the Namdhari leader Baba Kesar Singh Mohawewale. It was at Namdhari congregations or *holas* that he imbibed *ishwar-bhagati* (meditation on the name of God) and *desh-bhagati* (patriotism). He learnt that meditation on the name of God was not a sectarian exercise. He also learnt that a communal individual could not become a true follower of God. Under the influence of Namdhari philosophy he formed a society called Prem-Sangat which comprised Christians, Muslims, Hindus, and Sikhs. Sohan Singh Bhakna disclosed that he learnt from Baba Kesar Singh that religious meditation alone was not enough for a man to survive. He required bread, clothes and shelter. Sohan Singh and his fellow Sikhs went abroad in thousands to earn these things.[18]

Baba Kesar Singh, Thathgarh, Amritsar, vice-president of the Ghadar Party, was also attached to the Namdhari movement. Baba Jawala Singh, another Ghadarite, imbibed the Namdhari lifestyle.

The Ghadar poets lauded the Kuka-heroes and their patriotism. In the one issue of *Ghadar Gunj*, a revolutionary periodical, they wrote:[19]

Keeta Kukian kath Punjab andar
Ram Singh Bhai Mohri aan ho gae
Bandobast sara unah theek keeta
Ghadar karan de theek saman ho gae
Ram Singh Bhai jalawatan keete
Naal hor vi kai kurban ho gae
Bache aurtan kai hazar Kuke
Khatar desh de lai lahu lohan ho gae.

The exigencies of First World War compelled the British to seek cooperation and support in India for funds and recruits. It is said that the deputy commissioner of Ludhiana district approached Namdhari Guru Partap Singh and asked him if he could provide recruits. Namdhari guru declined. However, under certain compulsions he contributed some money to the War Fund.

The Jallianwala Bagh tragedy on 13 April 1919 left a deep impact on Maharaj Nihal Singh and Maharaj Gurdial Singh, brothers of Namdhari Guru Partap Singh. For them the tragedy was the re-enactment of the Kuka tragedy of 1872, in which more than sixty-six Kukas had been blown up by canons. Since the Uprising of 1857 a racial hatred worked towards Indians. The only difference was that the tragedy of 1872 was justified by the allies of the raj whereas after 1900 patriots and nationalists questioned the moral authority of the raj to rule India.

In response to these developments, the Namdhari Sikhs resolved to resurrect their image and shake off the British surveillance particularly at Bhaini Sahib where a police post had been set in 1872. They launched a campaign for the removal of this post and organized conferences to explain their position. Some of these conferences were organized in Hoshiarpur district also.[20] For articulating their communitarian and national concerns, they launched *Satjug* from Lahore in March 1920. Its editor Nirankar Singh Chetan, dedicated this Gurmukhi weekly to the service of the Namdhari community and the country. According to him, *Satjug* aimed to address: (a) the concerns of the people and bring the same to the notice of the government, (b) to censure those policies and programmes of the government that affect adversely the countrymen, (c) to promote communal harmony and unity, (d) to advocate the opening of *pathshalas* (schools) for dispelling ignorance, and (e) to accelerate the struggle for achieving *swaraj* (self-rule).[21]

However, the immediate concern of *Satjug* was to mobilize public opinion and build up pressure on the Punjab government to remove the police post from the Bhaini Sahib headquarters. The newspaper highlighted injustice done to the Namdhari Sikhs in this context. It also underlined the futility of police surveillance when vigorous communitarian, nationalist and revolutionary movements (the Akali and Babbar Akali and Non-Cooperation movements) had been on since 1919.[22] Giani Kala Singh wrote a patriotic poem entitled 'Kuka Singh Ate Angrej Jaat' which was published in 1922. For him the Kuka struggle was actually the struggle for the country's independence. The Kuka Singhs were real Singhs who practised *gurbani* whereas Sodhis, Bedis and native rulers were imposters and supported the British who committed excesses on the people.[23] The *Satjug* published the statements and resolutions of the national leaders with regard to the Non-Cooperation movement. Thus the British banned its circulation among soldiers and then when it consistently articulated anti-British sentiments,[24] proscribed it.

In 1923 Bishan Singh published a book entitled *Inqalabi Kuka* (A Kuka Revolutionary) which asserted that the Kuka movement was for the liberation of the country. He recalled memories of the Kuka *subas* and leaders like Gian Singh, Giani Rattan Singh and Hira Singh, who had laid down their lives for liberating Hindustan. Bishan Singh was vocal in demanding complete freedom.[25]

Advocating the programme of the Non-Cooperation movement, *Satjug* asked the people to boycott imported goods and use only articles manufactured locally; and to boycott the British courts and settle their suits in the panchayats. Moreover, it advocated shunning the type of education which made people dependent on government services. For the Namdharis government service implied slavery. Above all, *Satjug* advocated that since the Non-Cooperation movement was actually started by their Satguru Ram Singh, the Namdhari Sikhs were morally bound to carry it forward.[26] Maharaj Gurdial Singh and Sant Nidhan Singh Alam participated in the political conferences organized by the Congress and were members of the committee which drafted resolutions. In one of such resolutions, Sant Nidhan Singh Alam argued that only those people could take the credit of promoting *swaraj* who themselves participated in the bonfire of imported clothes.[27] Sardul Singh Kavishar, a young Sikh Congress leader, too remembered Namdhari Guru Ram Singh as the '*sardar*' of the Non-Cooperation and Swadeshi movements. As early as 1921, Kavishar argued that 'Hindi' brothers should remember the fact that in the political arena 'Baba Ram Singh was the first Punjabi non-cooperator. When Baba Ji came to realize the evil nature of alien rulers he had launched a campaign against it in full swing.'

The rapport between the Namdhari Sikhs and Congress was further strengthened when Maharaj Nihal Singh, the younger brother of Namdhari Guru Partap Singh, attended the Lahore Congress session. He led a *jatha* (group) of a few hundred Namdharis to join the Congress procession. Mata Jiwan Kaur, mother of Namdhari Guru Partap Singh, also took part in this session. She was in-charge of the community kitchen for delegates.[28] In 1930 Nihal Singh was appointed 'Dictator' of the programme of Civil Disobedience movement which was to be carried on in the Punjab. Nihal Singh's appointment as Dictator was an important step towards Namdhari–Congress rapport. Maharaj Nihal Singh, along with a few Kukas, courted arrest during the course of Civil Disobedience movement.[29] The Namdhari activists also formed the Kuka Congress Dal to take part in the Congress movement against the British.[30]

In the 1930s, the Indian revolutionaries and nationalists began to appreciate the contribution of the Namdhari Sikhs to the anti-imperialist struggle. Bhagat Singh, the beau ideal of the revolutionary movement, 'attached considerable significance to the Kuka happenings which may quite possibly be traceable to his grandfather and his brother Arjun Singh and Surjan Singh'.[31] Bhagat Singh believed that the Kuka movement was the first rebellion in Punjab against the British. He also believed that Baba Ram Singh was the harbinger of the Non-Cooperation movement. Bhagat Singh stated that 'In Punjab, the freedom struggle began with the Kuka movement.[32] Subsequently, the Congress leaders like Jawaharlal Nehru and Rajendra Prasad too visited the Bhaini Sahib headquarters and eulogized the sacrifices of the Kuka Sikhs.

The Namdhari Guru and his confidants took note of the crisis of Punjab economy in the wake of great depression and the false claims made by the then Unionist Party with regard to the problem of the peasants. In the 1930s, the Unionists organized several conferences of the zamindars in the Punjab. *Satjug* exposed the agrarian policy of the Punjab government. It gave the statistics on increased volume of land revenue in Punjab. The volume of land revenue had increased to the tune of 30 to 40 per cent. In 1922, the volume of land revenue was Rs. 5 crore 54 lakh which increased to Rs. 7 crore 37 lakh in 1938. Moreover, the periodical gave coverage to the peasant agitations. According to its information, 30,000 to 40,000 peasants participated in the processions taken out in Amritsar and Lahore in 1938. The peasants demanded an improvement in the system of distribution of canal water and reduction in land revenue. The periodical condemned the ruthless lathi-charge on the peasant *satyagrahis*. Commenting on government policy, the periodical stated that its repression had exposed a false sympathy with peasants. The *Satjug* argued that the recent *Act Intkal Arazi* was intended to divide agriculturists from non-agriculturists. The latter were discriminated against by the government. They were not allowed to purchase agricultural land. Moreover, the Act imposed several restrictions on moneylenders, who were asked to obtain licenses from the government. The periodical expressed a serious concern over the indifferentce of the Sikh and Hindu MLAs when the bill was debated. The *Satjug* found the *Act Intkal Arazi* to be anti-Hindu and Sikh since traders and businessmen largely came from them.[33] As we shall discuss in the following chapter, Namdhari Guru Partap Singh also espoused a concept of social order in response to the new concept of socialism advocated by the Kirti Kisan organizations in Punjab. He allowed some of his followers to join these organizations.

In response to the politics about Partition, the Namdhari Sikhs supported the Congress and opposed the separatist politics of the Muslim League under Mohammed Ali Jinnah. In this context, the *Satjug* analysed the speeches made by Jinnah on different occasions and came to the conclusion that he was determined to destroy the Congress. The periodical commented that the singing of *Bande Matram* in the Congress ruled states could in no way endanger Islam as alleged by the Muslim League. In fact, the *Satjug* saw that the fissiparous ideology of the Muslim League was a threat to Indian unity. Thus the periodical was not happy with the Congress policy of appeasing Jinnah and his League in 1938. This policy, *Satjug* apprehended, would alienate the Hindus from the Congress.[34]

At the same time, *Satjug* supported Hindu nationalists like Veer Savarkar who championed the concept of Hindu Rashtra. Namdhari Guru Partap Singh floated the idea of Sikh-Hindu Sangathan in 1943 at Bhaini Sahib. Namdhari Guru saw a chance of uniting Sikhs and Hindus as they shared a cultural heritage. He believed that an alliance between Sikhs and Hindus was essential at the time.[35] Namdhari Guru's confidants, Nidhan Singh Alam and Inder Singh Chakarvarti wrote articles to expose the non-viability of this scheme. Simultaneously, the Namdhari Sikhs joined hands with the Shiromani Akali Dal in the wake of the proposals of the Cabinet Mission in May 1946. Tragically, mounting violence in Punjab forced non-Muslims to accept the partition of Punjab in 1947.

In the post-Independence era, Namdhari Guru Jagjit Singh and his followers had been committed to protect and promote national unity and integrity, communal harmony and world peace. Whenever communal violence broke out in Punjab, they persuaded people to shun violence and resolve issues amicably. They maintained a distance from the fundamentalists and fissiparous forces. Like their counterparts—Hindus and Sikhs—some of the Namdhari families became victims of the terrorism in in the last quarter of the twentieth century. Moreover, they are also very committed in promoting Punjabi language and literature, classical devotional music, health services and sports. They supported the formation of a Punjabi-speaking province; sponsored several national and international conferences and seminars for the promotion of Punjabi language and literature and patronized a number of writers and artists. However, in recent years, they are struggling hard to protect and promote the identity of their community and its cohesion in the wake of adverse impact of industrialization and urbanization on the one hand and of diaspora on the other. They are also facing a challenge from Sikh hardliners in the mainstream.

METHODOLOGY

This work emanates from a project I launched in 2008, on Demographic, Occupational, Social, and Cultural Changes among the Namdhari Sikhs of the Punjab. While studying published historical work on the Namdhari Sikhs I came to know that research questions were restricted to the socio-religious and political mission of the Namdhari gurus. Most studies dealt with the nature and scope of the Kuka movement in late nineteenth century, but a few studied its continuity and various changes since inception.

I took up this project to explore some new dimensions of the past and present of the Namdhari Sikhs. My query started with the core and subordinate questions: who were and are these Sikhs in terms of caste and occupational background? How many Sikhs of different occupations joined this movement? What demographic, socio-religious, and cultural changes have taken place among them during this period? Another set of core and subordinate questions was related to patterns of migration and resettlement (a) from western Punjab (Pakistan) to the east in 1947, (b) from rural to urban areas, and (c) occupational changes since Independence. What has been the impact of these changes on their lifestyle? How far do their practices today conform to the Namdhari *maryada*?

We are fortunate to have official reports on the Kuka movement which furnish information about the occupational castes of this group Fauja Singh and W.H. McLeod inform us that the Kuka movement derived its following from the lower classes of the countryside. However, Fauja Singh merely says that 'all Kukas, big and small, were from the countryside and in one way or the other drawn from the Jat Sikhs'.[36] Since Fauja Singh does not see any economic factor as the main cause of rise of the Kukas movement, he does not analyse the social background of the Kukas. On the other hand, McLeod constructs his thesis of 'The Kukas: A Millenarian Sect of the Punjab' on the premise that the Kuka Sikhs comprised Jat agriculturists and artisans who were the victim of agrarian crisis. A general social discontent was prevalent among these classes. McLeod quotes the occupational list of the prominent Kukas prepared by the police in 1878. This shows that Kuka converts chiefly came from Jats, Tarkhans (carpenters), Chamars (leather tanners and workers), and Mazhabis who had given up their traditional calling. Among them, Jat Sikhs were in the majority. Meanwhile, Nahar Singh edited documents on Guru Ram Singh and Kukas from the period 1863 to 1871 in 1965. Jaswinder Singh too edited documents on the Kukas of subsequent period in 1984. These documents show ample evidence of the occupational background of the Kukas: prominent Kuka leaders and activists came from the agriculturist, artisan, and menial castes.[37] It is on the basis of these documents that Kuldip Singh analysed the occupational background of the Kuka Sikhs according to region (Malwa, Doaba, and Majha).[38] He too came to the conclusion that among the agriculturists, Jat Sikhs were in the majority. Then came the Saini, Rajput, and Kamboj Sikhs. Similarly, the majority of the artisan Namdharis were Lohars (iron smiths), masons, and Tarkhans. They were popularly known as Ramgarhias who traced links to the eighteenth-century Sardar Jassa Singh Ramgarhia. Only a small number of Jhiwars (water carriers/cooks), Chhimbas (calico-dyers), Ghumiars (potters) and Julahas (weavers) were Namdharis. Among the menial castes were the Chamar and Mazhabi Namdharis. It may be mentioned here that the total Kuka population ran into lakhs. The magnitude of the Namdhari masses can be gauged from the fact that some of the congregations of Namdhari Guru Ram Singh reached to 40,000.[39]

Most of these studies do not extend the question to occupational backgrounds in the twentieth century. Although the Census Reports of 1911, 1921 and 1931 mention the total numbers of these Sikhs, they do not mention their caste. However, when scholars began to equate Namdhari sect with Ramgarhias my query deepened. I posed a simple but essential question: what has been the caste and occupational status of the Namdhari Sikhs of Punjab since the inception of the Namdhari mission in the nineteenth century? Allied to this is the number of agriculturists, especially Jat Sikhs, whose number declined during the subsequent 150 years. Conversely I raised the question, when did the numbers of Namdhari Lohars and Tarkhans overtake the Namdhari Jat Sikhs in the twentieth century? What are the variables which have changed the numerical strength of the occupational castes among Namdharis? It became necessary to examine the impact of the Sikh movements: the Singh Sabha, the Akali and Babbar Akali movements (1920-5) and the Kirti Kisan movement (1926-36). These movements not only marginalized the Kuka movement but also forced the Namdhari gurus to review their relationship with contemporary organizations and parties. They built up rapport with the Hindu organizations and the Congress, but in the process distanced themselves from the Shiromani Gurdwara Parbhandhak Committee and the Shiromani Akali Dal in the early twentieth century.

Another question was directed to the changes in numbers in rural and urban areas of Punjab. As noted above, the majority of the Kuka Sikhs were rural Sikhs in the late nineteenth century. There was a marginal response from urban occupational castes. By the end of the twentieth century, the concentrations of these Sikhs are found in the cities and towns of Batala, Amritsar, Jalandhar, Phagwara, Goraya, Ludhiana, Mohali, and Chandigarh. This means that a large rural to urban migration

I find in this study that rural to urban migration was essentially determined by the partition of Punjab in 1947, the formation of the

Indo-Pakistan border, the Green Revolution, industrial development, and the Khalistan movement. These developments served as major push in and pull out factors. While analysing these factors I have tried to comprehend patterns of migration and rehabilitation in the cities.

Similarly, I have also attempted to know the factors responsible for occupational changes. The process of occupational changes has given rise to new classes within the Namdhari community which have established their hegemony over its administrative hierarchy.

What has been the impact of these historical and demographic developments on the lifestyle of the Namdhari Sikhs? How far do they conform to their normative *maryada*? Has there been a problem of incompatibility between Namdhari orthodoxy and the modern life? How far are Namdhari Sikhs free of social evils like female foeticide, suicide, dowry, and drug addiction? Inferences drawn by this study are very revealing.

For the analysis of demographic, socio-religious and cultural changes among these Sikhs, there are several ideological and methodological problems. One of the major problems is the absence of demographic data of the Kuka Sikhs of the twentieth century. After suppressing the Kuka movement, the British officials gave more attention to emerging Sikh social reformers, especially militant Tat Khalsa, Ghadarites, Akalis and Babbar Akalis. Archival sources are available on the social background of the leaders, and the nature and scope of these movements. Yet no such sources particularly on the Namdhari Sikhs of the post-Independence period are available. Moreover, Namdhari literature is inadequate to the comprehending task of these changes. We were told that the Bhaini Sahib headquarters launched a census operation on its own, but no consolidated report was made public. Incidentally, we could get only a section of this report, one pertaining to the Namdhari families of Amritsar. It contains some vital statistics: postal addresses, numbers of males and females, age-groups, level of education, caste and occupation, frequency of visits to Bhaini Sahib, and quantum of *daswand*. But this statistical information does not cover all the Namdhari families of Amritsar. Moreover, the report has inflated the number of Namdhari families. And the single page proforma does not include data on rituals and their practice.

The only alternative was a fresh random survey of contemporary rural and urban Namdhari Sikhs in Punjab. It was a difficult task in the sense that there were thousands of villages and hundreds of cities and towns in this state. However, there are some villages, towns and cities in which Namdhari families live in substantial number. We travelled to locate these families and conduct interviews with the heads of these families. Scanty Namdhari families in the villages left little choice for a sample survey. The position of these families in the urban centres, however, was better for sampling Namdhari families. The cities of Amritsar, Jalandhar, Ludhiana, Chandigarh, and Mohali proved ideal for sampling as hundreds of Namdhari families are found there. In spite of their haphazard demography, we tried to rationalize their rural and urban representation on the one hand and caste and occupational representation on the other. For instance, the number of Namdhari Jat families was larger than their counterparts of other occupational castes in rural areas, whereas the number of the Namdhari Ramgarhias was bigger than their coreligionists in the urban centres. We were helped by local leaders in locating the families, and are conscious of the fact that our dependence on the Namdhari leadership might have restricted our choice or skewed our sample.

Sociologists inform us that

> in practice two types of error will arise from any sampling procedure; first, sampling bias may arise in the way the selection is carried out; and second, random sampling error may arise in the sample obtained, due to chance differences between the members of the population included, or excluded, from the sample. Total sampling error in the sample issued for interviewing consists of these two taken together.[40]

I am acutely aware of these biases and errors in the case study of Namdhari Sikhs of India and of overseas countries. The statistical inferences with regard to the present status of the occupational castes of Namdhari Sikhs of districts of Haryana and Himachal Pradesh will not be complementary due to their different demographic status. In Haryana we are told that the Namdhari agriculturists are in majority whereas the Namdhari artisans and traders are in a minority. On the other hand, in Himachal Pradesh, the Namdhari traders and businessmen (Khatri and Arora—mercantile castes) are in the majority. In Delhi the number of Namdhari Ramgarhias is larger than other castes. Similarly, the status of occupational castes of Namdhari Sikhs overseas varies from country to country. In Thailand, the Namdhari traders and businessmen are in majority. In the United Kingdom, the Namdhari Ramgarhias are in majority.[41] In USA and Canada, the Namdhari Sikhs belong to several occupational castes. The study of the diaspora thus requires different paradigms and methodologies because its past and present are radically different from those of the Punjab.

Given a limited budget I was able to collect data on 1,545 Namdhari families of 18 districts of Punjab. These families belong to 150 villages and 48 towns. While collecting the data we attempted to give due representation to the occupational castes. Nevertheless, one is aware of the limitations of this survey, since Punjab state comprises more than 12,278 villages and 141 towns.[42] The survey was facilitated by students. Simarjit Kaur and Anuradha who collected data for their respective M.Phil. dissertations in 2004 and 2006 respectively. On my request, the Namdhari leaders and scholars helped these scholars in their fieldwork. Encouraged by their results I submitted a major project to the Guru Nanak Dev University in 2008. Again Namdhari leaders and scholars helped us to locate Namdhari families in rural and urban centres.

The questionnaire comprised 17 core-questions and each core-question contains several subordinate questions. The entire data was tabulated into the following categories: (i) number of Namdhari families in each village and city/town; caste-wise number of these families (agriculturist, artisan, business and menial castes); variables responsible for increase or decrease in the number; (ii) the patterns of migration of Namdhari families from west Punjab to east Punjab during 1947 and from rural to urban centres in the post-Independence period and patterns of their rehabilitation; (iii) caste-wise variables affecting the occupational changes; (iv) impact of demographic change; and (v) Namdhari beliefs and practices.

This data is as authentic as the census reports. However, we are aware of the intentions and biases of the Namdhari respondents. The vital statistics like the names of persons, places, castes and sub-castes, number of males/females, age-groups, qualifications, nature of family callings and present status of occupations are unintentional. However, the information related to income, property/landed assets, debts, and involvement in civil and criminal cases suffer from under- or over-statement of these Namdhari respondents. Similarly, a substantial number of respondents could not remember when and how their great grandfathers became Namdhari Sikhs. Most of them could not state the exact size of their landholdings before Partition. Their statements on the practice of Namdhari *maryada* are not free of bias because of a natural tendency to hide failings and project a good image. Nevertheless, a large number of Namdhari respondents were not pretentious, and were free and frank in admitting the prevalence of social evils among them. At the same time, we tried on our own to ascertain the actual mode of their living from the structures of their houses, presence or absence of Namdhari symbols, means of transportation and communication and entertainment, dress-code and use of cosmetics. To our surprise, a few respondents including office-bearers were outspoken. On condition of anonymity, they disclosed ground level social reality which served as tools of cross-examination and moderated our explanation of variables of demographic, socio-religious and cultural changes. Moreover, published primary and secondary works have also helped us to check the reliability of our data and corroborate our inferences drawn from this data.

On the basis of data provided by the Namdhari respondents, several tables have been constructed. However, the number of the respondents of the Namdhari families vary from one category of tables to another because respondents did not always answer core and subsidiary questions. Several of them answered these questions partially. Moreover, their information on several issues was notional. It became difficult for us either to quantify or corroborate their information. Due to these limitations, several tables have been constructed as sample analysis.

NOTES

1. *Chandi di Var* (the Ballad of Goddess Chandi) or, to give it its exact title, *Var Sri Bhagauti Ji Ki*, by Guru Gobind Singh, included in the *Dasam Granth*, is the story of the titantic contest between Chandi and other gods on the one hand and the demons on the other. The poem allegorizes the eternal conflict between good and evil. The source of the legend is the *Devi Mahatmya*, a section of the *Markandeya Purana*. The narrative follows the latter in the main, though the dominant interest lies in the character of Chandi which, through the creative genius of the poet, attains reality and firmness belying its mythical origin. The *var* is in Punjabi; the other two poems about Chandi in the *Dasam Granth* are in Braj, *The Encyclopaedia of Sikhism*, ed. Harbans Singh, vol. I, 1995, p. 434.
2. For details of this ceremony, see, M.M. Ahluwalia, *Kukas: The Freedom Fighters of the Punjab*, 1965, pp. 48-9.
3. Fauja Singh, *Kuka Movement: An Important Phase in Punjab's Role in India's Struggle for Freedom*, 1965, p. 34.

4. M.M. Ahluwalia, 1965, p. 54, also see weekly Urdu newspaper, *Ashruf-ul-Akhbar*, Delhi, 19 December 1866, p. 20.
5. Nahar Singh and Kirpal Singh (eds.), *Rebels Against the British Rule*, 1995, pp. 6-7; as early as 1860, the British government had become very suspicious of the activities of Kuka Sikhs. It instructed its intelligence department to gather information about the activities of the Namdhari Sikhs. It is in this context that Captain Millar, Cantonment Magistrate, Jalandhar deputed Gaindah Singh, a Sikh informer, to the headquarters of the Namdhari Guru. Although Gaindah Singh did not succeed in seeing the Namdhari Guru, he was able to carry two papers which were given by the disciples to him, for the Namdhari Guru. However, Gaindah Singh managed to bring back these papers and handed them over to the Magistrate.
6. The number of these Kukas varies from 125 to 200, see Bhai Nahar Singh and Kirpal Singh, p. XX; Jaswinder Singh, *Kuka Movement*, 1985, p. VII.
7 M.M. Ahluwalia, *Kukas,* 1965, pp. 78-93.
8 Ibid, pp. 141-50.
9 Jaswinder Singh, *Kuka Movement: Freedom Struggle in Punjab-Documents 1880-1903*, pp. 95-188.
10. P.C. Roy, 'Gurcharan Singh's Mission in Central Asia', in *The Punjab Past and Present*, ed. Ganda Singh, vol. VIII, April 1974, p. 207.
11. Jaswinder Sing*h, Kuka Movement, Document 1880-1903*, p. 108.
12. Ganda Singh (ed.), *Maharaja Duleep Singh Correspondence,* 1977, pp. 83, 90, 95, 105.
13. Ibid., p. 104.
14. M.M. Ahluwalia, *Kukas,* 1965, p. 33.
15. Percival Spear, *A History of India,* vol. II, 1977, pp. 153-4.
16. Joginder Singh, *A Short History of Namdhari Sikhs*, 2010, p. 10.
17. Ibid., pp. 10-11.
18. Baba Sohan Singh Bhakna, 'Namdhari Movement', *Satjug,* March-Apnl 2002, pp. 36-7.
19. Cited by Bhagat Singh Bilga, 'Ghadar Party Te Kuka Lehar', *Mera Vatan.* See *Satjug*, March-April 2002, p. 38.
20. *Kuka*, 11 October 1922, Nihal Singh, *Lord of Virtues and Fortunes*, pp. 36-7.
21. First editorial note cited in *Satjug*, 2001, p. 8.
22. Ibid.
23. Kala Singh, *Kuka Singh Ate Angrez Jaat,* 1922, p. 42.
24. Sohan Singh Josh, *Akali Morchian Da Itihas*, 1972, p. 513.
25. Joginder Singh, 2010, p. 74.
26. Ibid., p. 75.
27. Ibid., pp. 75-6.

28. *Satjug*, November 1934, p. 4.
29. His interest in the National Movement remained unabated until the country won Independence. Fauja Singh. *The Kuka Movement,* 1965, p. 193.
30. Tarn Singh Vahmi, *Jas Jiwan*, vol. II, Hissar, 1974, p. 225.
31. Ibid.
32. Cited in *Namdhari Sikhs: The Pioneer Freedom Fighters,* ed. H.S. Hanspal, 2006, pp. 10, 21.
33. For details, see *Satjug*, 17 June 1938, pp. 6-7, 30 July 1938, pp. 6-10, 1 September 1938, pp. 6-7.
34. *Satjug,* 29 April 1938, p. 5.
35. *Satjug,* 8 December 1943, p. 3.
36. Fauja Singh, *Kuka Movement,* 1965, p. 185.
37. Nahar Singh, *Gooro Ram Singh and the Kuka Sikhs: Documents 1863-1871,* vol. I, 1965, pp. 36-46; Jaswinder Singh, *Kukas of Note in Punjab: Documents 1881,* 1984, pp. 12-72.
38. Kuldeep Singh, *The Namdhari Movement: Continuity and Change,* 2000, pp. 173-83.
39. Nahar Singh and Kirpal Singh, *Rebels Against the British Rule,* 1995, pp. 37-8.
40. *Oxford Dictionary of Sociology*, Oxford University Press, New Delhi, 2006, p. 577.
41. For variations of statistical inferences, see, Arvind Sehgal, 'Assimilation of an Ethnic Group: A Case Study of Namdharis in Mandi Town in Himachal Pradesh', PhD. thesis, 1990; Gurharpal Singh and Darshan Tatla, *Sikhs in Britain: The Making of Community,* 2008, pp. 79-81, 91-110, 173.
42. *Punjab-at-a-Glance, District-Wise, 2009,* Government of Punjab, p. 1.

CHAPTER 1

The Social Order

This chapter examines the social order of the Namdhari Sikhs of contemporary Punjab in terms of their occupational castes and their caste-wise status in the community hierarchy. The chapter also examines caste-wise responses of these Sikhs during the period of 150 years. The relevance of this preliminary exercise lies on the assumption that caste systems are 'systems of cumulative inequality' where the advantages of status tend to be combined with advantages of wealth and power, and those who are socially under-privileged also tend to be at the bottom of the economic and political scales'.[1] Moreover, an analysis of occupational background of followers gives a basic understanding of the demographic structure of the Namdhari community. It is on the basis of class or caste background of the followers of a movement that historians and sociologists characterize the nature of that movement. Changed perception, of class/Namdharis we are sure, is going to give a different image among the caste-conscious people of Punjab. At the same time, it also obliges us to answer a host of questions which are fundamental for writing a social and political history of a religious community. For instance, one of these questions relates to the dialectical relationship between social background and the articulation of ideas since the inception of the movement. Our survey shows that for the last hundred years, if not earlier, the Sikh agriculturists and artisans constituted the major section of the Namdhari following. What was the ideological commonality in leadership and organization of the Namdhari community for which these two categories of Namdhari followers co-existed and worked harmoniously? Good studies are available on this type of relationship on several movements including Sikh movements.[2] But no work is available on the Namdhari movement since the last quarter of the nineteenth century.

PRESENT CASTE-WISE NUMERICAL STATUS

I conducted a survey of 1545 Namdhari families of 18 districts of Punjab state and found that the Namdhari Sikhs come from agriculturist, artisan, and business castes. On the basis of information provided by the respondents of these families this chapter ascertains the occupational status of the Namdhari Sikhs of districts of Gurdaspur, Amritsar, Tarn Taran, Kapurthala, Hoshiarpur, Jalandhar, Nawan Shahr, Ferozepur, Ludhiana, Rupnagar, Fatehgarh Sahib, Patiala, Bathinda, Muktsar, Moga, Sangrur, Mohali and Union Territory of Chandigarh.

For historians of Punjab it may sound incredible that the Namdhari Sikhs comprise 16 occupational castes. Nearly half of them are agriculturists and the rest artisans and traders. The agriculturists comprise Jat, Saini, and Rajput Sikhs. The artisans include Ramgarhias, Parjapats/Ghumiars, Chhembas, Mehras/Jhiwars, Swarankar/Suniara (gold-smiths), Julahas, Nais (barbers/match makers), Ramdasias (Sikhs of the Chamar Caste) and menial castes like Mahashas/ Mazahbis. The business groups include Khatris and Aroras. The Namdhari Brahmins are exceptions.[3] Our random survey shows that the Namdhari Jats form the single largest ethnic group, i.e. 50 per cent. If we include Sainis (3 per cent) and Rajputs (1 per cent) agriculturists outnumber (54 per cent.) their *gurbhais* (co-religionists) of other occupational castes. Like the agriculturists of Punjab, the Namdhari agriculturists form a differentiated class. In terms of the size of their landholdings, they can be put into four categories. Marginal agriculturists whose landholdings are less than 5 acres of land constitute 27 per cent of the total Namdhari agriculturists. The second category comprises those whose landholdings vary from 5 to 9.99 acres and they comprise 27 per cent also. The third category includes medium agriculturists whose landholdings vary from 10 to 24.99 acres of land. Interestingly, they form 32 per cent of the Namdhari agriculturist families. The last category comprises the big Namdhari agriculturists whose holdings are more than 25 acres and they constitute 14 per cent of the total Namdhari agriculturist families (Table 1.1).

Next to the agriculturists are Ramgarhias who constitute 37 per cent of the Namdhari population. They also form an ethnic group in terms of their 'common characteristics' which differentiate them from the other groups in Punjab. They are known for their skilled labour and distinct social customs. Besides them, there is a marginal number of other artisans like Suniaras, Chhembas, Parjapats, Julahas, Mehras, Nais and Mazhabis who are 1 or 2 per cent (Table 1.2).

TABLE 1.1: DIFFERENTIATED STATUS OF NAMDHARI AGRICULTURISTS*

Districts		A 0 to 4.99 acres of land	B 5 to 9.99 acres of land	C 10 to 24.99 acres of land	D 25 and onward acres of land	Total
Moga		26	12	8	7	53 + 7(NA**)
Barnala		20	6	21	1	48 + 14(NA)
Bathinda		2	5	7	3	17
Ferozepur		2	11	25	6	44 + 2(NA)
Patiala		3	7	2	2	14 + 3(NA)
Sangrur		11	7	17	26	61 + 5(NA)
Hoshiarpur		10	21	17	2	50 + 4(NA)
Muktsar		–	1	3	6	10 + 2(NA)
Nawan Shahr (Saini)		15	12	8	1	36 + 1(NA)
Ludhiana	Jat	2	4	4	2	12 + 8(NA)
	Rajput	7	3	3	2	15 + 2(NA)
Fatehgarh Sahib		2	14	17	4	37 + 1(NA)
Amritsar		8	7	7	3	25 + 2(NA)
Chandigarh & Mohali		2	8	5	1	16 + 11(NA)
Tarn Taran		20	9	9	3	41
Total		130 27%	127 27%	153 32%	69 14%	479

Notes: * Data provided by Namdhari respondents
** No answer

Before we analyse the demographic variables, a brief note on some details of the Namdhari families of occupational castes of each district. Table 1.2 shows that the Namdhari Sikhs of several occupational castes are spread over the entire districts of the present Punjab state. At the same time, numbers vary. The basic reason, as stated in the introduction, is accessibility. The highest number of these families as per Table 1.2 are in the districts of Gurdaspur and Kapurthala (244 and 197 respectively). Random survey of these districts was conducted in 2004 and 2005. The survey of rest of districts of Punjab was conducted during the period 2008-9. However, major Namdhari concentrations are certainly found in the districts of Gurdaspur, Amritsar, Kapurthala, Ludhiana, Barnala, Ferozepur, Moga, Tarn Taran, Sangrur and Mohali & Chandigarh. The caste-wise split of

TABLE 1.2: CASTE-WISE BREAKUP OF NAMDHARI FAMILIES

Name of distt.	Jat	Ram-garhia	Saini	Parja-pat	Arora/ Khatri	Ra-jput	Meh-ras/ Kohar	Maha-sha/ Ma-zhabi	Chhe-mba	Sun-iara	Ram-dasia	Kam-boj	Brah-min	Nai	Ju-laha	Bania	Total
Amritsar	36	69	–	4	9	1	4	1	–	4	–	–	–	–	–	–	128
Barnala	64	18	–	–	–	–	–	–	1	–	–	–	–	–	–	–	83
Bathinda	18	9	–	–	–	–	–	–	–	–	–	–	–	–	–	–	27
Mohali & CHD	27	35	–	1	6	–	–	1	1	1	–	1	–	–	–	–	73
Fatehgarh Sahib	38	6	2	–	–	–	–	–	–	–	7	–	–	–	–	–	53
Ferozepur	46	15	–	–	2	2	–	–	5	–	–	1	–	1	–	–	72
Gurdaspur	154	63	–	6	–	2	7	6	1	2	–	–	1	2	–	–	244
Hoshiarpur	54	–	–	3	–	–	–	–	–	–	–	–	–	–	–	–	57
Jalandhar	9	105	–	1	1	–	–	–	–	–	–	–	–	–	–	–	116
Kapurthala	107	83	1	–	4	–	1	–	–	–	–	3	–	1	–	–	200
Ludhiana	21	64	–	2	–	17	–	2	–	1	–	–	–	–	–	–	107
Moga	63	42	–	–	1	–	1	2	1	1	–	–	1	–	1	1	114
Muktsar	12	1	–	–	2	–	–	–	1	1	–	–	–	–	–	–	17
Nawan Shahr	1	11	37	–	1	–	–	–	–	–	–	–	–	–	–	–	50
Patiala	18	12	1	3	–	–	–	–	–	–	–	–	2	–	–	–	36
Rupnagar	–	17	3	–	1	–	–	–	–	–	–	1	–	–	–	–	22
Sangrur	66	–	–	–	–	–	4	1	–	–	–	–	1	–	–	–	72
Tarn Taran	41	21	–	8	1	–	–	2	1	–	–	–	–	–	–	–	74
Total	775	571	44	28	28	22	17	15	11	10	7	6	5	4	1	1	1545
%age	50.16	37	3	2	2	1.42	1.10	0.97	0.71	0.64	0.45	0.38	0.32	0.25	0.06	0.06	%age

Note: Data provided by Namdhari respondents.

these families in these districts gives their more specific demographic status.

MAJHA REGION

Gurdaspur: Data on 244 Namdhari families of this district was collected. These families come from several occupational castes, Jat 154, Ramgarhia 63, Rajput 2, Parjapat 6, Suniara 2, Chhemba 1, Mehra 7, Nai 2 and Mazhabi or Mahashe 6. Jats and Ramgarhias form 85 per cent of the Namdhari following. The rest of the occupational castes constitute a small portion. It was found that 100 families were migrants from the West Punjab of Pakistan (1947) more than 60 of them from villages and towns of district Sialkot. A small number came from Lahore, Lyallpur, Gujranwala, and Multan. These migrants were Jat Sikh agriculturists and artisans. Migrant agriculturists constitute 77 and the rest are Ramgarhias (18 per cent), Parjapats (2 per cent), Chhembas (1 per cent) and Mahashe (2 per cent). Out of 244 families, 158 are living in the rural area. Eighty-six families are in the urban centres of district Gurdaspur. The Ramgarhias are in a majority in urban centres.

Amritsar: The 128 Namdhari families of district Amritsar on whom data was collected comprise: 36 Jat, 69 Ramgarhia, 4 Parjapat, 9 Arora/Khatri, 1 Rajput, 4 Mehra/Kohar, 1 Mazhabi and 4 Suniara. The Namdhari Sikhs of rural area of this district mainly belong to Jat and Ramgarhia castes. The former constitute 53 per cent whereas Ramgarhia form 37.25 per cent. of the total rural population of this district. The Parjapats are 6 per cent. Mehras and Mazhabis are less then 2 per cent each. The majority of these families belong to two villages, Mohawa and Mahadipur, where Namdhari *deras* (seminaries) have been functioning since the mid-twentieth century.

At present there are more than 200 Namdhari families spread over different localities in Amritsar city, with major concentrations found in and around Chheharta, Putlighar, Sultanwind, Tarn Taran and Batala Roads and Khazana Gate. Most of these Namdhari families (50) belong to the Ramgarhia caste. They are followed by 10 agriculturist families Excepting two the rest of these agriculturists are migrants from West Punjab. Nine families are Khatris and Aroras. The rest of the artisans are 4 Suniaras (goldsmiths), 3 Parjapats and 1 Mehra.

Tarn Taran: Data on 74 Namdhari families was collected. More than 91 per cent are from to rural areas. Most of the Namdhari Sikhs are agriculturists: 41 Jat Sikh families. Next to them are artisan families: 21 Ramgharia, 8 Parjapat, 1 Arora/Khatri caste and 2 Mazhabi.

Doaba Region

Hoshiarpur: Data on 57 Namdhari families of Hoshiarpur district was collected. It is interesting to note that 55 out of 57 are migrants from district Sialkot, West Punjab, Pakistan. Only two of the agriculturist families moved from a village of district Gurdaspur to district Hoshiarpur. Similarly, 3 Parjapat families also came from the villages of district Sialkot. At present, these families are found in the villages of Fatehullah (3), Ladpur (1), Hardokhla (4), Mehmudpur (16), Budhobarkat (7), Dugri (6), Khokhran (5), Kaintha (1), Bhangala (2) and Marasgarh (2) in teshils of Mukerian and Dasuya. Only four families are residing in the towns of Mukarian and Dasuya. This means that only 7 per cent families are live in the urban area whereas 93 per cement in the rural area.

Jalandhar: We have data of 116 Namdhari families of the Ramgarhia, Jat, Arora and Parjapat castes of district Jalandhar. Approximately 80 per cent are migrants from the West Punjab (Pakistan). According to our survey, out of 116 Namdhari families, 105 are Ramgarhia, 9 Jat, one each Arora/Khatri and Parjapat. Their major concentration is in Jalandhar city and industrial towns of Goraya and villages of Padi Khalsa, Bara Pind, Boparai, Muthada Kalan and Loharan. More than 90 per cent of these families live in the urban centres of this district. The Namdhari Ramgarhias are in the majority both in rural and urban areas.

Nawan Shahr (*Shaheed Bhagat Singh Nagar*): Fifty Namdhari families of district Nawan Shahr (now Shahid Bhagat Singh Nagar) come mainly from Saini agriculturist caste and the marginal from Ramgarhia, Jat, and Arora castes. This is the only district of Punjab in which Namdhari families of Saini caste dominate (37 out of 50). Next are 11 families of Ramgarhias. There is one family each of Jats and Aroras. Ramgarhias constitute 22 per cent of the Namdhari population of this district. The percentage of the Namdhari Sikhs of other agriculturists and artisan classes is negligible.

Kapurthala: Data on 200 Namdhari families of district Kapurthala shows that these families belong to Jat, Ramgarhia, Saini, Arora/Khatri, Nai, Kamboj and Mehra castes. Statistically speaking, Jat and Ramgarhia families dominate. The number of families of each caste is as follows: Jat 107, Ramgarhia 83, Kamboj 3, Arora/Khatri 4, and Nai, Mehra, and Saini one each. Out of 200 families, 110 are in rural areas whereas 90 families in urban centres. These 90 Namdhari families are found in the following urban centres of district Kapurthala: 14 Phagwara, 43 Sultanpur, 4 Lodhi, 27 Bhulath, 2 Hussainpur (Railway Coach Factory). Among the 200 families 53.5 per cent are Jats and 41.5 per cent Ramgarhias. Majority of the migrants are from districts Sialkot and Lahore.

MALWA REGION

Ludhiana: There are approximately 300 to 400 Namdhari families in Ludhiana district but we could collect data of 107 only. We found that 60 per cent of them are Ramgarhias. Next, Jat families constitute 20 per cent. The Rajput families form 16 per cent. Numerically marginals are: Parjapat 2 per cent, Mazhabis 2 per cent and Suniaras 1 per cent. The rural-urban divide is as follows. In the city, there are 54 Ramgarhia, 1 Jat and 1 Suniara families whereas in the rural area, there are 20 Jat, 17 Rajput, 10 Ramgarhia and two each of Parjapat and Mazhabi families. It may further be noted that 6 Jat, 8 Ramgarhia and 1 Parjatpat families came from Pakistan. Besides, several families in Ludhiana city came from towns and villages of districts of Jalandhar, Amritsar, Nawan Shahr, Patiala, Sangrur, Kapurthala and Sirsa. Similarly, there are several agriculturist families of villages of Bathinda, Amritsar, Sangrur, Jalandhar and Sirsa who have ultimately settled in the villages of Ludhiana.

Fatehgarh Sahib: The 53 Namdhari families here belong to Jat, Ramgarhia, Saini and Ramdasia castes, Jat being 38, Ramdasia 7, Ramgarhia 6 and Saini 2. Of 53 Namdhari families, 33 are in living Bir Bhamarsi; 8 in Dera Mir Miran; 4 each in Jhalkheri and Bahadurgarh and 3 in village Rajinder Nagar. 19 families of the agriculturists and 5 of Ramgarhias came from the West Punjab in 1947.

Rupnagar: The Namdhari Sikhs of district Rupnagar comprise Ramgarhias, Sainis, Aroras, and Kambojs. However, the total number of urban Namdhari families, according to Suba Mani Singh, is 35. We collected the data of 22 families. Of which 17 are Ramgarhias, three Sainis and one each Aroras and Kambojs. The Ramgarhias constitute 77 per cent of the total Namdhari population of this district, Sainis 14 per cent, Aroras and Kambojs constitute 5 per cent each. Two families are migrants from West Punjab. The rural-urban divide is as follows: Urban—12 Ramgarhia, 2 Saini and 1 Arora; Rural—5 Ramgarhia, 1 Saini and 1 Kamboj.

Patiala: Data on 36 Namdhari families of district Patiala was collected, 18 Jat, 12 Ramgarhia, 3 Parjapat, 2 Brahmin and one Saini. Approximately 61 per cent (22 families: Jat 12, Ramgarhia 6, Parjapat 3 and Brahmin 1) are migrants from West Punjab. Similarly, five families are migrants from the districts of Amritsar, Ludhiana, Sangrur, Kainthal (Haryana). Thus the number of native Namdhari families is very small. Nevertheless, of the total Namdhari population, Namdhari Jats constitute 50 per cent, Ramgarhias 33 per cent, Brahmins 6 per cent and Parjapat 8 per cent and Saini 3 per cent. Urban families comprise Jat 10, Ramgarhia 11, Brahmin 1, Parjapat 1 and Saini 1; and rural, Jat 8, Ramgarhia 1, Brahmin 1 and Parjapat 2.

Barnala: 83 Namdhari families of Barnala district were studied, 64 Jat, 18 Ramgarhia and one Chhemba. The Namdhari Jats and Ramgarhias constitute 77 and 22 per cent of the total Namdhari population respectively. Another distinct demographic feature of this district is that, excepting three Jat Sikh families, the rest are natives of this district. Major concentrations of the Namdhari Sikhs of this district are in the villages like Raisar, Jangiana, Bhadaur, Gehal, Sehna, Alkra and Tapa. Twenty-one out of 62 Namdhari families are found in village Raisar. Incidentally, this survey does not include the Namdhari families of urban centres of this district.

Moga: Among 114 Namdhari families of district Moga Jats constitute 63, Ramgarhias 42, Brahmin 1, Arora 1, Aggarwal 1, Julaha 1, Darji 1, Mehra 1, Swarankar 1 and 2 Mazhabi families. Numerically, the Namdhari Jat and Ramgarhia families form 55 and 37 per cent respectively. Incidentally, our sample of this district could include only three urban families of Ramgarhia and one of Arora. This is one of the districts where all Namdhari families are natives.

Ferozepur: In district Ferozepur, we are informed that there are hundreds of Namdhari families who migrated from West Punjab in

1947. Our random survey of 72 families shows that more than 60 per cent of these families are migrants from Pakistan (Jat 23, Ramgarhia 14, Chhemba 4, Nai 1 and Rajput 1 families). It is interesting to note that most of the Ramgarhia families are agriculturists. At present, these families are inhabitants of Sabuana, Pathewala, Gatta Badshah, Fatehwal, Rajiwala, Assal, Maluwaliawala, Wasti Namdev, and Rode villages. There are a few families who actually belong to the villages of this district but have shifted to urban centres like Makhu, Zira and Ferozepur and Ferozepur Cantt. (Jat 2, Ramgarhia 1 and Chhemba 1).

Bathinda: Due to several limitations, we could collect the data on 27 Namdhari families only. We were told by the respondents that their approximate number is 400. Sant Hardev Singh, Pardhan Shaheed Wariyam Singh Yadgar Committee, Rampura Phull, asserted that the number was greater. He informed us that approximately 80 per cent were Namdhari Jats in the rural areas. Next were Ramgarhias forming 18 per cent.

The Namdhari Jats belong to three villages: Bhagta Bhai Ka 3; Parash Nagar 1; Kotha Guru 11 and Burj Tharor 3. The Namdhari Ramgarhias of this district come from both rural and urban areas. However, their number in the urban centres is bigger than their counterparts in the rural areas. We were also informed that in Rampura Phull alone there were 39 Namdhari families. There are only 4 Namdhari agriculturist families. Most of the Namdhari Ramgarhias belong to the villages like Saidoke, Bhagta Bhai Ka, Rampura Phul, Kotha Guru and Dallewal and most of them are marginal agriculturists.

Sangrur: The Namdhari Sikhs of district Sangrur are predominantly Jat agriculturists. Out of 72, Namdhari Jat families are 66. Next to them are 4 Namdhari Mehra families, one Brahmin Sikh and one Mahasha family. Excepting the Mehra families, the rest belong to the villages Jhall and Chakk Sheikhupra Kalan. Incidentally the survey could not include urban residents. It may further be pointed out that half these families are migrants from West Punjab.

Mohali and Chandigarh: Since the towns of Mohali and Chandigarh are similar in layout and class background of their inhabitants, the Namdhari Sikhs of these towns are placed into a single category. Although there may be several hundred Namdhari families of these two towns and adjoining areas, we could collect the data on only 73 families. According to this data 27 are Jat, 35 Ramgarhia, 6 Arora/ Khatri and one each Parjapat, Suniara, Chhemba, Mazhabi and Kamboj. Almost all these families are migrants either from West Punjab, or East Punjab.

CASTE-WISE RESPONSE AND NUMERICAL STATUS: HISTORICAL CONTEXT

An interesting demographic feature of these Namdhari Sikhs is that the number of each caste joining the Namdhari sect changed over-time. One of the questions asked to each Namdhari family was this: when did your great grandfather become Namdhari Sikh? About 24 per cent of the respondents said that their families became Namdhari during Namdhari Satguru Ram Singh's time (1816-85). Only 10 per cent referred to Namdhari Satguru Hari Singh's time (1872-1906). However, 49.5 per sent stated that their grandfathers or fathers became Namdhari Sikhs during Satguru Partap Singh's time (1906-59). Similarly, 17 per cent became Namdhari Sikhs during Satguru Jagjit Singh's time. In other words, nearly half of the total conversion took place during Satguru Partap Singh's time. Low conversions in the late nineteenth and early twentieth centuries was largely due to the fact that the Namdhari Sikhs were undergoing ruthless colonial repression. Gurus Hari Singh and Partap Singh were not allowed to carry on their *maryada* and propagate of the Namdhari mission in the early years of the twentieth century. They could not hold their religious congregations. The local officials humiliated the 'Kukas' whenever they came across them. However, as we shall note, when the political scenario in Punjab changed in favour of the Kukas, the Namdhari guru availed that opportunity to revamp techniques of propagation. Our respondents confirm the stories of conversion of Sikhs by the Namdhari guru, *sants*, *mahants* and *babas* and their *deras*. However, before we take up some other dimensions of a big or poor response of occupational castes, it is essential to point out that at present there is stagnation in the expansion of Namdhari mission. Statistically speaking, in the last quarter of nineteeth century the rate of conversion was 24 per cent. Around 1950 it shot up 49.5 per cent but towards 2000 it declined to 17 per cent (Table 1.3).

Namdhari agriculturists are in the majority in rural area of Punjab.

TABLE 1.3: CASTE-WISE CONVERSION OF NAMDHARI FAMILIES IN EACH DISTRICT OF PUNJAB*

Namdhari Gurus	Jat	Ram-garhia	Arora/ Khatri	Chhem-ba	Parja-pat	Nai	Ram-dasia	Suni-ara	Mehra	Maha-sha/ Mazhabi	Saini	Raj-put	Kam-boj	Ju-laha	Brah-min	Jhi-war	Total
Ram Singh	221 (31.79 %)	63 (11.90 %)	7 (25 %)	1 (11.11 %)	5 (16.12 %)	1 (25 %)		2 (25 %)	–	1 (7.69 %)	26 (63.41 %)	4 (20 %)	–	1 (100 %)	–	–	332 (23.52 %)
Hari Singh	75 (10 79 %)	44 (8.31 %)	2 (7.14 %)	–	2 (6.45 %)	–	1 (14.28 %)	1 (12.5 %)	–	4 (30.76 %)	3 (7.31 %)	–	–	–	–	–	132 (9.35 %)
Partap Singh	304 (43 74 %)	307 (58.03 %)	14 (50 %)	5 (55.55 %)	18 (58.06 %)	–	6 (85.71 %)	3 (37.5 %)	6 (50 %)	6 (46.15 %)	9 (21.95 %)	11 (55 %)	4 (50 %)	–	1 (50 %)	3 (100 %)	697 (49.39 %)
Jagjit Singh	95 (13.66 %)	115 (21.73 %)	5 (17.85 %)	3 (33.33 %)	6 (19.35 %)	3 (75 %)		2 (25 %)	6 (50 %)	2 (15.38 %)	3 (7.31 %)	5 (25 %)	4 (50 %)	–	1 (50 %)	–	250 (17.71 %)
Total	695	529	28	9	31	4	7	8	12	13	41	20	8	1	2	3	1411
% age	49.25	37.49	1.98	0.63	2.19	0.28	0.49	0.56	0.85	0.92	2.90	1.41	0.56	0.07	0.14	0.21	

Note: *Data provided by Namdhari respondents.

Their number in each occupational caste varies from district to district. It was the Partition of Punjab 1947 and resettlement of the people subsequently which established the majority of the Namdhari agriculturists in the districts of Gurdaspur, Tarn Taran, Kapurthala, Hoshiarpur, Fatehgarh Sahib, Sangrur, Muktsar, Moga, Barnala and Ferozepur. In the districts of Sangrur, Moga, Muktsar and Bathinda, Namdhari Jat agriculturists have had been in the majority since the founding of the villages of these districts. Namdhari Ramgarhias outnumber their co-religionists in the urban centres of Batala, Amritsar, Jalandhar and Ludhiana cities. As we shall see it is the industrial development of these towns and cities which encouraged the migration of artisans to urban centres. Similarly, the Partition of Punjab 1947 was the second major variable for the concentrations of the Namdhari artisans in the urban centres.

As noted, the response of agriculturists, Jat Sikhs and Ramgarhias, was bigger than that of the other castes. However, the numerical status of these two castes shows a converse graph. Our random survey indicates an upward graph of Namdhari Ramgarhias. Over a period of 150 years their percentage doubled 12 to 22 whereas the percentage of the Namdhari Jats declined from 32 to 14 per cent. The Namdhari Jats are in majority in districts of Ferozepur, Tarn Taran, Kapurthala and Gurdaspur whereas Namdhari Ramgarhias have an edge over their co-religionists in Amritsar, Jalandhar and Ludhiana.[4]

CONCEPT OF RELATIVE DEPRIVATION

The big entry of agrarian and artisan classes into the Namdhari sect in the mid-twentieth century can be analysed from different perspectives. In the given social and economic status of the artisan classes in the Punjab agrarian society under the colonial and post-colonial rule, the concept of relative deprivation can provide insights into this phenomenal entry of agriculturists and artisan classes.

> The concept of relative deprivation can be applied to the members of all social classes. Relative deprivation refers to subjectively perceived deprivation that which people actually feel. In objective terms the poor are more deprived than middle class. However, in subjective terms certain members of the middle class may feel more deprivation than the poor.[5]

Before we precede with the illustration of sense of deprivation prevalent among these Namdhari classes, it is essential to point out that the theory of relative deprivation too 'suffers from serious limitations'. Shah informs us that theory, developed by American scholars (Gurr 1970), has guided some studies on agitation and mass movements. The limitations of this theory are pointed out by a number of Indian scholars. M.S.A. Rao asserts that relative deprivation is a necessary but not a sufficient condition for protest movements. He argues, 'a sufficient level of understanding and reflection is required on the part of the participants, and they must be able to observe and perceive the contrast between the social and cultural conditions of the privileged and those of the deprived and must realize that it is possible to do something about it' (1979: 207). Shah (1979) argues that the theory of relative deprivation ignores the importance of the consciousness and ideology of the participants. It explains protests and movements of revolt, but does not analyse revolutionary movements. Protest does not necessarily lead to a movement. T.K. Oommen (1977) also argues that the deprivation theorists view movements as 'temporary aberrations' rather than as 'ongoing process of change'. Moreover, they do not deal with the sources of deprivation. For T.R. Gurr (1977) 'deprivation' is primarily psychological, therefore, he does not deal with the socio-economic structure which is the source of deprivation.[6] It is in this sense that the concept of deprivation has been applied to the Namdhari Sikhs.

HISTORICAL CONTEXT

As part of the agrarian society of Punjab, the Namdhari agriculturist and artisan classes suffered under the colonial rule. They nurtured a sense of socio-economic deprivation and cultural alienation. Discontent and alienation among these classes were prevalent after 1850. Neither had benefits of colonial rule percolated to these sections of the Sikh community nor did it supplant nostalgia for the Khalsa raj. McLeod analyses the social discontent among the Namdhari agriculturists and artisans who were in the central tract of the Punjab province whose density of the population increased by 16.3 per cent after 1850. The re-occurrence of famine forced the peasantry to borrow from money-lenders and left them indebted. Indebtedness forced the peasantry to either mortgage or sell their landholdings. Consequently, land alienation became a universal phenomenon. McLeod observes that the Jat Sikh peasantry also became its victim.[7] As our random survey shows, Jat Sikh peasants constituted more than 60 per cent of the

Namdhari following. The condition of artisans also went from bad to worse since they were dependent on the agrarian economy of the Punjab.

Namdhari Guru Ram Singh appeared on the scene. The peasant, artisan, and menial castes responded to his message in the thousands. The Namdhari guru and his *subas* assured a kingdom which was to be free of suffering and exploitation. The Namdhari followers, an unprivileged class, were exploited by the privileged *pirs, sodhis, bedis*, and the *mahants* and *pujaris.* Ram Singh and his deputies launched a tirade against the privileged and their falsehoods. The Namdhari guru, being an incarnation of Guru Gobind Singh, formed his Sant Khalsa to attack ungodly issues like the killing of cattle. Sant Khalsa made Muslim butchers a target. Moreover, for them the British were *mlechhas* as they ate beef, destroyed the Khalsa raj, and patronized the privileged classes. McLeod argues that it was economic distress which made the Jat Sikh peasantry and subsidiary castes to join the Namdhari movement and this movement stood for the new social order.[8] It may also be stated here that the Namdhari movement also rekindled of nostalgia for the Khalsa raj. The official reports give statistical information about the social background of the Namdhari leaders and activists. They were Jat Sikhs, Tarkhans and Lohars, Nais, Jhinwars, Chhembas, Ghumiars and Mazhabis. The Inspector General of Police had prepared a report on the Kuka sect in 1867, submitted by the secretary, Punjab government to the secretary, Government of India. The report stated

> all castes of Hindoos, and even Mahomedans, may become Kookas. Major Perkins, District Superintendent of Police at Loodiana, writes that converts are chiefly made from Juts, Tirkhan, Chumars, and Muzbees; very few are obtained from and amongst Khuttrees, Brahmins, Bunneas; and he only knows of two Mahomedans who have embraced this faith. Mr. Kinchant in June 1869, when in the Goordaspur District, found that the following classes furnished most Kooka disciples viz., Tirkhan, Lohar, Libanee, Saynee, Bhattee, Kohars, Jhewars, and the lower orders of the Juts. Captain Menzies, District Superintendent of Umritsar in a report dated 22nd September 1866, speaks of the Tirkhans, Aroras, and Jhuthrass [*sic*] as castes amongst which the doctrines are gaining ground. Captain Parsons, then District Superintendent of Umballa also notices that converts are only obtained from the poorer classes.[9]

During the period of Namdhari Guru Hari Singh (1872-1906), the response of the agriculturist and artisan castes declined drastically (from 24 to 9.37 per cent). Excepting Ludhiana, this inference is substantiated by the statistical figures of the Namdhari leaders and activists tabulated (Table 1.4) by the police reports of 1881.[10]

The basic reason was that the British government and its allies (landed gentry and the priestly clan) crushed the Kuka movement ruthlessly. The British government put the Kuka Sikhs under surveillance. *Zaildars* and headmen of villages were instructed to punish the Kuka Sikhs for holding religious congregations, even an assembly of five Kuka Sikhs. The government forbade the Kuka Sikhs to carry axes, sticks, and other weapons. Inspite of such repression, the Namdhari guru tried to keep up the morale of his followers and around 1,900 Namdhari writers worked out a mechanism to keep up the morale of *gur-bhais* (co-religionists). They wrote *sakhis* (hagiographic narratives) of their *satgurus* and *gathas* (legends) of heroic deeds of the Kuka Singhs who had laid down their lives during the Kuka movement. The *sakhis* also ensured the Kuka Sikhs that ultimately Khalsa would rule. Nevertheless, the number of followers declined drastically. The Census of 1891 and 1901 recorded Kuka population just 10,541 and 13,788 respectively. In the wake of state repression, *sehajdhari* Namdhari Sikhs did not disclose their identity and so many of them remained unaccounted for.

In early twentieth century, the population of Kuka Sikhs remained stagnant. The Census of 1931 recorded merely 13,000 Kukas. This was most probably due to the rise of other movements in Punjab. The Akali movement (1920-5) systematically mobilized rural Sikhs.

> The bulk of the Akali volunteers came from the Sikh peasantry—especially from the Districts of Lyallpur, Sheikhupura, Amritsar, Jullundur and Hoshiarpur. Thus out of a total of 15,506 Akali volunteers in different areas

TABLE 1.4: PROMINENT KUKA SIKHS

Malwa Region			Central Punjab		
Districts	1867	1881	Districts	1867	1881
Ambala	12	9	Jalandhar	48	8
Ludhiana	5	152	Hoshiarpur	2	2
Ferozepur	37	17	Gurdaspur	7	5
Patiala, Nabha, Jind	39	N.A.	Amritsar	53	10
			Lahore	N.A.	14
Total	93	178	Total	110	39

in early 1922 (these figures are incomplete as Akali volunteers from the Sikh States and South-East and South-West of the then Panjab are not included) the number of Jat Sikhs was 10,200 or almost 66 per cent of the total. Rawalpindi division provided the highest proportion of non-agriculturist (mainly traders) Akali volunteers (1,269 out of a total of 2,907). Next to them, low caste agricultural labourers and other rural non-Jats made up 2,399 volunteers. 1,270 volunteers were Military pensioners and discharged soldiers. Returned emigrants numbered 248.[11]

The discontented Sikh peasantry swelled the rank and file of the Akali movement. Moreover, the militant Sikh leadership of the Akali movement joined the Babbar Akali movement. The Babbar leadership comprised a large number of returned emigrants, retired and demobilized soldiers, many of them Jats. Similarly, the rank and file of the Babbar Akalis too came from the Jat Sikh peasants of Hoshiarpur and Jalandhar districts,[12] thus shrinking the social base of the Namdharis in rural Punjab.

In late 1920s and early 1930s, the Great Depression generated a crisis in the agrarian economy of Punjab. It brought agricultural prices crashing down to half or less of their normal levels. This was a severe crisis for already impoverished peasants burdened with high taxes and rents.

> The Government was obdurate in refusing to scale down its own rates of taxation or in asking *zamindars* to bring down their rents. The prices of manufactured goods, too, didn't register comparable decreases. All told, the peasants were placed in a situation where they had to continue to pay taxes, rents, and debts at pre-Depression rates while their incomes continued to spiral steadily downward.[13]

It was against the backdrop of this Depression, that at the all-India level Left-wing organizations and Congress mobilized peasantry and workers. In Punjab, the Naujawan Bharat Sabha, Kirti Kisan Party, Punjab Kisan Sabha and Punjab Congress Socialist Party mobilized the peasantry and held conferences at the provincial level. Their agenda was the 'reduction of taxes and a moratorium on debts'. They also built-up anti-imperial and feudal movement and advocated a new socialist order. Much of the leadership and rank and file of those organizations came from the Jat Sikh peasantry. Consequently, this development posed a new ideological challenge to the Namdhari leadership.

Meanwhile, the radical organisations attacked the Unionist Ministry dominated by the big landlords of Western Punjab.[14] The impact of

Second World War had wide socio-economic and political ramifications for the Punjabis. The beginning of this war boosted the economic prospect of the agriculturists. Faithfully serving the British, the Unionist Party mobilized human and financial sources. The 'martial' and non-martial classes enlisted in the army in a big way. In return, the soldiers from abroad sent large sums of money to their relatives in the villages. Moreover, the 'grow more food campaign' increased the total cropped area of the province from 30 million acres in 1939-40 to nearly 35 million acres in 1942-3. Thus increasing the agriculture production which was sold on higher prices. There was relief for agriculturists, but it was temporary. The war brought considerable hardships in the shape of inflation and a growing shortage of consumer goods. As the war progressed, inflation wiped out the surplus savings of the agriculturists. The agriculturists got a further setback when the British demobilized soldiers, which closed the additional source of income for many families.[15] The unholy alliance between the British and the Unionists comprising the rural elites was exposed and the latter were defeated in the elections. The British left the Unionists in the lurch and patronized the Muslim League. The Muslim League under Jinnah over took the reins of the Muslim landed gentry and religious classes. The emergence of the Muslim League as spokesman of the Muslims had wide ramifications for the Hindus and Sikhs in Punjab.[16]

As noted in the introduction, Namdhari Guru Partap Singh was aware of the problems and challenges posed by official hostility on the one hand and antipathy of the Sikh organizations on the other. In addition, the new challenges were also thrown by the emerging nationalists and revolutionaries who had evolved their new political ideologies and strategies to fight the British raj. With his team of scholars and writers and administrative personnel, Namdhari Guru Partap Singh launched a programme to institutionalize beliefs and practices and a strict code of behaviour for its members. He enforced Namdhari *maryada* rigorously. More importantly he canonized it. To begin with, he asked his followers to wear white *kurta* (loose shirt) and *pajama* (trouser), and *gurmukhi dastar* (traditional turban of the Gursikh—a true Sikh of the Guru). The dress was to be made of handspun cloth. Each follower was to get up early in the morning and after ablutions, perform *nam-simran* (meditation on the name of God) The *nam-simran* and woollen rosary were to be integral part of daily life of a Namdhari Sikh. Throughout the day, a Namdhari

Sikh was expected to remember and recite God's name. Moreover, the Namdhari guru regularized the rituals and customs for the occasions of birth, marriage, and death. Detailed instructions were given for *akhand paths* and *havans* (ritual fire ceremonies). Moreover, Bhaini Sahib headquarters was developed into pilgrimage centre as *satguru's* abode. A sacred pond called *Ramsar* was constructed here. A an attempt was made to seek legitimacy for each Namdhari concept and institution in Sikh history and religion. One such concept was *sodh*, according to which a Namdhari Sikh used water from a well and cooked his or her food observing strict principles of purity, his own utensils of metal that no other Namdhari could touch.

Primary emphasis of the Namdhari *maryada* was simplicity, the avoidance of ostentation. Each ceremony related to birth, marriage, and death was to be performed with minimum expenditure. The marriages of the Namdhari Sikhs were to be held at Bhaini Sahib or Namdhari *dharamsalas* and there would be no feasts all the Namdharis were to be vegetarians and teetollers. They were not to eat food outside homes or in bazaars. In a sense, Partap Singh and Jagjit Singh worked out the social and religious ethics for building the community, which made a special appeal to the deprived section of Sikhs, agriculturists and artisans. The Namdharis were not, however, perceived as true Sikhs by the Singh Sabhas, the Chief Khalsa Diwan, or the SGPC. The protagonists of these organizations often ostracized the Namdhari Sikhs on account of latter's faith in *deh-dhari* guru (embodied spiritual master) and their Sanatan practices like *havan* and *yagya*.[17] The Namdhari guru and his scholars believed that the practice of *havan* and *yagya*, *jap paryog* and *varnia* (recitation of the *Adi-Granth* or meditation) could give the Namdhari Sikhs an aura of the Sanatan Sikhs. They wrote several articles and books to contextualize the Namdhari *maryada* in Sikh history.[18] Namdhari Guru Partap Singh made special efforts to organize and consolidate his following. He undertook several tours in the districts and organized *holas* (religious festivals) with the help of his followers.[19] During his tours, he met and stayed in the houses of his followers which enhanced the image of his followers among the local people. Friends and relatives rallied around and shared their personal problems. Moreover, some people were impressed by the Namdhari guru's religious discourse and became Namdharis. For his part the guru concentrated his missionary efforts in district Sialkot. According to a Namdhari belief,

Satguru Partap Singh administered *bhajan* (initiation of the mystic word) to hundreds of Sikhs of this district.[20]

The Namdhari *sants*, *mahants*, and *babas* too played a role in bringing people into their fold. They founded *deras* in their respective areas. Among the founders of *deras*, the prominent men were Sant Baba Kesar Singh Muhave Wale, Sant Harnam Singh of Nangle Dhab Malwa, Sant Kesar Singh ji Chawinda, Sant Baba Harnam Singh ji Ghardiwala, Baba Sada Singh ji Iban Kukian, Sant Jaimal Singh ji Tiba Manga, Bhai Natha Singh Sirhali, Sant Jiwan Singh Jhabar and Bhai Ball Singh (Gurdaspur). Their major contribution was that they kept alive *sufiana* (mystic) form of the Namdhari mission in the local areas in the late nineteenth and early twentieth century. Namdhari Guru Hari Singh and his successor Satguru Partap Singh often interacted with them and recognized services rendered by them to the Namdhari community in the face of state-hostility.[21]

As noted above, the left-wing organizations and Congress took up the issues of peasants and workers in the wake of World Economic Depression and anti-peasantry policies of the Unionist Government Punjab. Both had resolved to mobilize the peasants and workers and make them a part of freedom struggle in Punjab. Moreover, the left-wing organizations advocated socialism. Responding to this concept, Namdhari Guru Partap Singh thought of evolving that social order which was free of social discrimination and based on egalitarian principles. Articulating this type of social order, *Satjug* published several editorials and articles by political activists. One such editorial note was 'Hindustani Socialism' in which Balwant Singh argued that the brand of socialism which was being propagated in the West as an alternative to capitalism was not suited to the Indian social, religious and cultural milieu. The popular brand of socialism had resulted in confrontation and disorder, he argued that this socialism did not give space to the Indian *dharma* and spiritual contentment. The editor gave a brief sketch of the socialism advocated by Satguru Ram Singh:

> Reminding Satguru's message, he told the Namdharis to observe ethics, earn livelihood by honest means and share earnings with the needy people. He further told them to offer surplus earnings to Satguru who was true custodian of their resources or they should spend their earnings for the charity purposes. The editor believed that property and income actually belonged to true lord.

> Editor took pride in telling his fellow-religionists that Satguru Chiniwala blessed Namdharis with the spirit of brotherhood, contentment and love. These virtues were not found elsewhere. The Namdharis did not indulge in political praxis. On the other hand, they followed their Satguru's orders and lived according to His will and rendered services to the needy people. In response, Satguru took care of their requirements and problems. Namdharis lived in that state of spiritual socialism where the mundane affairs did not matter under Satguru's shelter, they were free from anxiety and troubles.
>
> Such brand of socialism could be prosperous only in the Indian soil and could be helpful in promoting the peace in the world. The world would continue to remain in the state of utter dejection and confusion till it followed spiritual socialism advocated by the Namdhari spiritual lord.[22]

In fact, the editor was trying to advocate utopian socialism as an alternative to the scientific socialism of Marx and Engels. The utopian socialism sought salvation of the Kirtis-Kisans from the dehumanizing and exploitative effects of agrarian policies of the Unionist government. The editor's advocacy of utopian socialism was based on moral and ethical values.[23] The editor argued that Marxian socialism did not go with Namdhari spiritual teachings since Namdhari Guru Partap Singh and his confidants had become protagonists of the non-violence philosophy.

Namdhari Guru Partap Singh was aware about the hard fact that agrarian legislation, particularly Land Alienation Act of 1900, was not intended to ameliorate the problems of peasantry. It was intended to perpetuate a social division between the agriculturist and non-agriculturist castes. The implementation of this Act in 1901 had far-reaching ramifications. The Act accentuated caste-communities as it legalized the occupational castes. Whether a person was an agriculturist was now to be decided not by his livelihood but by his caste. The people of these castes who had recently adopted agriculture or had been carrying on this profession along with their traditional occupations began to organize and strengthen their caste-associations when they were declared non-agriculturists by this Act. In this context, the Aroras, Bedis and Ramgarhias held their respective conferences. It was important for those castes which had been traditionally engaged in agriculture or whose elites possessed sizeable landholdings, to get themselves included in the list of agriculturists.[24] The Namdhari guru was absolutely clear that the amendments made by the Unionist govenment, Punjab under Sir Fazl-e-Hussain in the late 1920s had a far-reaching impact in terms of depriving non-agriculturist castes of their right to invest their surplus capital in land. He was also conscious of the fact that the artisans as well as business communities too owned land and were agriculturists. This consciousness is reflected in the files of *Satjug*. The periodical consistently protested against the legalized discrimination by the allies of the colonial rule. The aim of this protest was to remove social discrimination. The Ramgarhias, the elite among lohars and tarkhans, and the more fortunate among the artisans were struggling against the Alienation Act. The Ramgarhias, who had possessed sizeable landholdings since the founding of Sikh rule, felt their openings for better occupations had been blocked. They also found that the Act blocked their entry into electoral politics, as the franchise was based on the payment of revenue and income tax. The Ramgarhia Sabhas and Conferences passed resolutions and petitions, submitted the same to the government asking the latter to rectify the wrongs done by the Act. Moreover, they established their caste associations like Sewak Sabha Amritsar (1904) and Vishvakarma Vansha Sudhar Sabha (1908). They also opened their educational institutions. For espousing the concerns of the Ramgarhia *biradari* (caste community) they started a monthly periodical *The Ramgarhia Patrika* (1902) and after two years *Sewak Sangh Patrika*. In 1922-3, they started *Ramgarhia Gazette* in Shimla. These associations and institutions asserted the distinct identity of the Ramgarhias. Subsequently, they began to identify themselves with those *sants* and *babas* who belonged to their own *biradari* and sought religious/ spiritual quest. Since the Namdhari sect was led by 'Ramgarhia' Guru Partap Singh they began to respond to his sect which was close to the orthodox rules of Sikhism.[25] It was in the 1930s that Namdhari Guru Partap Singh introduced several religious practices in which the Namdharis participated collectively. These were *havan*, *varnia* and *jap parjog*. The structure of each ritual was meant for purification of the Namdhari Sikhs and inculcating a spirit in them as if they were a chosen people. In 1937, *Satjug* told the Namdhari Sikhs that they should believe that Satguru Ram Singh was a spiritual lord, sent for their liberation from cycles of births and deaths, liberation from the sorrows and pains of the Kalyuga and from slavery. The collective participation of the Namdhari Sikhs removed a feeling of social inequality and strengthened brotherhood among them.[26] Bhaini was declared the *gurudham* (guru's abode), an abode of peace and heaven on earth.

The Namdhari mission appealed to the deprived section of the agriculturist class when it stated that the *zamindar sahukars* (landed-proprietor bankers) took full advantage of the Alienation Act and appropriated the land of the agriculturists. In the early twentieth century, the number of *zamindar sahukars* multiplied into thousands and they started appropriating the role of *bania-sahukars* (traditional bankers) in the villages. The *Satjug* posed a serious question:

> Doesn't Sir Sikander Hayat [the then Punjab Premier] know that, taking advantage of this Act, several zamindars have become *maliks* (owners) of the villages while others have been reduced to beggars? Aren't the classes of zamindars producing those moneylenders who have appropriated the lands of the peasants on a large scale? Since the introduction of this Act, the condition of the peasants have worsened because these moneylenders pilfering thousands of rupees from the earnings of workers whose average monthly wages are below Rs. 2. The moneylenders have unlimited sources of income.[27]

While *Satjug* was clear that the Land Alienation Act was a slur on the face of Punjab, its annulment was a remote possibility unless the rule of big zamindars were supplanted by the 'proletariat' class. The paper stated:

> It is paradox that the victims of this act were pinning their hopes for its annulment on those people who themselves are beneficiaries of this act. For these people, this act was God-send opportunity. The only alternative for its annulment is that the workers should understand the nefarious designs of the capitalist class and end its rule. In six provincial states, the rule of such people has been finished (it refers to the victory of Congress in the six Provincial Assembly elections). The Punjab should follow their example if it wishes to end its agony.[28]

There were several prominent Namdhari writers and activists who were victims of the agrarian depression. They came in contact with the *kirti-kisan* (workers and peasants) leadership and took part in peasant agitations. One of them was Gurbakash Singh popularly known as Goda Singh Jat (1900-70). He was resident of village Jia-Bagga near Kh[illegible]dpur, district Lahore. When he was a school-teacher, he came in the contact with liberal nationalists like Kedar Nath Sehgal, Nidhan Singh Alam, and young Bhagat Singh who espoused the cause of the peasantry. He took part in the conferences of the Zamindara League and composed verses in Punjabi, articulating the hardships of the *kirti-kisans*. He wrote plays which were staged first by the Punjab Conference Bhangali, district Lahore and then the

Socialist Punjab Conference, Gujranwala, All India Kisan Conference Lyallpur, Punjab Kisan Conference Jia Bagga and Akali and Congress Conferences. He was one of those Namdhari activists who launched tirades against the exploitation of the *kirti-kisans,* social discrimination, religious fanaticism, communalism, and the obscurantism of *sants* and *babas.*[29]

Pritam Singh Kavi (1910–2002) was one of the Namdhari Sikhs who had imbibed socialist ideology and was a member of the Communist Party of India. With dedication he worked for the party from 1945 to 1947 and from 1966 to 1977. He was the son of Suba Phulla Singh and Dial Kaur, a peasant couple of village Dafferke, Lahore. Under the impact of Bolshevik ideology, he discovered anti-imperialist overtones in the Namdhari mission and he evolved by Satgurus Ram Singh and Partap Singh. With his like-minded colleagues, Pritam Singh Kavi formed Namdhari Progressive Party which worked for a few months. In spite of ideological contradictions Namdhari Guru Jagjit Singh was generous with financial support to Pritam Singh's family. After the partition of Punjab in 1947 his family lived in Malout tahsil (district Ferozepur) for some time and then settled in New Delhi. For nine years, he edited the weekly *Satjug* from Sri Jiwan Nagar, Sirsa (Haryana).[30]

Pritam Singh informs us that 'Satguru' Partap Singh kept *dharam-karam* (religious ethics and virtues) free of futile ritualism so that his followers could get enough time for their mundane affairs. In the life struggle, an hour's meditation on the Name of God was sufficient for the common Namdhari Sikhs. Moreover, Pritam Singh Kavi's writings also inform us that he appreciated links between Namdhari gurus and Comrades like Harkishan Singh Surjit, Avtar Singh Malhotra, and Phuman Singh who had been working among the peasantry of district Sirsa. Namdhari Guru Partap Singh allowed the comrades to carry on their political campaign among the Namdharis of this district. Namdhari Guru's financial support for Kisan Conferences and for candidates of the Communist Party in the elections of the Punjab Assembly dismayed the Congress leaders. The Namdhari-Communist rapport was continued by Namdhari Guru Jagjit Singh. As a result of this mutual interaction, the focus of the Namdhari mission remained on the problems of the peasants and artisans.[31] The legacy of the duality of being Communist and Namdhari Sikh is still seen in Suwaran Singh Virk's personality. He is both Namdhari and member of the Communist Party of India. For him the Namdhari mission is essentially concerned about the uplift of the struggling peasants and artisans, and social justice of the common man and he seeks inspiration from Namdhari Guru Jagjit Singh.

Pritam Singh Panchi (1922-2004) was another Namdhari activist-cum-writer who espoused the problems and aspirations of peasants and artisans. He participated in the peasants' agitations for irrigational facilities in Doaba region and Kalsia state in 1939. He was arrested and put into the Multan Jail for six months. He edited *Satjug* from 1944 to 46 and *Prem-Sandesh*, a progressive weekly of Lahore, in 1947. For some time, he assisted Comrades Sohan Singh Josh and Arjan Singh Gadgaj in editing and publishing *Jang-i-Azadi*, a mouthpiece of the Communist Party of India. He also worked for *Nawan Zamana* and *Ajit*, daily newspapers of Jalandhar. He himself published a monthly, *Safar*, for some time. He translated and edited several books. He wrote *Zamin-ka-Tukda* in 1954-5. At the end of his life, he thought of writing a novel on the Kuka movement.[32]

Namdhari Guru Partap Singh was conscious of the implications of direct confrontration with the colonial rulers. He was aware of the fact that the repression let loose by the alien rulers and their allies decreased the numerical strength of his followers considerably. He came to think that if he wanted to launch a programme of consolidation, moderate politics was the only alternative. He successfully tested his *satyagrahi* strategy in checking the opening of slaughter house at Lahore. He revived the concepts of *swadeshi* and non-cooperation which helped him to build up rapport with the Congress when the latter launched the Non-Violence Non-Cooperation movement in 1920. The Congress too wanted allies in Punjab to successfully launch movement against the British raj. As noted above, the Namdhari Sikhs under the leadership of Maharaj Nihal Singh participated in the Congress session at Lahore and in the Civil Disobedience movement. In the 1930s, Congress leaders would visit Bhaini Sahib headquarters. Simultaneously, the Namdhari Guru and his followers welcomed Indian revolutionaries at Bhaini Sahib. So the Namdhari Sikhs were recognized as patriots and nationalists. The Namdhari Sikhs supported the Congress in electoral politics.

Namdhari Guru Partap Singh was an exceptional religious leader of the twentieth century. He warned his followers, about the impending danger of a partition of Punjab. He made best possible efforts to listen and share the grief of thousands of his followers. He also made all possible efforts to rehabilitate refugees. Major Namdhari concentrations in Mandi town of Himachal Pradesh and founding of Jiwan Nagar in Sirsa are the best examples of rehabilitation. Beside, he resolved the personal problems of a substantial number of his followers and gave them financial help. His son and successor Satguru Jagjit Singh carried on the work which went a long way in the process of consolidation of the community. For instance, he rehabilitated more than 400 migrant Namdhari agriculturists of West Punjab in Jiwan Nagar and elsewhere. The rehabilitated families and subsequently their next generation were morally bound to follow Namdhari beliefs and practices. Several of them motivated their kith and kin to do the same. However, the second generation bear a lesser degree of gratitude to the Namdhari faith.

LUKEWARM ATTITUDE OF MARGINAL CASTES

Throughout the period of hundred fifty years, artisan groups such as the Suniaras, Parjapats, Mehras, and Nais did not respond to the Namdhari mission in a substantial way. Their lack of enthusiasm requires some explanation. They did not enjoy a good social status in the social hierarchy of the Punjab castes and were inferior to lohars and tarkhans. Similarly, their wages were lower than the wages of lohars and tarkhans. Moreover, like Ramgarhias they could not benefit from the new job avenues provided by the colonial rule because they were skilled labourers. Being a part of the deprived section of the Punjabi society, they too aspired for the elevation of their social status.

However, their marginal response to the puritan Namdhari sect can tentatively be explained in the following ways. First and foremost is that they were numerically insignificant. If the population of the Sikh lohars and tarkhans was from 5 to 7 per cent under colonial rule, the population of Sikh Suniars, Parjapats, Mehras, and Nais was less than 2 per cent of the Sikh population respectively. Their combined population was about 5 per cent of the total Sikh population.[33] Secondly, like Namdhari Jats and Ramgarhias, the Namdhari Sunars, Parjapats, Mehras, and Nais did not have peers either in their own *biradaris* or in the Namdhari hierarchy who could inspire them to join the Namdhari sect to elevate their social status. Right from the inception of the Namdhari movement, several *subas*, *pardhans*, and *jathedars* belonged to Jat and Ramgarhia castes. Ramgarhias could perceive that their spiritual master belonged to their own caste therefore, they could have more 'say' in the community affairs. The Namdhari Suniars, Parjapats, Mehras, and Nais, however, had no such social affinity.[34] Lastly, the Namdhari Jats and Ramgarhias have made some special efforts to mobilize the people of their own *biradaris* to bring them under the Namdhari fold. For instance, the Namdhari parents in some circumstances marry their sons and daughters in the non-Namdhari families. These parents consistently persuade their in-laws to come into the Namdhari fold. We have data of some such families. Similarly, the Namdhari Jats and Ramgarhias interact with the people of their own *biradaris* and try to persuade them to become Namdharis. Several Namdhari Sikhs attributed their conversion to their mothers. In fact, the stature of the in-laws family also exercised a decisive influence on their conversion. Sant Kuldeep Singh of New Santoshpura (Sarabha Nagar), Jalandhar, admitted that he became Namdhari under the influence of his in-laws.[35] On the other hand, there were several families who accepted daughters of Akali families in marriage. Gradually these daughters-in-law adapted themselves to the Namdhari *maryada* while their parents remained Akalis.[36] The Namdhari Suniaras, Parjapats, Mehras and Nais are yet to gain that position in the Namdhari hierarchy. Nevertheless, the Namdhari community can take pride in the diverse social background of its following.

DIMINISHING INFLUENCE

The majority of the Namdhari shopkeepers, *sahukars* and traders of late nineteenth and early twentieth centuries came from the Khatri and Arora castes. Official reports of late nineteenth century do not state the caste background of the Namdhari shopkeepers, *sahukars* and traders but in traditional Punjabi society the majority of them belonged to Khatri and Arora castes. Shopkeepers, *sahukars*, and traders in the villages of the West Punjab were Aroras. Their numerical strength among Namdharis can be attributed to the fact that Guru Balak Singh, the founder of the Namdhari movement, was himself an Arora. Under his spiritual leadership, the first headquarters was at Hazro in Peshawar district where traders happened to be largely the Aroras. In a recent PhD thesis on the Namdharis of Mandi town, it is stated that the Khatri Namdharis have been in the majority.[37] This may be true in cases of Namdhari Sikhs in the towns/cities of Himachal Pradesh, Haryana and Delhi. Concentrations of the

Namdhari business and artisan classes in urban centres of the north, however, is largely due to immigration and resettlement post-1947. My random survey shows that the Namdhari Khatri families are exceptional cases. Most probably their marginal number was due to the emergence of peer-groups of the Khatri and Arora Sikhs and establishing their own *dera* under Sant Baba Harnam Singh of Kilewale. There is a probability that a large chunk of Khatris and Aroras in the post-Independence period shifted their loyalty to Sant Baba Harnam Singh. However, there are twenty-nine families which form 2 per cent of the total Namdhari families. The Namdhari Arora families whom we could interview live in the following urban centres: 9 Amritsar; 6 Chandigarh and Mohali; 4 Kapurthala, 2 Ferozepur; 1 each in Rupnagar, Tarn Taran, Moga and Muktsar (Table 1.2).

From the beginning of the Namdhari movement, the response of the low castes known as Chamars and Chuhras was very poor. In the late nineteenth century, when police officials compiled reports about the castes and occupations and religio-political affiliations of the notable Kukas working according to the instructions of Namdhari Guru Ram Singh and his successor Guru Hari Singh, we come across some references to the Chamars and Mazhabis as followers of these gurus. In 1866, the District Superintendent of Police, Ambala, noted that in the villages around, the majority of the people belonged to lower castes. Among these castes were the Ramdasias. It implied that some of the Ramdasias might have become followers of the Kuka sect.[38] Similar references about Kukas of menial castes in other districts of the British Punjab are mentioned in police reports. Some of them were described as fanatics. The Deputy Inspectors of Police at Dehlon and Khanna in district Ludhiana noted that several Mazhabi Kukas were involved in the demolition of Muslim graveyards and *pirkhanas* (Muslim shrines): Mazhabi Kukas Megh Singh, Sher Singh, Jota Singh and Gulaba held a midnight meeting in the house of Megh Singh, resident of Punadi village in Khanna Police Station and resolved to demolish the graveyard of a *pirkhana*. Gulaba was one of the convicted Kukas in this case.[39] In 1872, R.H. Wall Major, District Superintendent of Police, Ferozepur, noted the incidents of Suba Jawahar Singh. This police official informs us that Jawahar Singh himself belonged to Mullah (Muhial or Moyal – a Brahman caste). He made 400 converts who were zamindars, chamars, carpenters, Mazhabis, Dhobis (washer men) and Musalmans.[40] It seems that Namdhari Chamars, Ramdasias and Mazhabis actively participated in the Kuka movement but their number was marginal. Moreover, none of them was appointed *suba, naib-suba, jathedar* or *granthi* during this movement. Among them was Mastan Singh, who was sweeper at the Dera Bhaini Sahib, but neither official reports nor the Namdhari literature mentions Namdhari Chamars or Mazhabis in the context of socio-religious discourses. In fact, throughout the previous century the Namdhari Sikhs of low castes remained unnoticed. During this survey, I came across Namdhari Mazhabi and Ramdasia families in the following cities/towns: 6 in Gurdaspur, 7 in Fatehgarh Sahib, 2 Mazhabi families at Bhaini Sahib Headquarters, 2 in Moga, 2 in Tarn Taran and one each in Sangrur, Amritsar and Chandigarh. As Table 1.3 shows, the majority of these families became Namdharis during the period of Namdhari Guru Ram Singh and Namdhari Guru Partap Singh. Only one or two families became Namdharis after 1975.

Mazhabis and Ramdasias, before taking *naam* (sacred word), kept unshorn hair and beards and tied turbans like other Sikhs. Going by the meaning of the word Mazhabi, some of the Chuhras took *khande-di-pahul* (Khalsa initiation) and became Singhs to elevate their social status. Similarly, those Chamars who took this *pahul* (baptism) were known as Ramdasias. Both of them left the occupations that made them *achut* (untouchables). By the time the Kuka movement came into being, the Mazhabis and Ramdasia Sikhs had been recognized as part of the Sikh community.[41] It was for this reason that the Namdhari Mazhabis and Ramdasias of Gurdaspur and Fatehgarh Sahib districts recorded that their parents worked as labourers and Julahas. They stated that their grandparents came in contact with the Namdhari *sants* and *gurus* and became Namdharis. The Namdhari Ravidasias (originally followers of Guru Ravi Das) of Fatehgarh Sahib still express their gratitude to Namdhari Guru Partap Singh, who allotted 5 to 10 acres of land to each of their families in Bir Bhamarsi and put them on a par with other Namdhari agriculturists who also received land from this Guru.

This apart, Chamars, Mazhabis, and Ramdasias did not show any keenness to become Namdharis. Two fundamental reasons can be attributed for this. First and foremost is that the Namdhari gurus and their confidants were not particularly egalitarian and Ramdasias and Mazhabis did not believe they were integral to the Namdhari community. Several of them have recorded their resentment in terms of social and religious discrimination shown to them in the *sangat*.

They feel that they are outcastes within the Namdhari community. On the other hand, the Mazhabi Singhs, Rangreta Singhs and Rangreta Dal have had been given due respect and honour by the Sikh gurus and Singhs.[42] Similarly, the Radha Soami sect also welcomed the entry of the low caste people and tried to raise their social status. Above all, the *Ad-Dharm* movement in the early twentieth century tried to assert this distinct identity and due share in the social order. The movement also espoused their political rights.[43]

The Namdhari *maryada*, when it assumed Sanatanist values and ethics over a period of 150 years, discouraged the entry of the low castes. Parallel to the Sanatanist Namdhari social order, these Sikhs had options either to join Dalit organizations or become Mazhabi Singhs and assert their respective identities. They got adequate legitimacy and appreciation in electoral politics.

Under the aegis of Namdhari Guru Jagjit Singh, the Namdhari community has made progress in terms of building of an administrative structure, modern means of transportation and communication, trained teams of propaganda, and a flow of finances and means. Yet the paradox is a stagnation in the expansion of the community. As hinted above, an often given Namdhari explanation is that the Namdhari *maryada* is too rigid to be observed by a common man in his day-to-day life. But all religious communities face the problem of compatibility between the orthodox *maryada* and modern life-style. There is another reason for this stagnation. Since about 1975 the network of Namdhari propaganda has been urban-centric. The Namdhari missionary tours cover towns and cities in India and in other countries. But rural Punjab has been left open to other *sants* and *babas*.

Several other factors too discourage the Sikh masses to become Namdharis: demographic change, coalition politics, a phenomenal rise of Sikh *sants* and *babas*, and the emergence of the Khalistani militant movement. To begin in 1947, the Namdhari concentration in some of the villages and towns of the East Punjab helped to form socio-religious organizations and establish *dharamsalas* for collective activities. The continuous process of socio-religious intercourse among the Namdhari Sikhs at the local level strengthened their brotherhood. They could also interact with their counterparts, the Sikhs and Hindus and share beliefs and practices. Nevertheless, advantages of their concentration were marginalized by the Sikhs of the mainstream. The Partition of

Punjab 1947 made the Sikhs a majority community in the districts of Amritsar, Jalandhar, Gurdaspur, Ferozepur. The formation of the Punjabi-speaking province in 1966 transformed the Sikh minority into a majority. The rural area was dominated by the Jat Sikh agriculturists whereas Hindus were predominant in the urban centres. The latter were engaged in banking, shopkeeping, trade and business. The Shiromani Akali Dal could now think of forming an independent government. Its leadership, dominated by the rural elites, made an alliance with urban Hindu elites. Their combine supplanted Congress domination in electoral politics and formed governments alternatively. Consequently, the Namdhari Sikhs, traditional supporters of the Congress party, lost their weightage in electoral coalition politics. Above all, the emergence of the Khalistan movement after 1975 put the Namdhari Sikhs on their defence. The Khalistan militants seriously questioned the Namdhari concept of embodied guru. Although the Namdhari Sikhs stood fast to their beliefs and practices, yet the Khalistan movement did not allow Sikh sects to grow. They were further marginalized in communal politics.

In the post-Khalistan movement period, the campaign against the concept of embodied guru took serious overtones. Several Sikh publications, and leaders and activists, associated with the Shiromani Gurdwara Parbhandak Committee; radical Sikh organizations have consistently opposed the concept of embodied guru. The most vocal have been weekly periodicals like *Sikh Spokesman* and now *Rozana Spokesman*, Chandigarh; *Khalsa Fatehnama*, Amritsar; *Khalsa Khandedhar*, Amritsar. Scholars like Giani Partap Singh, Giani Narian Singh and Bhai Sukhwinder Singh Sabhra have been aggressively condemning Namdhari belief in the living guru. They have been putting pressure on the SGPC to take effective steps to stop the worship of a living guru. They have been arguing that the practice of embodied guru is contrary to the *gurmat*.[44] Besides, they have accentuated as well as popularized the Sikh tradition of *guru manyo granth*. Apart from the network of the SGPC, there is powerful class of *sants* and *babas* who are the protagonists of the concepts of the *Guru Granth* and Khalsa traditions.

Namdhari respondents in several districts mentioned to us the role of *sants*, *mahants*, and *babas* in bringing hundreds of Sikh families into the fold of the Namdhari *maryada*. They could attract a large number of agriculturist and artisan followers because they themselves practised simplicity and some degree of asceticism. They shared the social concerns of the local people irrespective of religion. In this context, some of the respondents of Gurdaspur and Jalandhar stated the names of *sants* Jawala Singh, Kartar Singh and Mohan Singh. At one stage or another, they were known for their close rapport with Namdhari Gurus Partap Singh and Jagjit Singh. For instance, several Namdhari families of Goraya attributed their conversion to Sant Kartar Singh who was grandfather of Manjit Singh, President of Goraya Sangat.[45] However, since the founding of their respective *deras*, they have tended to develop *maryadas* which deviate from the Namdhari *maryada* of Bhaini Sahib. The founding of Gurdwara Sahib at Dera Baba Nanak Road Bhagowal, Batala Gurdaspur, in the name of Sant Baba Mohan Singh by his devotees indicates such a partial deviation. Sant Baba was born in village Bhagowal in the late nineteenth century and died in December 1974. During his life-time he meditated on the name of God and attained spiritual elevation to *braham giani*—a holy man in communion with God. He performed miracles. His devotees believe he was messenger of God. Namdhari Guru Partap Singh himself appreciated Sant Mohan Singh's spiritual attainments and ecstasy. Sant Mohan Singh administered *nam* (holy word) to a large number of Sikh families in Dera Baba Nanak and Batala, district Gurdaspur. However, his devotees arrange *akhand paths* and hold an annual fair at Gurdwara Sant Mohan Singh. Some of his devotees arrange *akhand paths* in his name at their respective places.[46]

Persistent deviation resulted in the founding of independent *deras* like Bhagowal and Neeldhari Sant Khalsa of Naushera Majha Singh Gurdaspur. Some of these *deras* are becoming popular and their followers are increasing rapidly.[47] This is more true in case of Neeldhari Sant Khalsa. The headquarters of the Neeldhari Sant Khalsa of Punjab is located in Naushehra Majha Singh, a small town on Amritsar-Pathankot Road. This headquarters is known as Dera Sant Harnam Singh. For their particular dress code, the followers of this *dera* are known Neeldhari Sikhs. The dress is called *neela-bana* (blue dress) which comprises white *kurta-pajama*, blue scarf known as *chakuta* and blue *kamarkassa* (guarding lion with blue scarf). The devotees also keep on their person a *saila* (small-stick), *gadva* (iron vessel), and rosary. The Neeldhari Sikhs claim that they form a *teesra panth* (community). *Teesra panth* comes from a couplet in the *Ughardanti*—a composition of the *Dasam Granth* (Granth of Tenth Master, Guru Gobind Singh). In the post-colonial period, a substantial number of

Namdhari Sikhs left their parent-body and became followers of this schism. Many of these followers comprise Khatri/Arora Sikhs who belonged to urban centres of Gurdaspur, Naushehra Majha Singh, Batala, Jalandhar, and Amritsar.

The emergence of dissenting Namdhari *sants* further eroded traditional Namdhari *maryada* and marginalized the Namdhari followers. Kukian-da-dera of Sasrali, Ludhiana indicates this development. There are fifteen Namdhari Rajputs in Sasrali. Only two Rajput belongs to Boothgarh and Mangali villages of Ludhiana district. Eleven out of seventeen became Namdhari Sikhs during Satguru Partap Singh's time; four families during Satguru Jagjit Singh and two families during Satguru Ram Singh's time. The Namdhari Sikhs have built a *dharamsala* at Sasrali which is under the supervision of Sant Satnam Singh. He is 28 years old and son of Karam Singh. The *dharamsala* comprises five rooms, two for performing the ritual of *varnia* and an adjoining room for the accommodation of Sant Satnam Singh and his *sevaks* (attendants). Another room is a congregational hall. This *dharamsala* is called Kukian-da-dera and known for drug de-addiction. Satnam Singh claimed that the drug addicts of different ages come from afar and he and associates cure them with the help of meditation alone. Sant further told us that the de-addiction is effected free of cost. He also disclosed that this *dera* did not accept any financial aid from Satguru Partap Singh or Satguru Jagjit Singh. The *dera* is thriving on the offerings of its followers. The *dera* is evolving its own *maryada*: like Namdhari *maryada* the *Adi-Granth* or *Granth Sahib* is kept for recitation only; *varnia* and *jap-paryog* are also performed; *langar* (community meal) is also arranged. Most of *dera's* following is youth. No woman is allowed to stay a night in the *dera*. Morality is strictly maintained.

The *dera* is an autonomous organization in terms of its management of religious activities and finances. The offerings and donation of the followers are utilized by Sant Satnam Singh and his aides. No share of income is forwarded to the Bhaini Sahib headquarters. Although Sant Satnam Singh shows reverence to Satguru Jagjit Singh and attribute the *dera's* success to Satguru's blessings, he is critical of the activities of Namdhari administrative personnel of Bhaini Sahib headquarters.

Sant Satnam Singh and aides took pride in telling us that they are better Namdhari Sikhs and are spreading Namdhari mission. He claims that popularity of the *dera* is increasing day by day due to its humanitarian activities. However, we did not find increasing enrolment here much less of people belonging to other occupational castes.

The phenomenal rise of Sikh *deras* since 1980 has attracted thousands of Sikh agriculturists, artisans and business communities. The *sants* and *babas* of these *deras* have adapted Sikhism and its traditions to current needs. They have also appropriated Sikh history for legitimizing the *maryada* of their respective *deras*. The Nanaksar Sampardai can be cited as a case in this context. This sampardai was founded by Baba Nand Singh (1872-1943). During his lifetime, he himself identified secluded places for meditation which eventually emerged as the preaching centres. It was Sant Baba Nand Singh's successor, Sant Baba Ishar Singh, who had constructed gurdwara complexes popularly known as Nanaksar Thaaths. The prominent *thaaths* are located in the districts of Moga, Faridkot, Sangrur, and Gurdaspur. According to the *sant babas* of these *thaaths*, the number of their followers runs into lakhs. It is estimated that the majority of these followers are Jat Sikh agriculturists.

In summing up, we can say that the Namdhari Sikhs come from sixteen occupational castes. In terms of numerical strength, they constitute the following social order: Jats 50.16 per cent, Ramgarhias 37 per cent, Sainis 3 per cent, Parjapats 2 per cent, Aroras/Khatris 2 per cent, Rajputs 1.42 per cent, Mehras 1.10 per cent, Mazhabis 0.97 per cent, Chhembas 0.71 per cent, Suniaras 0.64 per cent, Ramdasias 0.45 per cent, Kambojs 0.38 per cent, Brahmins 0.32 per cent, Nais 0.25 per cent, Julahas 0.06 and Banias 0.06 per cent respectively. It is obvious that the Namdhari Jats and Ramgarhias constitute 87 per cent per cent of the total Namdhari following. The Namdhari Sikhs of the rest of the castes are insignificant in terms of their numerical strength. However, the Namdhari Sikhs of above-mentioned occupational castes belong to both rural and urban areas of 18 districts of Punjab. The Namdhari artisans are in a majority in urban areas whereas the agriculturists dominate the rural areas. Moreover, the major concentrations of these families are found in Amritsar, Jalandhar, Ludhiana, and Batala (Gurdaspur). Over the period of hundred fifty years, the population of each Namdhari caste varied from time to time. For instance, the proportion of Namdhari Jats has declined (from 32 to 14 per cent) whereas the proportion the Namdhari Ramgarhias has doubled, i.e. 12 to 22 per cent during this period. However, there is an overall decline in the Namdhari population (from 24 to 18 per cent). A substantial number of traditional Namdhari families are disintegrating. Their members, particularly the youth, are not interested in observing The Namdhari *maryada*. Several of them either are becoming *amritdharis* (taking initiation of *khande-di-pahul*) or joining other sects like Radha Soami.

Nevertheless, in the wake of rapid social and demographic changes, Namdhari Guru Partap Singh revived religious rituals which prepared followers of diverse social background for social life by imposing self-discipline and a certain measure of asceticism. The Namdhari religious ceremony brought members together and reaffirmed their common bonds and solidarity. The Namdhari guru evolved religious observances that revitalized the social heritage and helped transmit its enduring values to future generations. Finally, since the following was economically deprived and alienated from contemporary society, the Namdhari gurus sermonized in a manner which helped to dissipate feelings of frustration and loss of faith. They also succeeded in offering the believers' sense of well-being and righteousness of their moral world. By countering the sense of loss, the Namdhari gurus reestablished the balance of private and public confidence. However, phenomenal rise of the *sants* and *babas* (including the former Namdhari *sants*) who promised to liberate Sikhs from their temporal frustration and lured them to the spiritual world. A substantial number of the Sikhs of all shades have shifted their loyalties to these holy persons in the last quarter of the twentieth century. As a result, the social base of the Namdhari community has considerably shrunk. Thus a substantial number of the Namdhari families have given up the orthodox Namdhari *maryada* and its dress-code. These families have shifted their religious affiliations to other sects or merged into the mainstream of the Sikhs.

NOTES

1. Andre Beteille, 'Race, Caste, and Ethnic Identity', 2006, p. 129.
2. For a review of literature on social movements, see, Ghanshyam Shah, *Social Movements in India*, 2005; Mark Juergensmeyer, *Religion as Social Vision*, 1982; Kenneth W. Jones, *Arya Dharm Hindu Consciousness in 19th-Century Punjab*, 1976; W.H. McLeod, *The Evolution of the Sikh Community*, 1976; Gurdarshan Singh Dhillon, *Character and Impact of the Singh Sabha Movement*, 1973; Richard G. Fox, *Lions of the Punjab: Culture in the Making*, 1985; Mohinder Singh, *The Akali Movement*, 1997.

3. In the late nineteenth century, British ethnographers, anthropologists, and Census officials perceived the people of Punjab in terms of 'descent' and hereditary 'calling'.
4. We have worked out the caste-wise numerical status of Namdhari Sikhs of these districts in Table 1.2.
5. M Haralambos and Robin Hearld, *Sociology: Themes and Perspective*, 2007, p. 470.
6. Ghanshyam Shah, 2005, pp. 28-9.
7. For detail, see, Kuldip Singh, *The Namdhari Movement: Continuity and Change 1857-1959*, 2000, pp. 82-3.
8. Ibid.
9. Jaswinder Singh (comp.), *Kuka Documents*, 1985, p. 30.
10. For detail, see Nahar Singh, *Gooroo Ram Singh and Kuka Sikhs Documents, 1863-1871*, vol. 1, 1965, pp. 38-46.
11. Mohinder Singh, *The Akali Movement*, 1997, p. 97.
12. Ibid., pp. 113-15.
13. Bipan Chandra, *India's Struggle for Independence*, 1989, p. 343.
14. Op. cit., p. 344.
15. For details, Ian Talbot, *Punjab and the Raj 1849-1947*, 1988, pp. 143-4.
16. Ibid., pp. 185-200.
17. In the 1930s, a controversy between editors of the *Khalsa Samachar* and of the *Satjug* erupted on this issue. Joginder Singh, *A Short History of the Namdhari Sikhs*, 2010, pp. 66-93.
18. Joginder Singh, *Namdhari Guru Ram Singh: A Biography*, 2010.
19. *Namdhari Hola Mohala, Satguru Ram Singh Ji* (booklet), 1985; from the beginning of Namdhari mission, the Namdhari gurus organized *Holas* (religious festival) in different places.
20. Namdhari Sikhs believe that Satguru Partap Singh administered *bhajan* to 80,000 Sikhs. We do not have any evidence to corroborate this number.
21. For details, see Suwaran Singh Virk, *Namdhari Mat Nu Harmanpiara Banaon Vich Santan, Mahantan and Babian da Yogdan (p)*, Paper presented to Seminar, Namdhari Lehar, Namdhari Guru Ram Singh Chair, Guru Nanak Dev University, 17 September 2008.
22. ਸਤਿਗੁਰਾ ਦੀ ਆਗਿਆ ਹੈ ਕਿ ਆਪਣੇ ਅਹਾਰ ਵਿਹਾਰ ਅਚਾਰ ਨੂੰ ਸ਼ੁਧ ਰਖੋ। ਦਸਾਂ ਨੁਵਾਂ ਦੀ ਧਰਮ ਅਨੁਸਾਰ ਕਿਰਤ ਕਰੋ। ਅਤੇ ਉਸਨੂੰ ਵੰਡਕੇ ਛਕੋ। ਜੇ ਫੇਰ ਭੀ ਸੰਪੱਤੀ ਜਮਾਂ ਹੋ ਜਾਵੇ ਤਾਂ ਉਸਨੂੰ ਸਤਿਗੁਰੂ ਦੀ ਦਾਤ ਅਰ ਇਮਾਨਤ ਸਮਝਕੇ ਉਸਦੀ ਹਿਫਾਜ਼ਤ ਕਰੋ। ਧਰਮ ਯਾ ਪਰ ਉਪਕਾਰ ਵਾਸਤੇ ਉਸਦੀ ਲੋੜ ਪਵੇ ਤਾਂ ਇਸ ਪ੍ਰਸੰਨਤਾ ਨਾਲ ਅਰਪਣ ਕਰ ਦਿਓ ਕਿ ਤੇਰਾ ਤੁਝਕੋ ਸੋਂਪਤੇ ਕਿਆ ਲਾਗੈ ਮੇਰਾ।
    ਸਾਨੂੰ ਇਸ ਬਾਤ ਦਾ ਗਰਵ ਅਤੇ ਅਭਿਮਾਨ ਹੈ ਕਿ ਇਸ ਸੋਸ਼ਲਿਜ਼ਮ ਦਾ ਪਾਲਨ ਕਰਨ ਵਾਲੇ ਸਤਿਗੁਰੂ ਚੀਨੀ ਵਾਲਿਆਂ ਦੇ ਨਾਮ ਲੇਵਾ ਨਾਮਧਾਰੀਆਂ ਵਿਚ ਜੋ ਏਕਤਾ, ਸ਼ਾਂਤੀ ਸੰਤੋਖ, ਪ੍ਰੇਮ ਅਰ ਦਿਲੀ ਪ੍ਰਸੰਨਤਾ ਹੈ ਓਹ ਹੋਰ ਕਿਸੇ ਜਗਹ ਦਿਖਾਈ ਨਹੀਂ ਦਿੰਦੀ। ਅਸੀ ਨਾਮਧਾਰੀ ਬਹੁਤੀਆਂ ਰਾਜਨੀਤਕ ਉਲਝਨਾਂ ਵਿਚ ਨਹੀਂ ਪੈਂਦੇ, ਸਤਿਗੁਰੂ ਸਚੇ ਪਾਤਸ਼ਾਹ ਦੇ ਹੁਕਮ ਦੀ

ਪਾਲਨਾ ਕਰਨਾ, ਦੂਸਰੇ ਨੂੰ ਪਾਣੀ ਪਿਲਾਣ ਦੀ ਭੀ ਖੇਚਲ ਨਹੀਂ ਦੇਣੀ, ਦਸਾਂ ਨੂਵਾਂ ਦੀ ਪਵਿਤ੍ਰ ਕਮਾਈ ਵਿਚੋਂ ਜੋ ਹੋ ਸਕੇ ਦੂਸਰਿਆਂ ਦੀ ਭੀ ਸੇਵਾ ਕਰ ਦੇਣੀ। ਸਤਿਗੁਰੂ ਦੇ ਹੁਕਮ ਦੀ ਪਾਲਨਾ ਵਿਚ ਹੀ ਸਭ ਕੁਝ ਆ ਜਾਂਦਾ ਹੈ। ਉਹਨਾਂ ਦੇ ਸਪੁਰਦ ਆਪਣੇ ਆਪ ਨੂੰ ਕਰ ਦੇਣ ਵਾਲਿਆਂ ਦੇ ਯੋਗਖੇਮ ਦੀ ਚਿੰਤਾ ਆਪ ਸਤਿਗੁਰੂ ਕਰਦੇ ਹਨ। ਐਸੇ ਸੋਸ਼ਲਿਸਜ਼ਮ ਨੂੰ ਧਨ ਜਮਾਂ ਕਰਨ ਦੀ ਕੀ ਪਰਵਾਹ ਹੈ, ਜਿਸਦੇ ਲੋਕ ਪਰਲੋਕ ਦਾ ਸਾਰਾ ਪ੍ਰਬੰਧ ਸਭ ਤੋਂ ਬੜੀ ਸ਼ਕਤੀ ਆਪ ਕਰ ਰਹੀ ਹੋਵੇ। ਉਹ ਤਾਂ ਮਾਂ ਦੀ ਗੋਦ ਵਿਚ ਬੈਠੇ ਬਚੇ ਵਾਂਗ ਹਰ ਮੁਸੀਬਤ ਅਰ ਚਿੰਤਾ ਫਿਕਰ ਤੋਂ ਬਿਲਕੁਲ ਨਿਸ਼ਚਿੰਤ ਹੋ ਜਾਂਦਾ ਹੈ।

ਏਹ ਸੋਸ਼ਲਿਜ਼ਮ ਹੈ ਜੋ ਸਿਰਫ ਹਿੰਦੋਸਤਾਨ ਵਿਚ ਹੀ ਸਫਲ ਹੋ ਸਕਦਾ ਹੈ ਬਲਕਿ ਸਾਰੀ ਦੁਨੀਆਂ ਵਿਚ ਨਿਸ਼ਚੇ ਹੀ ਅਮਨ ਅਤੇ ਸ਼ਾਂਤੀ ਵਰਤ ਸਕਦੀ ਹੈ। ਜਦ ਤਕ ਇਸ ਨੂੰ ਦੁਨੀਆਂ ਨਹੀਂ ਅਪਣੌਂਦੀ ਏਸੇ ਤਰਾਂ ਭੰਬਲ ਭੂਸੇ ਖਾਂਦੀ ਰਹੇਗੀ ਅਤੇ ਦੁਖ ਨਿਵਰਤੀ ਦੇ ਯਤਨ ਹੀ ਸੰਸਾਰ ਦੇ ਦੁਖਾਂ ਵਿਚ ਵਾਧਾ ਕਰੀ ਜਾਣਗੇ। *Satjug*, 28 May 1937, p. 3.

23. See Utopianism, *Oxford Concise Dictionary of Politics*, 2006, pp. 554-6.
24. Joginder Singh, *The Sikh Resurgence*, 1997, pp. 58-9.
25. Ibid., p. 60.
26. *Satjug*, 22 ਮਘਰ ਸੰਮਤ/1996, ਸਫਾ 3; 19 ਮਘਰ ਸਮਤ, 1996, ਸਫਾ 3.
27. "ਕੀ ਸਰ ਸਿਕੰਦਰ ਹਯਾਤ ਨਹੀਂ ਜਾਣਦੇ ਕਿ ਇਸ ਐਕਟਦੇ ਸਬਬ ਹੀ ਕਿਤਨੇ ਜ਼ਿਮੀਦਾਰ ਕੌਡੀਆਂ ਦੇ ਮੁਲ ਪਿੰਡਾ ਦੇ ਮਾਲਕ ਬਣ ਗਏ ਅਤੇ ਕਿਤਨੇ ਦਰ ਦਰ ਦੇ ਭਿਖਾਰੀ ਬਣ ਗਏ ਹੈਨ? ਕੀ ਜ਼ਿਮੀਦਾਰ ਸ਼੍ਰੇਨੀਆਂ ਵਿਚ ਐਸੇ ਸਾਹੂਕਾਰ ਇਸ ਐਕਟ ਨੇ ਹੀ ਪੈਦਾ ਨਹੀਂ ਕੀਤੇ ਜੋ ਇਕ ਇਕ ਹੀ ਸੈਕੜਿਆਂ ਦੀਆਂ ਜਮੀਨਾਂ ਹਜ਼ਮ ਕਰ ਗਏ ਹਨ? ਭਲਾ ਜੇ ਇਸ ਹੁਜਤ ਨੂੰ ਕੁਝ ਵਜ਼ਨ ਭੀ ਦਿਤਾ ਜਾਵੇ ਕਿ ਕਾਨੂੰਨ ਪਾਸ ਨ ਹੋਣ ਦੀ ਸੂਰਤ ਵਿਚ ਪਤਾ ਨਹੀਂ ਕੀ ਅਨਰਥ ਹੋ ਜਾਂਦਾ। ਤਦ ਭੀ ਇਸਤੋਂ ਜ਼ਿਆਦਾ ਕੋਈ ਅਨਰਥ ਤਾਂ ਨਹੀਂ ਹੋ ਸਕਦਾ ਸੀ ਜੋ ਲਗ ਭਗ ਦੋ ਰੁਪਏ ਮਹੀਨਾ ਔਸਤ ਆਮਦਨ ਵਾਲੇ ਦੇਸ਼ ਦੇ ਮੇਹਨਤੀਆਂ ਦੀ ਕਮਾਈ ਵਿਚੋਂ ਸਾਢੇ ਤਿਨ ਤਿਨ ਹਜ਼ਾਰ ਇਕ ਇਕ ਆਦਮੀ ਦੇ ਹੂੰਝ ਲੈ ਜਾਣ ਦੀ ਸੂਤ ਵਿਚ ਹੋ ਰਿਹਾ ਹੈ। ਹਾਲਾਂਕਿ ਓਹਨਾਂ ਦੀਆਂ ਹੋਰ ਆਮਦਨੀਆਂ ਦਾ ਭੀ ਕੋਈ ਅੰਤ ਨਹੀਂ। *Satjug*, vol. 12, 28 May 1937, p. 3.
28. Ibid., p. 4: ਹੈਰਾਨੀ ਏਹ ਹੈ ਕਿ ਐਕਟ ਦੇ ਸ਼ਿਕਾਰ ਓਹਨਾਂ ਪਾਸੋਂ ਇਸਦੀ ਮਨਸੂਖੀ ਦੀਆਂ ਆਸਾਂ ਰਖਦੇ ਹਨ ਜਿਨਾਂ ਨੂੰ ਐਕਟ ਖੁਦਾਈ ਬਰਕਤ ਸਾਬਤ ਹੋਯਾ ਹੈ। ਇਸ ਬੇਇਨਸਾਫੀ ਤੋਂ ਬਚਣ ਦਾ ਢੰਗ ਇਕ ਹੀ ਹੈ ਕਿ ਮਾਲ ਦਾਰ ਸ਼੍ਰੇਣੀ ਦੇ ਭਾਵਾਂ ਨੂੰ ਸਮਝ ਕੇ ਦੇਸ ਦਾ ਪ੍ਰਬੰਧ ਓਹਨਾਂ ਲੋਕਾਂ ਦੇ ਸਪੁਰਦ ਕੀਤਾ ਜਾਵੇ ਜੋ ਆਪ ਮੇਹਨਤੀ ਹਨ ਤੇ ਜਾਣ ਦੇ ਹਨ ਕਿ ਕਮਾਈ ਕਿਵੇਂ ਹੁੰਦੀ ਹੈ ਅਤੇ ਸਾਧਨਾਂ ਤੋਂ ਵੰਚਿਤ ਲੋਕਾਂ ਵਾਸਤੇ ਕੀ ਕੀ ਮੁਸ਼ਕਲਾਂ ਹੁੰਦੀਆਂ ਹਨ। ਹਿੰਦੁਸਤਾਨ ਦੇ 6 ਸੂਬਿਆਂ ਨੇ ਇਸ ਭੇਤ ਨੂੰ ਪਾਲਿਆ ਹੈ ਜਦ ਤਕ ਪੰਜਾਬ ਇਸਨੂੰ ਨਹੀ ਸਮਝਦਾ ਠੋਕਰਾਂ ਖਾਂਦਾ ਰਹੇਗਾ।
29. Suwaran Singh Virk, *Kuka Lehar Da Punjabi Sahit*, 2009, pp. 197-207.
30. Ibid., pp. 292-6.
31. Ibid., pp. 297-8.
32. Ibid., pp. 302-2.
33. Joginder Singh, *The Sikh Resurgence*, 1997, pp. 41-3.
34. It has been noticed that even in a religious community whose egalitarian principles are upheld, members belonging to a particular *jati* have tendency to regroup and form pressure groups.
35. Interviews with Jarnail Singh and Baldev Singh of Fatehgarh Sahib on 27 June 2008; Sant Makhan Singh of Padi Khalsa (Goraya) Jalandhar on 29 October 2007; Lakhwinder Singh of Jalandhar city, on 28 October

2007; Harminder Singh of Village Fatehpur Khera, Jalandhar on 20 February 2007; Lakhwinder Singh of Namdhari Dharamsala Muktasar on 26 October 2008; Preet Singh of Abohar City on 2 October 2008.

36. Ibid.
37. Arvind Sehgal, 'Assimilation of An Ethnic Group: A Case Study of Namdharis of Mandi Town in Himachal Pradesh', 1990, p. 108.
38. Nahar Singh and Kirpal Singh, *Rebels Against the British Rule,* 1995, p. 67.
39. Ibid., p. 73.
40. Ibid., p. 479.
41. For details, see, Denzil C.J. Ibbetson, *Punjab Castes,* 1883, pp. 268-9.
42. It was Guru Gobind Singh who honoured Bhai Jaita, a Rangreta Sikh, and called him Rangreta Guru Ka Beta for bringing the severed head of Guru Tegh Bahadur from Delhi to Kiratpur Sahib in 1675. Guru Tegh Bahadur had been martyred on 11 November 1675. Since then the Rangreta Sikhs played an important role in the Sikh struggle. Recognizing their martial spirit, the British admitted Mazhabi Singhs in the army into new regiments. Some of them were awarded with land for their services to the British raj: Harbans Singh (ed.), *Encyclopaedia of Sikhism,* vol. III, 1997, pp. 74-5.
43. For details, Mark Juergensmayer, *Religious Rebels in the Punjab,* 1988, pp. 107, 123, 208-20.
44. For details, *Khalsa Khandedhar*, Amritsar, *Dehdhari Guru Dam nu Biparvad di Sheh,* Amritsar, November 2005, p. 25.; *Khalsa Fatehnama*, Amritsar, October 2007, pp. 29-30 February 2008, p. 28, December 2008, p. 40; *Sada Virsa Sada Gaurav*, Sikh Study Circle, Ludhiana, 2007, pp. 17-18.; also Sukhwinder Singh Sabhra, *Santan De Kautak,* vols. I to IV, 2006.
45. Interviews with Bibi Amar Kaur, Bibi Balwinder Kaur, Mohan Singh, Surinder Singh and Manjit Singh of Goraya town on 27-8 October 2007 and Gurnam Singh, village Jagral, Jalandhar on 20 February 2008.
46. Booklet on Sant Baba Mohan Singh, Batala, n.d.
47. Sant Jagdish Singh Namdhari, *Satguru Te Jo Muh Phere,* 1998; Simarjeet Kaur, 'Nildhari Sikhan Da Uthaan Ate Sansthawan Da Adhyan', *Proceedings of Punjab History Conference,* March 2007, Punjabi University, Patiala, pp. 861-6.

CHAPTER 2

Partition of Punjab 1947: The Dispersal of Agriculturists and Artisans of West Punjab and their Resettlement in East Punjab

The partition of Punjab (1947) uprooted 10 million Punjabis. Hindus and Sikhs of the West Punjab were rehabilitated in India whereas the Muslims of the East Punjab were rehabilitated in Pakistan. A large number of studies highlight the communal violence and sufferings of these migrants; the quantum of destruction of the economies of East and West Punjab; and the fracture of composite culture of the united Punjab. Studies on rehabilitation give details of problems about resettlement, property-claims, and allotments of houses, shops, and land by the Government of India. Many Hindu/Sikh migrants were rehabilitated on the landed-property and houses vacated by Muslims.

This chapter examines the processes and patterns of dispersal and rehabilitation of the Namdhari agriculturists, artisans and businessmen. Data on nearly 500 migrant families of this community of thirteen districts of Punjab state have been tabulated. Table 2.1 of these migrant families shows that among them were 68 and 27 per cent the Namdhari Jats and Ramgarhias respectively. The Parjapats and Aroras/Khatris were two other occupational groups who constituted 2.42 and 1.21 per cent of these migrant families respectively. The percentage of the rest of the families was insignificant. Table 2.1 also shows that the majority of these migrant families are found in the districts of Kapurthala, Gurdaspur, Jalandhar, Hoshiarpur, Sangrur, Ferozepur, Fatehgarh Sahib, Patiala, Ludhiana, Amritsar and Chandigarh and Mohali (Table 2.1).

Of all the migrant Namdhari Sikhs, more than 90 per cent came from district Sialkot. In Namdhari literature, this district is a major centre of concentration of Namdhari Sikhs. Namdhari Guru Ram Singh and his successors held several religious festivals in this district.

TABLE 2.1: THE MIGRANT NAMDHARI FAMILIES FROM PAKISTAN*

Districts	Jat	Ramgar-hias	Parjapats	Mahashes	Chhembas	Aroras Khatri	Sainis	Mehras	Brahmins	Swarankars	Total
Kapurthala	92 + 4 Kamboj	35	–	–	–	2	2	1	1	–	137
Gurdaspur	77	18	3	2	1	–	–	–	–	–	101
Jalandhar	6	56	–	–	–	–	–	–	–	–	62
Hoshiarpur	52	–	3	–	–	–	–	–	–	–	55
Sangrur	30	–	–	–	–	–	–	–	–	–	30
Firozepur	23	–	–	–	–	–	–	–	–	–	23
Fatehgarh Sahib	19	–	–	–	–	–	–	–	–	–	19
Patiala	12	6	3	–	–	–	–	–	1	–	22
Chandigarh & Mohali	10	–	–	–	–	–	–	–	–	–	10
Ludhiana	6	8	1	–	–	–	–	–	–	–	15
Amritsar	3	4	2	–	–	2	–	–	–	1	12
Muktasar	2	1	–	–	–	2	–	–	–	–	5
Tarn Taran	–	4	–	–	–	–	–	–	–	–	4
Total	336	132	12	2	1	6	2	1	1	1	494
%age	68	27	2.42			1.21					

According to tradition, thousands of Namdharis attended these festivals. In one of such, it is said that Satguru Ram Singh distributed 80,000 woollen rosaries to the people. The Namdhari tradition gives the impression that 80,000 people became Namdharis Sikhs. However, the official report gives a different version. Captain Thulloch's report of 27 October 1866, stated that 'the sect in this district (Sialkot) do not muster more than 200 . . . 80,000 necklaces have been given away by Ram Singh to a like number of admitted disciples. In 1863 the Native Inspector thought the Sect numbered 300, whilst Lieutenant McNeille considered 3000, nearer the mark.'[1] According to the assessment of the census officials, 'the Kuka movement appears to be on the decline owing obviously to the disfavour with which the followers of this sect are looked upon in political circles, and the opening created by the Tat Khalsa movement for religious zeal. The number has decreased from 13,788 in 1901 to 4,706 in 1931.'[2]

According to our data, the numerical strength of the migrant Namdhari agriculturists and artisans was equal in proportion. The reason for major concentration of the artisans in this district was that the city of Sialkot was 'full of industries' such as sports goods, surgical, EPNS, rubber, and leather goods. It was called the Japan of India. Its population was 1,10,000 out of which 90,000 were engaged in manufacturers.[3] However, in terms of landed property as well as social status, the Namdhari agriculturists were superior to the artisans. Data on 120 families of Sialkot and Lahore districts shows that more than 42 per cent agriculturists were big farmers and owned 25 acres or more. Approximately a dozen families owned more than 100 acres. 19.16 per cent were medium farmers who owned 10 to 24.99 acres of land. Only 10 per cent were small and marginal farmers.

EVACUATION PLAN OF GOVERNMENT OF INDIA

The massacres and migrations forced the Governments of India and Pakistan to make arrangements for the exchange of population. Within a few months of partition, approximately 5.2 million Muslims entered West Pakistan and about 3.8 to 4.2 non-Muslims from both urban and rural areas, entered East Punjab. To meet this exigency, the Punjab Boundary Force was constituted to maintain peace in the Punjab during evacuation. Unfortunately, this force miserably failed to control the situation. Nevertheless, both governments set up a machinery to evacuate these displaced persons. At the central level, the first Inter-Dominion Conference was held on 17 August 1947.

Subsequently, several such meetings were held for providing facilities and other amelioration for the refugees. The Government of East Punjab appointed the East Punjab Liaison Agency which was set up at Lahore under a Chief Liaison Officer. District Liaison Officers were also appointed in a number of districts of West Punjab under this agency. This agency worked for more than a year and was finally withdrawn on 30 November 1948. The East Punjab Liaison Agency was assisted by a Military Evacuation Organization whose main task was to facilitate the movements of refugees and to protect them from marauding groups. Routes were planned for the convoys.[4]

Hindus and Sikhs made for the Indian border by the shortest possible routes—from Narowal to Dera Baba Nanak, from Lahore to Amritsar, from Kasur to Ferozepur, from Montgomery to Fazilka, from Bahawalpur to Bikaner, from Mirpur Khas to Jodhpur. This they did by air, train, car, and bus, as well as in foot convoys.

Six hundred seventy-three over-crowded refugee trains ran between 27 August 1947 and 6 November 1947 and ferried 13,62,000 refugees. These trains were risky and sometimes proved to be death cages. Several were held at Lahore, Amritsar, Sialkot, and Multan and not a single passenger was spared.

Nearly, 4,00,000 Hindus and Sikhs were evacuated mainly from countryside, through motor transport provided by the M.E.O., provincial governments, and private organizations.

Trekking on the foot was the quickest means of evacuation for the largest number of refugees. The M.E.O. and Liaison Agency organized 24 foot convoys, consisting 30,000 to 40,000 people each. The biggest one was from canal colonies of Lyallpur consisting of 4,00,000. It was 150 miles long and looked like a slow moving flood of utter human misery. In all about 10,36,000 people came on foot from West Pakistan.

Towards the end of August, air transport become operational. Aircraft were used mainly to transport government servants and army officers, on both sides, across the border. Aircrafts belonging to Indian Air Lines and BOAI were used for the speedy evacuation of nearly 50,000 Hindus and Sikhs from West Pakistan.[5]

RELIEF ARRANGEMENTS

Simultaneous with the evacuation work, arrangements began for the reception and relief of refugees. The Government of India created a new ministry on 6 September 1947 to look after the evacuation, reception, relief and rehabilitation of refugees. In East Punjab, the entire government machinery was mobilized for this work. Overall command was with the governor, chief minister, and chief secretary of the state. The Civil Supplies Department was entrusted with providing food, clothes, and basic necessities of life to the refugees. The PWD had to arrange for accommodation. Police, health and education departments were involved to maintain law and order, sanitary conditions and educational facilities for the children of refugees respectively. A Special Department of Rehabilitation was established to work exclusively for the relief and rehabilitation of the new arrivals. A large number of officials were appointed by this department to tackle the gigantic task of relief and rehabilitation.

A central plan was drawn up and the refugees were first to report at the transit camps opened at entry point like Fazilka, Ferozepur, Khemkaran, Atari, Amritsar, and Dera Baba Nanak. From there they were to proceed to the other relief camps or the area allocated to them under the central plan. The East Punjab government set-up a large number of such camps all over the state. There were more than 160 refugee camps all over the country, providing accommodation to 12,50,000 refugees. In the East Punjab alone, 7,21,397 refugees were accommodated in 85 camps towards the end of December 1947.

Out of remaining, 150,000 were in camps at Delhi, 53,000 in Punjab and Rajasthan states, 13,000 in Bombay Presidency, 30,000 in United Provinces, 500 in Madras and 1,500 in the Central

TABLE 2.2: DESCRIPTION OF REFUGEES CAMPS AND REFUGEES IN EAST PUNJAB UPTO DECEMBER 1947

Name of District	No. of Camps	No. of Refugees
Amritsar	5	1,29,398
Gurdaspur	4	3,500
Ferozepur	5	5,300
Ludhiana	1	2,500
Jalandhar	19	60,000
Hoshiarpur	1	11,701
Hissar	3	3,797
Rohtak	2	50,000
Ambala	1	40,000
Karnal, including Kurukshetra	4	3,25,000
Gurgaon	40	20,000
Total	85	7,21,396

Provinces. According to the Punjab government, the total number of refugees from the West Punjab was 40,85,386. These included 19,03,042 Hindus and 14,83,165 Sikhs, and 6,99,179 others. 42,96,805 Muslims had gone away from the East Punjab.[6]

DISPERSAL

In terms of dispersal and migration, the Namdhari Sikhs can be put into two categories. In the first were those agriculturists who had left their native villages and towns in West Punjab much before the disturbances (*raula*) took place. A substantial number of them informed us that their Satguru Partap Singh informed them in advance that the partition of Punjab was going to take place and before the situation could take a bad turn they should cross the river Ravi and move to safer places. These agriculturists believe that they escaped violence since they followed their guru's advice. However, the second category comprise those Namdharis who did not take the advice of their guru seriously and left their places only when they were caught up by the marauding columns of anti-social elements. The pattern of their dispersal was not different than their counterparts—the Hindus and the Sikhs. A Namdhari respondent narrated the beginning of communal tension and violence at the village level. He is a Punjabi writer and his autobiography provides information about the rise of communal tension and experiences of the Namdhari families and of the village Hindu-Sikh *biradari*, the swelling number of the *kafilas* (convoys of refugees) and their advance from one village to another and then across river Ravi to dispers, different families opting for unknown destinies in independent India. Accordingly to this writer, the communal harmony of his village (in the Narowal tashil of district Gurdaspur) was disturbed all of a sudden when the slogans of *Pakistan Zindabad* and *Khalistan Zindabad* or *Pakistan Murdabad* were raised, manufacture of swords and spears began and when members of each community formed defence-committees. The situation took a bad turn when the village ties were supplanted by 'mistrust' and rumours. The Muslims of the other villages started attacking Sikhs and Hindus. Within a short time, the villages were burnt, forcing Sikhs and Hindus to take shelter in those villages where Sikhs/Hindus were dominant in number and resources. In the atmosphere of insecurity, the Sikhs of nearby villages assembled in one place and moved collectively. The *kafila* in which some Namdhari families were included was 5 miles long. It reached Narowal Railway Station, then crossed the river Ravi and made its first stay at Dera Baba Nanak, a historic town.[7]

There were exceptional families that escaped unhurt and did not lose members, or whose women were not assaulted. The Namdhari families of Jalandhar city belong to this category. Out of 72 families, only one or two families disclosed that they suffered causalities. They had traditional weapons for protecting themselves, but none of the respondents narrated sordid stories of killings or assaults or their women, or being picked up forcefully by the anti-social elements. It was at Dera Baba Nanak that they heard such stories. At the same time, they stated that on their way they saw dead bodies or that the river water was black or red due to slaughtered of men and women being thrown into the running water.

However, the experiences of Namdhari migrants of district Ferozepur and Patiala are more telling in this regard. The respondents of several families of Patiala admitted that they lost their relatives and members of their respective families in the communal violence. One of such respondent is Labh Singh who was witness to the killings of hundreds of people (Sikhs and Hindus). He lost his elder brother (retired Captain) Lal Singh. He also stated that the Sikhs (including his son) killed the women of their families lest they be dishonoured by the Muslim mob. Another respondent told us that he and his companion could save women from the Muslim mob. They also retaliated against Muslims in the communal violence, killing some. Nostalgia for their land and native culture has not faded out of their memory.[8] Similarly, a resident of village Jia Bagga Lahore came to know about the impending danger from a person in his own village. He was told that Sikhs and Hindus could not stay here.

Excepting a few families, The majority left their native villages when violence broke out. When questioned that why they had not left earlier, some disclosed that it was too hard to leave an ancestral home and habitat. One of the respondents of village Sabuana remembered the agony of leaving home for ever. It seems that most people were caught unawares. For instance, an agriculturist of village Khudpur, tehsil, Lahore, stated that the people of his village ran helter-skelter in the night and took shelter in the nearby fields. Several migrants admitted that it was the communal violence which forced them to vacate their villages and take shelter wherever it was available.[9]

Once driven out of their native places either by impending danger or by actual attacks by Muslim hooligans, Sikhs and Hindus gathered in groups and started a frantic search for safe routes and camps. Generally, the Sikhs and Hindus of the same village moved together in convoy. Since most migrants belonged to Lahore district which shared a boundary with districts Ferozepur and Amritsar, the Namdhari respondents disclosed that they did not take long to cross the broder. (which was yet to be demarcated). It was done in a day and a night. However, there were several Namdhari families, who like their counterparts, were trapped by Muslim hooligans. They had to take shelter in a Lahore camp and were escorted by the military to reach Indian Punjab. They stayed in the Khalsa College in Amritsar for some time. The refugee camps gave them a temporary relief and sense of safety, but they were haunted by the dark future. They thought of resettling in those places somewhere they could raise their own homes and find work. However, it was this goal that eluded them as the government policy of resettlement and rehabilitation of refugees took time to crystallize. Lands and urban properties left by Muslims were yet to be identified. Meanwhile life in camps too became hard. Most refugees approached their distant relatives. Only a few were lucky to stay in the houses of their relatives. For the agriculturists, the process of resettlement was marked by two phases. In the first phase, they stayed in those villages where they were allotted land temporarily. Most of the Namdhari agriculturists stayed in the villages like Pihewali (Fazilka), Rajoke (Tarn Taran) and Joian (Gurdaspur). In the beginning, they depended on the crops and tools left behind by Muslims. Apart from the problems being faced as 'strangers' in those villages, these agriculturists found that temporary allotted lands were less fertile, in some cases *banjar* (fallow-land) and there was a scarcity of water. Both the problems persisted even when they were allotted land permanently. Moreover, the size of the allotted land was small compared to the land-squares they had left behind in West Punjab. The formula of standard deduction was evolved and applied to the land squares of the agriculturist migrants.[10] The Namdhari agriculturists still regret the reduced size and bad quality of land allotted to them.[11] They are yet to overcome the experiences of hardship they bore in making these lands productive. For instance, Jagjit Singh, younger brother of Suba Jagir Singh (Muktsar), disclosed that his grandparents owned *25 murabas* (700 acres) of land in Chauhliwala, Bahawalpur, whereas the land allotted to him in the village Chhapianwali, Muktsar was 60 acres. He told us that it was a desert area and took 10 to 15 years to develop. Till 1976, he and his brothers lived in the *kacha* (made of mud) houses.[12] While farming on the temporary allotments for three to four years, some of them also cultivated land on contract to meet their requirements.

REHABILITATION

The process of rehabilitation of artisan *panahgeers* (refugees) was longer and more cumbersome than for agriculturists. It was the government policy which determined the pattern of their rehabilitation.[13] In the case of non-agriculturists, there was no specific official policy guiding them where to go. The only guideline followed by the officials was that the immigrants from cities and towns should be settled in towns and cities in the houses and land of the Muslim evacuees and later in colonies built for the rehabilitation of refugees. In Jalandhar were constructed the Bharghawa Camp, Gandhi Camp, and Model House. Preet Nagar was constructed as early as 1960. By 1950 the population of this city was about 1,68,000 showing an increase of 52 per cent over the previous decade. Jalandhar ranked fourth in accommodating the refugees from Pakistan.[14] In spite of the construction of colonies for refugees, the latter faced serious problems in getting reasonably suitable compensation for properties they had left behind in West Punjab.

Some of the Namdhari respondents stated that they had taken riots as a temporary phenomenon and stayed back in their respective villages. In fact, most had thought they would sooner or later go back, 'therefore, all that [they] wanted was temporary refuge in any corner of India'.

> . . . .The first wave of refugees from the North-West Frontier Province and the Rawalpindi Division was able to bring with it a part of their moveable property. There was at that time no restriction on taking out their cash, silver or gold and ornaments etc. . . . The second wave of the refugees consisted of those brave people who had stayed behind hoping for the best in the Rawalpindi Division and of the Hindus and Sikhs in the urban area of the Lahore Division.[15]

The second wave started after 2 June 1947. A heavy exodus of Lahore citizens took place only after the 21 July 1947. Wholesale shooting and murder of the Sikhs and Hindus with the active help or connivance of the Muslim Police and troops eroded the belief that the communal violence was a temporary phenomenon. This belief got further shattered when the convoys of the Sikhs and Hindus were looted by these personnel and Muslim marauders. The next wave of refugees consisted of rural Hindus and the Sikh population of canal colonies of Montgomery, Sheikhupura and Lyallpur. They thought that they would remain in Pakistan if they could be assured of an honourable living. But the Pakistan government had decided to get rid of them. The Muslim marauders supported by the Pakistani military troops hunted the Sikhs and Hindus in the villages and butchered their convoys on foot, motors and railways.[16] The intensity of riots increased, engulfing the villages and towns of the West Punjab. The 'rioting in rural areas started almost simultaneously'. In cases, when local Muslims promised safety and protection to the non-Muslims village would be attacked by men from neighbouring villages, and then 'these promises were forgotten'. In other cases,

> heavy bribes were demanded and paid, but this only increased the greed of the bribe-takers, and the non-Muslim residents were soon after-wards robbed of everything they had. Conversion to Islam was frequently offered as the price of safety, and if the victims exhibited any reluctance or religious scruples they were subjected to duress and torture. The hair of Sikhs was cut off, their beards were trimmed and beef was cooked and forced down their throats. Some of them were circumcised. Young women and girls were molested and carried away. Reason and decency were completely banished by fanatical zeal; and young innocent girls were raped in public.[17]

In *Stern Reckoning* G.D. Khosla has compiled names of the villages, dates, number of witnesses, nature of incidents, number of casualties, conversion, kidnappings or abduction of the districts of Punjab. He also narrates several horrible scenes of rapes and loot. Ninety-eight per cent of the Namdhari respondents expressed their ignorance of sufferings due to the communal violence. Only 2 per cent of the Namdhari respondents confirmed the forcible conversion of the Hindus and Sikhs. One respondent disclosed that Sikhs and Hindus of some villages who became Muslims under the threat.[18]However, almost all admitted the loss of hearth and home, livestock and money.

On the other hand, several families narrated incidents of sobriety and generosity shown by the Muslims when they were in the thick of communal violence. We cite only one case of Sardar Gurcharan Singh who was an eye witness to the tragic happenings of 1947.

Gurcharan Singh is, at present, Sarpanch of his village Hambowal, tahsil and post office Dhilwan, district Kapurthala, Punjab. His ancestral village was Nadali, tehsil Narowal, district Sialkot, Pakistan. His narrative runs like this. At the time of Partition of Punjab he was eight years old. He remembered horrible scenes of his family's escape. In the wake of riots, about 250-300 Sikh families of village Sair Bajwe and his own village were provided shelter by a Muslim *zaildar*, Said Khan, of his own village. *Zaildar's* brothers were also police and revenue officials and were equipped with licensed rifles. Sardar Gurcharan Singh disclosed that Zaildar Said Khan kept them safe in his house for three days. One day his in-laws, along with a gang, came to the village and wanted to kill *kafirs* (non-Muslims). In the face of such aggtession *zaildar* told them that those Sikhs were his own brothers. If they did any harm to them, his in-laws would have to take their two daughters back home. In the heat of exchanges *zaildar* threw down his rifle which suddenly released its bullet. Frightened, the in-laws and gang dispersed. Finding it difficult to control the situation, *zaildar* and his brothers then escorted the Sikhs to a refugee camp in Pasrur. They had fulfilled their moral obligation. It may be pointed out here that there were several such cases of decency and generosity shown by the Muslims.

This camp was arranged by the Bhrowale Sardars. The next morning, their *kafila* crossed Pasrur town with the help of the Pakistani military. When they reached the town of Narowal, they found the railway crossing locked. A Muslim mob wanted to kill and loot them. They flooded the streets with muddy water and sprinkled them with broken glass which injured several people. Luckily, the Maratha army appeared on the scene and broke the lock and helped the Sikhs to run away. The next day, the temporary refugee camp was raised by the army at village mound Chandowal. After a night over there, they crossed bridge over the river Ravi. They could cross it due to the patrolling units of Indian army. However, a tussle between the Pakistan army and Indian army broke out on the issue whether Indian refugees should cross the river-bridge first or their Pakistani counterparts. The will of the Indian army prevailed. In fact, whosoever was left.

Gurcharan Singh stated that their *kafila* reached Dera Baba Nanak but by crossing over the dead-bodies. Small or big ponds were in full flow of blood and dead bodies. Loot and murder were going on. He said that he himself, his father, and mother saw the dead bodies of his aunt and uncle, their two sons, and a daughter near the rivulet under the Jassran' bridge.

After spending some days at Dera Baba Nanak, they moved to Mangal Sain near Gurdas Nangal. Here they used to collect fodder, crush sugar cane, and prepare jaggery which they sold in Gurdaspur. Some of them worked as daily-wagers. They passed three months in this manner. Then they started looking for relatives and friends. The family moved to Miani Bakurpur where sons of his sister were residing. Ultimately he shifted to Hambowal.

Such families did not receive any help from government. They had to work hard to rebuild their economies and houses.[19]

THE REHABILITATION POLICY OF THE GOVERNMENT OF INDIA

In the initial stage, the Government of India did not possess the required data on property left by the Hindu and Sikh refugees in West Punjab or evacuee property left by the Muslims in East Punjab. The government simply asked the refugees to proceed to the tahsils of their own choice, in groups.

> The migrant rural population was sustained for 2½ years, the interregnum between the migration and the quasi-permanent allotment of land, through a system of land allotments which later on came to be known as temporary allotments. Each family was given a plough unit, i.e. about 10 acres of land, regardless of its holding in Pakistan. No distinction was made between a tenant and a land-holder and both were equally eligible for allotment of evacuee land.[20]

It also thought of allotting a fixed area of land and a pair of bullocks to every adult family. Financial assistance was also given to displaced persons. Group allotments were to enable kinsfolk and villagers to remain together as far as possible so that resources could be pooled. 'These objects were largely secured and within two months, two million acres of land were occupied.'[21]

During their temporary stay in the agricultural fields, the Namdhari agriculturists faced very hard times. They had neither adequate live-stock nor agricultural implements. Most of them survived on the crops and dilapidated houses left behind by Muslims. Worse, several Namdhari families found that Muslim agriculturists had set their crop fields on fire. Moreover, what Muslims left behind in their houses was looted by local Sikhs and Hindus. In the wake of this situation, the refugee agriculturists took to manual labour.

REHABILITATION POLICY OF NAMDHARI GURUS

In the absence of government help, a large number of Namdhari agriculturists stated that they were supported either by their spiritual master or their own relatives. Satguru Partap Singh made arrangements for immediate relief. He directed his followers to move to Bhaini Sahib headquarters at Ludhiana or go else to straight to Sri Jiwan Nagar in Sirsa, Haryana or to the town of Mandi in Himachal Pradesh. It is stated that Satguru Partap Singh approached the ruler of Bilaspur for refuge for the Namdhari Sikhs in his territory, but he did not agree. Then he met the Raja of Mandi, Joginder Sen, with whom he had cordial relations and asked him to allow his followers to settle down at Mandi, who immediately agreed. The local people of the Mandi town and government supported the refugees. It may be pointed out here that the majority of the Namdhari refugees comprised artisans and businessmen (Khatris and Aroras). Most of them started their careers as labourers and kiosk owners. Gradually they established small shops. Subsequently, some professional Namdhari Sikhs (doctors, engineers and petty administrative personnel) came to this town to settle in. Similar patterns of resettlement of migrant Namdhari Sikhs are perceptible in the localities of Preet Nagar and Basti Bhure Khan of Jalandhar city. More than 80 per cent are artisans (lohars and tarkhans) who came from Sialkot district.[22] Such a policy of rehabilitation went a long way in maintaining the identity of the zat biradaris of these Sikhs.

Satguru Partap Singh's equally important action was to found Sri Jiwan Nagar for migrant Namdharis. He bought 12,430 acres of land in villages Chuchal Kotli (Jiwan Nagar), Jag Malera (Sant Nagar), Alipur (Haripur), and Kangran Wala (Damdamal) in tahsil Sirsa, district Hissar. He had taken permission from the then Commissioner, Department of Rehabilitation, Jalandhar to allow his followers to settle in district Hissar. As noted above, his followers comprised agriculturists, businessmen, and artisans. He made arrangements for the distribution of land among them. It is said that several hundred families of migrant agriculturists and non-agriculturists were resettled. Moreover, roads were constructed; means of irrigation, agricultural implements, and markets were developed. Besides, some manufacturing units for processing agriculture production were also established. In addition, educational institutions were founded.[23] Nevertheless, a study of the native places of these migrants, their occupational castes, volume of landed property they left in the West Punjab and volume of land allotted to each migrant family here is yet to be conducted.

Namdhari Guru Partap Singh and his son and successor Satguru Jagjit Singh initiated another project, on the land of Bir Bhamarsi. This land was donated by Maharaja Ripudaman Singh of Nabha state when he was blessed with a son. The Namdhari tradition claims that it was Satguru Partap Singh who blessed the Maharaja with a son. In a token of gratitude Maharaja donated this land. The total area of this land comprised 1,129 acres. Some of the Namdhari respondents disclosed that on Maharaja's order *navalid dheri* (landholdings of those parents who were 'issueless') was transferred and consolidated to this *bir*.[24]

Immediately after Idependence, the Congress expressed its concern for enacting legislation regarding land-ceilings.[25] There were peasants' struggles in different states of India. In Patiala and subsequently in PEPSU, Lal Communist Party led by Teja Singh Swantantar and Kirti-group had launched an armed struggle in 1948. In response the Congress ministry led by Brish Bhan enacted the PEPSU Tenancy (Temporary Provision) Act in 1952. Subsequently, the PEPSU Occupancy Tenants (vesting of Proprietary Rights) Act (1953) was passed. Most probably these developments influenced Namdhari Guru Partap Singh to speed up distribution of land in Bir Bhamarsi. Influenced by socialist ideas, he resolved to distribute land to his agriculturist as well as artisan followers. He made slabs of 10, 7 and 5 acres of land, verified the antecedents of the Namdhari Sikhs to whom it was to be given. According to a Namdhari respondent, Namdhari guru gave land to those of his followers who either had 5 or less than 5 acres of land. Some of these agriculturists themselves availed of this opportunity and encouraged their relatives to come to Bir Bhamarsi. Namdhari Gurnam Singh, Harjinder Singh, Bachitter Singh and Mrs. Bhajan Kaur w/o late Sant Bakhshish Singh were such beneficiaries. The Namdhari guru also gave land to artisans. One of the recipients disclosed that when their Satguru decided to allot landholdings to artisans, particularly Ramdasia families, the Namdhari agriculturists were surprised. One of the agriculturists enquired from his Satguru that how many acres were to be given to non-agriculturists.

The Namdhari guru told him that he was not going to discriminate among allottees according to their caste. On hearing this, the Namdhari Ramdasias felt as if their guru raised their social status. In fact, Namdhari guru was conscious of the hard social reality that people of artisan castes suffered from feelings of inferiority. Thus Sant Bishan Singh too was given five acres of land in village Damdama, Sirsa (district Hissar). Sant Bishan Singh was son of Giani Kahla Singh and was known as a historian.[26]

An interesting feature of land distribution was that out of 53 Namdhari families, 20 from the West Punjab got land from Namdhari Gurus Partap Singh and Jagjit Singh. The number of migrant recipients of landholdings were as follows: out of 23, Namdhari Jats were 17; Ramdasias 4 and Ramgarhias 2. Under the Land Alienation Act, non-agriculturists could not purchase land. It was a progressive act of the Namdhari gurus to provide land to lower caste families.

Recipients still express their gratitude to their spiritual masters when they state, 'It is the bounty of the guru what we eat today'. Moreover, some of the recipients became prosperous farmers. They increased their landholdings and increased production with the help of modern technology. On the other hand, the present generation of several recipient families has disposed of its lands and has migrated to the nearby towns and cities. Incidentally, most of them belong to the artisan castes.

PATTERNS OF RESETTLEMENT OF AGRICULTURISTS

The Namdhari migrant agriculturists of Sialkot, Lyallpur, and Lahore after crossing river Ravi and staying in the refugee camps, moved into different districts of East Punjab. Forty-eight agriculturist families of Sialkot and 4 of Lyallpur preferred to settle in district Hoshiarpur; 19 agriculturist families of Sialkot chose district Fatehgarh Sahib, 29 families of Sialkot went to district Sangrur (only one from Gujranwala in this district); 16 families of district Lahore, 6 of Sialkot and 1 of Gujranwala ultimately settled in district Ferozepur. Thus 145 migrant families from four districts of West Punjab were resettled in the four districts of Hoshiarpur, Sangrur, Fatehgarh Sahib, and Ferozepur. Excepting Hoshiarpur, which is in Doaba region, the rest of the districts are in Malwa region of Punjab.[27]

Some of these agriculturists faced serious hardship in ultimately settling on suitable land. The case of Namdhari Dalip Singh of village Fatehwali is worth quoting here as it refers to the zig-zag path of resettlement. After staying with his cousin, resident of Rataul village now in Tarn Taran district, Dalip Singh moved to Sirsa and worked as a share-cropper on the land owned by Thakur, brother of the then Namdhari Guru Partap Singh. It was a temporary arrangement. He was then allotted 36 acres in village Kandhwala Hazarkhan near Fazilka. Here canal-irrigation was available but insufficient for increasing production. He cultivated this land for 15 years. Then Dalip Singh was allotted of 40 acres by the Rehabilitation Department in Zira tahsil, Ferozepur, but found that it was actually owned by a Khatri. The latter, an influential man, got this allotment cancelled. When Dalip Singh reported back to the revenue officials he was told that he should go back and himself identify land squares in any village which could be given to him on a permanent basis. After a great hassle, he found 36 acres in Fatehwali, but only in 1970. Since then he is farming. His rehabilitation took 20 years. Dalip Singh is not an exception.[28]

The native village of Dalip Singh in Pakistan was Kudhpur teshil, district Lahore. There were six other Namdhari agriculturists there. All first took shelter with their distant relatives and then moved to Haripur, near Sirsa, and worked as share-croppers on the landholdings of Thakur. But like Dalip Singh, they faced similar problems. Then they were allotted landholdings in the villages of nearby Fazilka on a temporary basis. After some time, they moved to Fatehwali in the 1970s. One of these agriculturists is Dhara Singh. It was he who narrated the common experience of hardships borne by the migrants.[29]

Six Namdhari agriculturist families who belonged to Chak No. 33 in Pakistan went through the similar hardships. After reaching Indian Punjab, they were persuaded by Satguru Partap Singh to come to Sirsa and start cultivation there. Some of them went and stayed there till they were allotted landholdings in Paliwala village near Fazilka on a temporary basis. Afterwards, they were allotted land permanently in the village Sabuana, tahsil Fazilka. According to Phulla Singh, *pardhan* of Bhaini Sahib, all the agriculturists of Chak No. 33 have been resettled here, but were given smaller plots of land in compensation. In his case, he got 16 acres.[30]

Similarly, there are six more Namdhari families whose native village was Thinga Jattan, tahsil Chunia, district Lahore. Before their resettlement in village Rajiwala, tahsil Ferozepur, these families moved from one village to another for shelter and livelihood. After crossing the border, they took shelter with the distant relatives of villages in Muktsar. Some of these families were allotted land in Kharajke and Doda on a temporary basis, for two to three years. Then they were allotted lands in the present village of Rajiwala, permanently. One of these families was allotted land in village Assal (Ferozepur).[31] Besides, they were two more families who migrated from the native village Zia Bagga Khurd in Lahore district and ultimately settled in village Gatta Badshah (Ferozepur). They too had to work hard for survival.[32]

The migrant Namdhari agriculturists preferred to settle in those districts where they got social support from their relatives and where evacuee-property was available. For some of them, the resettlement in these districts was a rejoining of their relatives or coming back to ancestral 'homes'. This is true in the case of those agriculturists (including Namdharis) who were encouraged by the British to colonize lands in the West Punjab. According to an estimate, thousands of Sikh agriculturists of Sialkot, Gujranwala, Sheikhupura, Lyallpur, Lahore, and Montgomery came from the districts of Amritsar, Gurdaspur, Ferozepur, Ludhiana, Jalandhar and Hoshiarpur. For instance, in Lyallpur district, the Sikhs owned 75 per cent of the total holdings and in the colony area, they paid 80 per cent of the land revenue. In fact, often the land was mostly owned by the Sikh peasants 'who paid more than twice the land revenue paid by the Muslims'.[33] Nevertheless,

> Sialkot was a district of small holdings. According to the District Gazetteer it came second in order of population but only tenth with respect to cultivated area. The pressure of population on the soil is great and the consideration which goes furthest to stay the hand of the Settlement Officer in this well favoured district is the fact that holdings are minute and the people, as a rule, poor in consequences.
>
> The Jats were the most important agricultural clan in the district. They owned 65% of the cultivated area and constituted nearly a quarter of the total population. About two-thirds of them were Mussalmans and less than a fourth were Sikhs. Their clans are legion but the Bajwa, Basra, Bhindar, Chimma, Deo, Ghuman, Kahlon, Goraya, Malhi, Sahi, Sandhu and Varaich are the most important. In Sikh villages the Jat enlisted freely in the army, and made a sturdy soldier, but occasionally indulged a taste for liquor and for cheating the excise man.
>
> The Jats from the sub-montane tahsil of Pasrur are miserable specimens

of humanity; their half-starved appearance sallow complexion and untidy turbans easily mark them out from others. The Jats from Narowal tahsil are comparatively better-built and are fairly good colonists. Between the two extremes stand the Jats of Daska and Sialkot. Emigration except to the canal colonies or to the neighbouring cities of Amritsar and Lahore, is not generally popular, and money-lending or cattle dealing are the only enterprises indulged in outside the ordinary round of agriculture. Thanks to their small holdings, they were masters of intensive cultivation and rotation of crops.[34]

There were specific causes and circumstances that had led the migrant agriculturist families to resettle in specific villages of above-mentioned districts. The majority of them belonged to Sialkot district and their temporary stay was in district Gurdaspur where they waited for the temporary allotment of landholdings. Then they moved to those villages where they got temporary allotments. Nevertheless, there were a few families whose temporary allotments were converted into the permanent holdings and they felt satisfied with the quality of land. In majority of the cases, the migrant agriculturists thought of moving to the better agricultural land. It was in this state of influx that Satguru Partap Singh came to their rescue. As noted above, for his migrants he made arrangements for resettlement in Sirsa and Bir Bhamarsi, district Fatehgarh Sahib. The policy of resettlement complemented the official policy of rehabilitation. 'The evacuee-land available in Amritsar could not meet the demand of even the colonists of that district. The overflow was therefore accommodated in the neighbouring districts of Jullundur, Hoshiarpur and Ferozepur.' [35] Similarly, Namdhari guru accommodated the inflow of his migrant followers in the above mentioned places. The Namdhari allottees developed their respective landholdings subsequently.[36]

The pattern of resettlement of Namdhari agriculturists suggested that the common migrants had their own compulsions to move in groups and resettle collectively in one place. They could not settle according to the official directives.

Migrants from Lahore and non-colonists of Montgomery districts were asked to move to Ferozepur district. In case of the Namdhari migrants of Lahore district, out of 23 migrant families, 16 resettled in district Ferozepur. Six families came from Sialkot and one from Gujranwala district.

That kinship ties were major considerations for resettlement is corroborated by the fact that the migrant families belonging to the same sub-caste preferred to settle in those villages where there were

TABLE 2.3: RESETTLEMENT OF MIGRANT NAMDHARI AGRICULTURIST FAMILIES OF DISTRICT GURDASPUR

Number of families	Sub-caste	Native village of West Punjab	District	Number of same sub-caste	Settled at villages of East Punjab (District Gurdaspur)
7	Deo (Jat)	Vadian Rattian	Sialkot	7	Chak Yakub (Kahnuwan)
5	Bajwa	Mahar	Sialkot	5	Hardan
3	Bajwa	Budhia		3	Awan, Dhariwal
4	Malhi	Khana Malhi		4	Qadianwali (Dorangla)
9	Kahlon	Shania	Sialkot	9	Fajupur (Dhariwal)
3	Kahlon	Jhanda Jarmiya	Sialkot	3	Pakiwan (Kalanaur)
3	Goraya	Kake-ke-Pind	Sialkot	3	Kiri Afghana (Rajowal)
4	Randhawa	Kiapur	Sialkot	1	Dasua (Mukerian), Dalam
				2	Qadian Gujran (Shahpur Goraya)
				1	Kiri Afghana
3	Sara	29 Chak Dehar		3	Nawan Pind Milkhiwal (Bhagowal)

families of the sub-caste. The following table of the resettlement of migrant agriculturists of district Gurdaspur corroborates our arguments. We have data on 77 of these migrant families originally from villages of district Sialkot (Pakistan) who preferred to resettle in the villages of district Gurdaspur where their kin had settled. Out of 77 families, we quote the following cases of resettlement of cluster of such families:

There were 16 migrant families of the Randhawa sub-caste of village Kiampur of Sialkot district. When uprooted, 11 of them managed to resettle in Mehmudpur of district Hoshiarpur. In the initial stage, these families stayed in the different villages of district Gurdaspur. Most of these villages fell under the tashils of Dera Baba Nanak, Batala, and Gurdaspur. The most probable reason for their temporary stay in these villages was that they found close relatives in these tahsils. Another important feature of their settlement was that some of them got temporary as well as permanent land allotments in this district. Of course, there were several migrant families who got their permanent allotments in the villages of tahsil Dasua of district Hoshiarpur. Since the majority of these migrants preferred to settle in villages of tahsils Dasua and Mukerian of Hoshiarpur district, those left in Gurdaspur district, also joined their zat-biradari of native villages of district Sialkot.[37] Similarly, there were 30 agriculturist migrant families from 6 villages of district Sialkot and they settled in two villages of district Sangrur of the East Punjab. These villages are Bhattian (7 families) and Jhall (23 families).[38] Nineteen agriculturist families of villages of district Sialkot got themselves settled in just four villages of district Fategarh Sahib of the East Punjab.[39] Last, 16 agriculturist families of district Lahore migrated to district Ferozepur and settled in its four villages.[40]

Most probably, like their counterparts, the Namdhari agriculturists were too encouraged by the Group Allotment Policy of Government of India.

According to this policy, 'the temporary allotments of evacuee land were, as a rule, given to groups of families in preference to individuals. In the early phase of migration, friends and relatives, because of insecurity and uncertainty about the future, collected together and formed small groups. Government also found it easier to deal with these groups than dealing with individuals or single families. Each group selected an intelligent and influential person as its spokesman, who was called the Group Leader. It was through him that the Patwari of the village or the Halqa revenue officer dealt with that group. The advantages of the group system for quick distribution of land as well as for the happy and successful settlement of displaced persons in villages which they had never seen or heard of before are obvious. Living together among friends and relatives or in their own *Biradari* gave them a sense of security in these distant and foreign lands and helped in their mental rehabilitation. There was an advantage from the point of view of cultivation also. All of them did not individually have the wherewithal of agriculture like bullocks and implements. Working in groups they could pool together their manpower, bullocks and implements and thus, to a certain extent, overcome their shortages. Group allotments should not be confused with group-cultivation. The allottees were not obliged to cultivate jointly the area allotted to a group. If a particular allottee at any stage wanted to cultivate his share separately, he was at liberty to have it demarcated.

Unless the evacuee area in a village was very small, it was rarely that a whole village went to one group because the strength of groups generally did not exceed twenty families. Larger villages contained three or four or even more groups. At the time of the quasi-permanent allotment, a very large number of these temporary allottees were confirmed in the villages of their temporary allotment, and thus homogeneity was achieved in the rural resettlement.[41]

While some Sikhs faced physical and mental torture at the hands of marauding Muslim columns, it were also Muslims who protected and escorted others to safety. Second, agriculturists belonging to a particular village and *zat-biradaris* moved in groups and preferred to resettle in groups such as the Randhawas, Sandhus, Bajwas, Cheemas, Gorayas, Kahlons, and Blaggans. In a number of cases, the relatives of these migrants guided them to settle in those villages where evacuee property was available. The migrant agriculturists, like their counterparts, tried their best to retain their old *bhaichara* (community) while resettling in the villages of the East Punjab. It is not suggested here that the Group Allotment Policy of Government of India and kinship ties were the only variables of resettlement of the migrant agriculturists. There was a section of these agriculturists who were guided and attracted by the quality of land. When they found that the allotted land was of poor quality, they disposed it and bought more fertile land elsewhere. The Namdhari agriculturists too were guided by this dictum. There are several Namdhari agriculturists of district Kapurthala who left their land holdings of poor quality in Amritsar and Hoshiarpur districts.[42]

THE RESETTLEMENT OF ARTISANS

The process of rehabilitation of artisan *panahgeers* was essentially determined by the availability of homes for shelter, and work for livelihood. Many were skilled masons, carpenters and black-smiths. But they did not have implements for wood and iron working since they had left their native villages empty handed. In the initial stage, they shared or borrowed these implements from their relatives. Gradually, they raised money and purchased the required implements. However, those settled in the villages found that the adequate work was not available, as there were already lohars and the tarkhans there. Moreover, the communal disorder and violence had brought the construction and manufacturing work to stand still. The Muslim artisans who largely provided skilled labour in East Punjab had gone to West Punjab.[43] Meanwhile, 'sympathy' for the panahgeer relatives disappeared and they became unwanted for the host families. One Namdhari respondent narrated that they were thrown out of the house of their *nana* (father of his mother) and had a hard time resettling in Jalandhar city. Consequently, wherever these artisans could find work, they settled in those villages and towns. Table 2.4 and Table 2.5 show that unlike their counterparts (agriculturists), migrant artisans came from different villages and towns of district Sialkot, Gujranwala, and Lahore and resettled in different villages and towns of district Gurdaspur and Patiala. The majority of them ultimately preferred to settle in urban centres. However, they settled in different *mohallas* (localities) of these centres. These artisans belonged to different sub-castes of their respective biradaris. The partition of Punjab in 1947 certainly fractured their biradari-brotherhood.

On the other hand, village-kinship gave relief to several migrant families of artisans in the initial stage. Tarlok Singh's story of migration

TABLE 2.4: RESETTLEMENT OF MIGRANT NAMDHARI AGRICULTURIST FAMILIES OF DISTRICT GURDASPUR

Number of families	Sub-caste	Native village of West Punjab	District	Settled number of same sub-caste	Settled in villages of East Punjab (District Gurdaspur)
1	Deo (Jat)	Khara	Sialkot	1	Kalanaur
7	Deo (Jat)	Vadian Rattian	Sialkot	7	Chak Yakub (Kahnuwan)
1	Deo (Jat)	Vero Ke (Narowal)	Sialkot	1	Bahadur Hussain (Mesami) BTL
1	Bajwa	Chavinda Bajigar	Sialkot	1	Qadian
1	Bajwa	Chandowal Chota	Sialkot	1	Fatehgarh
2	Bajwa	Narowal	Sialkot	2	Sagarpur
1	Bajwa	Gajiwal	Sialkot	1	Deriwal (Kalanaur)
1	Bajwa	Chavinda	Sialkot	1	Masania
5	Bajwa	Mahar	Sialkot	5	Hardan
1	Bajwa	Kheva		1	Panj Gorayian
1	Bajwa	Narowal Chak	Sialkot	1	Sarwali (BTL)
1	Bajwa	Dadu Bajwa		1	Chak Yakub Kahnuwan
3	Bajwa	Budhia		3	Avan, Bhariwal
4	Malhi	Khana Malhi		4	Aadian (Dorangla)
1	Malhi	Khano Malhi		1	Aadian Dorangla

1	Cheema	Fatehpur		1	Qadian
1	Kahlon	Thamdal (Narowal)	Sialkot	1	Sangravan (BTL)
1	Kahlon	Jarmiya Singh	Sialkot	1	Athwal, Barila Khurd
9	Kahlon	Shania	Sialkot	9	Fajupur (Dhariwal)
3	Kahlon	Jhanda Jarmiya	Sialkot	3	Pakiwan (Lopo) (BTL)
1	Kahlon	Shania		1	Kamalpur (Kalanaur), Lakhan Kalan
1	Kahlon	Jarmiya Singh	Sialkot	1	Barila Khurd (Barila Kalan)
1	Kahlon	Wazerpur Qandhala		1	Bijliwal, Kila Lal Singh
3	Goraya	Kake-ke-Pind	Sialkot	3	Kiri Afghana (Rajowa)
1	Bhinder	Takia (Narowal)	Sialkot	1	Balalpur (BTL)
1	Bhinder	Milkhpur		1	Fajupur (Dhariwal)
1	Bhinder	Datewal	Sialkot	1	Munnan Kalan (Jagowal Bate)
4	Randhawa	Kiapur	Sialkot	1	Dasuha (Mukerian), Dalam (BTL)
				2	Qadian Gujran (Shahpur Goraya)
				1	Kiri Afgana
1	Randhawa	Ghatia	Lyallpur	1	Basrawan (Harchowal)
1	Randhawa	Ghania-ke-Bet		1	Chaura (Dera Baba Nanak)
1	Randhawa	Ghania-ke-Bangar		1	Nausehra Majha Singh
1	Randhawa	Ghama-ke-Bet		1	Ghanin-ke-Bet Batala (for last 8 yrs)
1	Hundal	Dugri Hundlan Di		1	Purowal Jattan (Dhariwal)
2	Mahal	Bina Daska	Sialkot	2	Kapura (Marhi Tanda) BTL
3	Sara	29 Chak Dehar		3	Nawan Pind Milkhiwal (Bhagowal)
1	Rajput	Vaddi Rattian (Narowal)	Sialkot	1	Chak Jakub (Kahnuwan)
1	Purewal	Lidhoke (Narowal)	Sialkot	1	Basant Kot (Dhianpur)

1	Bal	Milkhpur Shahan Da		1	Bajar (Jagowali Bet Pind)
1	Varaich	Madhogil (Narowal)	Sialkot	1	Qila Darshan Singh (BTL)
1	Wahale	Nangli Doaba (Narowal)	Sialkot	1	Bhagtana Tuliya (Dera Baba Nanak)
1	Pannu	Bala (Narowal)	Sialkot	1	Sarje Chak Baleem, P.O. Pakiwan
1	Tatle	Khusar (Narowal)	Sialkot	1	Santa Da Dera (Shehjada)
1	Sandhu	Kotli Sandhuan Di		1	Sarwali
77				77	

RESTETTLEMENT OF MIGRANT RAMGAHRIAS FAMILIES OF DISTRICT GURDASPUR

Number of families	Sub-caste	Native village of West Punjab	District	Settled number of same sub-caste	Settled in villages of East Punjab (District Gurdaspur)
1	Renu Bhullar		Sialkot	1	Qila Darshan Singh (BTL)
1		Kani Jafarwal	Sialkot	1	Ballaswar Mari Tanda
1	Nagi	Madogil (Narowal)	Sialkot	1	Dialgarh (BTL)
1	Sehmai	Mal (Narowal)	Sialkot	1	New Katra Kalanaur
1	Chalotra	Hazipur		1	Timo Road Sant Nagar GSR
1	Bhamra	Madogill (Narowal)	Sialkot	1	Kali Mata Mandir, Pathankot
1		Sarbkot	Sialkot	1	Fatehgarh Churian, BTL Road, GSR
1	Man-potra	Narang Chana (Narowal)	Sialkot	1	Fatehgarh Churian
1	Saggu	Siowal Gujran	Gujran-wala	1	Hathi Gate, BTL
1	Matharu	Khurpa	Sialkot	1	Umar Pura, Gupta Gali, BTL

1	Matharu	Shikarpur		1	Gurdaspur City, Shakarpura, Dera Baba Nanak Road, BTL
1	Malhotra	Vazirpur	Sialkot	1	Bulewal, P.O. Naushera Majha Singh
1	Bamrah (Ram-garhia)			1	Udowal, Dera Baba Nanak Rd. BTL
1	Bamrah	Bhura Dala		1	Rosa (Pakiwan); Zharianwala, BTL
2	Renu	Mauje-ke-Darap (Narowal)	Sialkot	1	Chaube, Shanti Nagar Kahnuwan Rd. BTL
				1	Bhath, Kahnuwan Rd. BTL
1	Marwah	Gaziabad (Narowal)	Sialkot	1	N. Foundry Kahnwan Rd. BTL
1	Shergill	Chak No 96, Khanewal	Multan	1	Tughalwal Gate Khuh-wali
18				18	
		MAHASHE FAMILIES			
2	Mahashe	Gamu Da Kot	Sialkot	2	Mustafapur, Prem Nagar GSR
2				2	
		PARJAPAT FAMILIES			
2	Sangar (Parja-pat)	Bugre (Daska)	Sialkot	2	Umarpur BTL
1	Bhikher	Kotli		1	Mohalla Tullian P.O. Kalanaur
3				3	
		CHHEMBA FAMILIES			
1	Chhemba	Gota (Narowal)	Sialkot	1	Fatehgarh Churian
1				1	
		TOTAL			
101				101	

TABLE 2.5: RESETTLEMENT OF NAMDHARI SIKHS IN DISTRICT PATIALA

Number of families	Sub-caste	Native village of West Punjab	District	Settled number of same sub-caste	Settled in villages of East Punjab (District Patiala)
		JAT FAMILIES			
3	Bajwa	Daduwal	Sialkot	3	Daulatpura, Patiala
1	Bajwa	Daduwal	Sialkot	1	Patiala
1	Dhillon	Isvian (Tappa)	Lahore	1	Patiala
1	Dhindsa	Dhindsa	Gujranwala	1	Patiala
1	Dhindsa			1	Dharamheri, Patiala
1	Hanjra	Lalepur	Gujranwala	1	Patiala
1	Lagra	Meerakpur	Sialkot	1	Daulatpura, Patiala
1	Maesh	Malookpura	Narowal/ Sialkot	1	Daulatpura
1	Maesh	Malookpura	Narowal/ Sialkot	1	Memad, Dasuha
1	Sandhu			1	Nabha
1	Virk	Kassoke	Hafizabad/ Gujranwala	1	Patiala
13				13	
		RAMGARHIA FAMILIES			
3	Slaich			3	Nabha
2	Sidhu	Santpura Babian da	Gujranwala	2	Patiala
1	Vasir			1	Nabha
1	Matharu		Sialkot	1	Patiala
1	Bamrah		Lahore	1	Patiala
1	Devgan		Gujranwala	1	Patiala
9				9	
		BRAHMIN FAMILIES			
1		Khanduwali	Daska, Sialkot	1	Nabha
1		Khaṇduwali	Daska, Sialkot	1	Bhattian, Nabha
2				2	
		PARJAPAT FAMILIES			
1	Khambh	Varan	Sheikhupura	1	Patiala

and resettlement is relevant. Tarlok Singh is a carpenter of Jaspal Nagar, Sultanwind Road, Amritsar. He said that the partition uprooted his family from Keeranwala village, Sialkot. When violence broke out, his family along with several Jat and artisan families moved to the dera of Sant Harnam Singh who was a prominent Namdhari leader. Near this dera, there was another village, Kanian. A Muslim mob had encircled this village and his father and other members of *bhaichara* suffered heavy casualties. To the good luck of the Sikhs, a Muslim *badmash* of a nearby village came to their rescue. He took the Sikhs to his village Malikpur and protected them. The Muslim escorted them to the ancestral well. They joined the *kafila* which crossed river Ravi and reached Dera Baba Nanak. For some time, all the artisan families stayed in the Refugee Camp at Amritsar. Meanwhile, the proprietor of Rohana Mill, Muzaffarnagar, UP, came to their help; he asked them to reach Rohana Mill. 'We worked in this mill for about two months when the Hindus of Samana town invited us to settle over there. These Hindus promised us to give free houses and some land.' Meanwhile, a large number of migrant artisan families moved to Samana. They worked as carpenters and black smiths. Tarlok Singh said that 30 to 40 families still live in Samana town. The invitation of the Hindus of Samana was not an act of charity. They were threatened by the Muslims of that area constantly and felt insecure. They thought that the Sikhs would shield them. Tarlok Singh stated that free houses and land given by Hindus went a long way in resettling and restarting life.[44]

Meanwhile, Tarlok Singh's family was allotted 2 acres of land in village Gharram in Patiala State. His father disposed of that land and moved from UP to Delhi which provided better avenues of employment. Tarlok Singh and other migrants established their households in Sahibpura colony, Tilak Nagar. He stayed there for 17 years. Tarlok Singh regretted that he had to leave Delhi for Amritsar due to a family dispute. It was in 1980 when he bought a plot of 125 yards in Jaspal Nagar, Sultanwind Road. Tarlok Singh did not disclose specific reasons for choosing Amritsar city. He simply said that he had relatives here and in-laws at Batala.[45]

The religious bond of the Namdhari Sikhs too played a role in selecting *mohalla* or locality for the resettlement in any city. For instance, in case of Jalandhar city, the migrants moved from Amritsar refugee camp to this city as the families of their 'mothers' and 'sisters' etc were already living here. Their *mamus* and cousins owned repair-

TABLE 2.6 RESETTLEMENT OF NAMDHARI SIKHS IN DISTRICT HOSHIARPUR

Number of families	Sub-caste	Native village of West Punjab	District	Settled number of same sub-caste	Settled in villages of East Punjab (District Hoshiarpur)
16	Randhawa	Kiampur	Sialkot	11	Mehmudpur
				2	Batala
				2	Bhangala
				1	Ladpur
4	Malhi	Kandiala	Sialkot	3	Mehmudpur
				1	Batala
4	Hundal	Kukranwala (Bandala)	Lyallpur	4	Hardokhla
2	Bajwa	Suzada	Sialkot	1	Mehmudpur
				1	Batala
1	Bajwa	Chak	Sialkot	1	Mukerian
1	Bajwa	Nangal	Sialkot	1	Fatehullapur
2	Bajwa	Chak 300	Sialkot	2	Budhobarkat
1	Bajwa	Rohi	Sialkot	1	Marasgarh
1	Bajwa	Chak 324	Sialkot	1	Budhobarkat
4	Bajwa	Chandowal	Sialkot	2	Fatehullapur
				1	Marasgarh
				1	Kaintha
4	Bajwa	Rachandpur	Sialkot	4	Khokhran
3	Goraya	Madogill	Narowal/ Sialkot	3	Dugri
1	Goraya	Ghakke Kiande	Sialkot	1	Budhobarkat
2	Cheema	Choon Cheema	Sialkot	2	Budhobarkat
4	Jathol	Mehmadwali	Sialkot	4	Dugri
1	Jathol	Mehmadwali	Sialkot	1	Khokhran
1	Maini	Kandiala	Sialkot	1	Budhobarkat
52				52	

Number of agricultural migrants from Sialkot 48
Lyallpur 04

workshops or wood workshops. It was in 1950-60 that most of the migrant Namdharis thought of going to Jalandhar city.

The 'host' Namdhari Sikhs helped migrant co-religionists to occupy empty houses of Muslims. A substantial number of co-religionists

TABLE 2.7: RESETTLEMENT OF NAMDHARI SIKHS IN DISTRICT SANGRUR

Number of families	Sub-caste	Native village of West Punjab	District	Settled number of same sub-caste	Settled in villages of East Punjab (District Sangrur)
3	Kahlon	Tianwali	Sialkot	3	Jhall
3	Blaggan	Rasada	Sialkot	4	Jhall
1	Blaggan	Khanduwali	Sialkot		
4	Goraya	Dugri	Sialkot	4	Bhattian
11	Sandhu	Khanduwali	Sialkot	3	Bhattian
				8	Jhall
2	Sandhu	Pakhowali	Sialkot	2	Jhall
4	Takhar	Tianwali	Sialkot	4	Jhall
1	Takhar	Khanduwali	Sialkot	1	Jhall
1	Hazran	Baure	Gujranwala	1	Jhall
30				30	

Number of agriculturists migrant from Sialkot 29
Gujranwala 01

settled in one place not only made the Namdhari migrants socially 'secure' but also enabled them to take 'collective action' for common problems. Their concentration also enabled them to start a community life. Subsequently, they founded their own religious-cum-social centres. Their earliest concentrations were in the localities of nearby Jalandhar Railway Station: on the Empress Garden Road; Gobindgarh Mohalla, and a collection of houses around Ghumar-Vali Maseet later known as Central Town and then Basti Bhure Khan, a Muslim locality outside city. It was during the decade of 1956-66 that the Punjab Government carved out a locality known as Preet Nagar around Basti Bhure Khan. This locality comprised small plots of 4 *marlas* and were given to the Namdhari migrants in lieu of their 'claims' Those who could not furnish claims purchased plots at low price.

Preet Nagar, Basti Bhure Khan, and the area around the Railway Station became safe places for the Namdhari artisans. Jalandhar city itself provided scope for shelter as well as jobs. Its twelve *bastis* (settlements) were dominated by Muslim artisans, whom Partition had forced to vacate.[46] In the early twentieth century Jalandhar (also Hoshiarpur) had a reputation for carpentry and sent its workmen to the Districts Hoshiarpur and Amritsar which supplied skilled labour

TABLE 2.8: RESETTLEMENT OF NAMDHARI SIKHS IN DISTRICT FATEHGARH SAHIB

Number of families	Sub-caste	Native village of West Punjab	District	Settled number of same sub-caste	Settled in villages of East Punjab (District Fatehgarh Sahib)
1	Randhawa	Nangli Doaba	Sialkot	1	Bir Bhamarsi
1	Bajwa	Nangli Doaba	Sialkot	1	Bir Bhamarsi
2	Bajwa	Gajiwal	Sialkot	2	Bir Bhamarsi
2	Sandhu	Khanduwala	Sialkot	2	Bir Bhamarsi
1	Sandhu	Khanduwali Chhianwali	Sialkot	1	Rajinder Nagar
2	Virk	Trigri	Sialkot	2	Bir Bhamarsi
1	Kang	Kang	Sialkot	1	Bir Bhamarsi
1	Cheema	Sialkot	Sialkot	1	Dera Mir Miran
1	Cheema	Maypur	Sialkot	1	Dera Mir Miran
1	Cheema	Cheema	Sialkot	1	Dera Mir Miran
4	Cheema	Man Suhawala	Sialkot	4	Dera Mir Miran
1	Blaggan	Pakistan	Sialkot	1	Dera Mir Miran
1	Waraich	Paida	Sialkot	1	Jalkheri
19				19	

Number of agricultural migrants from Sialkot 19

to the railway workshops. Kartarpur town came into being as a manufacturing centre of furniture.[47] Moreover, since Jalandhar city was connected by the railway lines and roads, migrants could easily come and go from this city to any other towns located on these routes. In fact, Jalandhar being one of the major rehabilitation centres of the refugees, gave them some sense of belonging. Some of the respondents disclosed that for some time, they tried their luck in other towns but ultimately came back.

There was another pattern of resettlement of village artisans including *sepidars* (artisans who provided skilled labour to the

TABLE 2.9: RESETTLEMENT OF NAMDHARI SIKHS IN DISTRICT FEROZEPUR

Number of families	Sub-caste	Native village of West Punjab	District	Settled number of same sub-caste	Settled in villages of East Punjab (District Ferozepur)
6	Sandhu	Chak 33	Sialkot	6	Sabuana
7	Sandhu	Khudpur	Lahore	7	Fathewali
2	Sandhu	Ziabagga Khurd	Lahore	2	Gatta Badshah
7	Sidhu	Dheeng Jattan	Lahore	6	Rajeewala
				1	Assal
1	Cheema	Behke Cheemian Vali	Gujranwala	1	Bhaval Basian Dhanian Sucha Singh/ Abohar
23				23	

Number of agriculturists migrant from Sialkot	06
Lahore	16
Gujranwala	01

zamindars of their own villages) in urban areas. The village artisans, by and large, moved along with the *kafilas* of their own native village men. Of course, in the *raula* (violence), several of them had to leave their own *kafilas* and were forced to take shelter in different places either with their relatives or friends. But ultimately they came to those villages of East Punjab where their native zamindars had settled. It may also be pointed out here that these artisans too preferred to stay with the people of their own village. The case of Namdhari artisans of tahsil Bhulath, district Kapurthala, is a typical case. Bhulath has still the distinction of 27 migrant Namdhari families from Pakistan. The caste wise breakup is as follow: 15 Ramgarhia, 11 Jat and 1 Arora. All these Namdhari Sikhs migrated from the village Miranpur where they had settled after 1955. They were forced to quit this village as it was thoroughly marooned by the floods. As a result, their households and *karkhanas* and fields were heavily damaged. Namdhari

Guru Partap Singh came to their rescue. He persuaded the then deputy commissioner of Kapurthala district to allot plots for households. The size of each plot was 6 *marlas*. Thus a small concentration of Namdhari Sikhs came into being in Bhulath. However, the Namdhari Jats carried on their ancestral calling of agriculture as their landholdings were not far of from Bhulath. The majority of the Ramgarhias too carried on their ancestral occupation but not as sepidars. At present they are carpenters and masons. Two or three families own workshops of wood-work. Namdhari Arora families run retail shops since they came to this place.

Nevertheless, the number of resettlement cases on the basis of biradari is not substantial. The majority of the Ramgarhia families shifted from one place to another according to the availability of job avenues. This pattern is more perceptible in the case of Ramgarhia families of district Gurdaspur. Among the 18 families, there are hardly 4 of the same *gotra* to be found in Batala town, district Gurdaspur. The rest belonging to different gotras of Ramgarhia castes. There is one family in Pathankot, 8 in Batala, 2 in Fatehgarh Churian and one family in village Rose (Gurdaspur), one family in village Bulewal (Gurdaspur), one family in Dialgarh (Batala), one family in Qila Darshan Singh (Batala), one family in Balarwal (Gurdaspur), one family in Kalanaur and one family in Tugalwal, etc.

To sum up, the following inferences can be drawn. Out of the sample survey of 1545 Namdhari families, 494 were migrants from the West Punjab. Like the other Hindu and Sikh migrants, the Namdhari migrants were too victims of communal violence, financial and physical hardships. However, the quantum of loss they suffered was comparatively small. The Namdhari migrants were fortunate to receive timely financial and moral support from Satguru Partap Singh who developed Jiwan Nagar, Sirsa (Haryana) solely for their rehabilitation and made similar arrangements in Bir Bhamarsi (Patiala). Namdhari guru also prevailed upon the raja of Mandi (Himachal Pradesh) to allow his migrants to settle in this town, thus maintaining a spirit of brotherhood and cohesion among his followers. However, the pattern of resettlement of the Namdhari agriculturist migrants in the districts of Hoshiarpur, Gurdaspur, Kapurthala, Fatehgarh Sahib and Ferozepur was mainly guided by the brotherhood of *zat-biradari* and availability of the evacuee land. Similarly, the concentration of the Namdhari artisan migrants in the cities/towns of Amritsar, Jalandhar and Ludhiana underlined the fact that the process of their resettlement was motivated by the spirit of brotherhood of the *zat-biradari* and by the religious bond. Of course, job and business avenues were also variables.

NOTES

1. Nahar Singh and Kirpal Singh, *Rebels Against the British Rule,* 1995, p. 38.
2. *Census of India, 1911: Punjab*, vol. XIV, pt. I, Lahore, Punjab, 1912, p. 158; According to the Census of 1941, the Sikh population was 11.7 per cent of the total. The Muslims formed 62.1 per cent: M.S. Randhawa, *Out of the Ashes,* 1954, p. 9.
3. Darbara Singh, *The Punjab Tragedy (1947)*, 1949, p. 241.
4. Kirpal Singh, *The Partition of Punjab*, 1972, pp. 95-114; Aiyar Swarna, pp. 15-38 cited by Narinder Kumar, *Post-Partition Rehabilitation Problem and State Policies*, 2002, pp. 3-4.
5. Ibid.
6. Ibid., pp. 26-7.
7. Jagdish Singh Waryam, *Khilre Patre,* 2005, pp. 43-72.
8. Interviews with Sant Labh Singh, aged 88, 2-C Malwa Colony Near Moti Mehal, Patiala and Amolak Singh, H.No. 1073, Urban Estate, Phase II, Patiala.
9. Interviews with Gurdip Singh, village Malowaliawale, Ferozepur district; Dalip Singh, village Fatewali, Ferozepur district; Jagjit Singh, Malaut town, Muktsar district.
10. Kirpal Singh, 1972, p. 19.
11. The problems of the Namdhari agriculturists were not exceptional. All non-Muslim agriculturists suffered this loss. It was estimated that out of 18.8 million cultivable acres in the West Punjab, about 6.7 million acres belonged to the non-Muslims who paid 34 per cent of the total land revenue. The Muslims in the East Punjab owned 4.7 million cultivable acres out of a total of 14.2 million acres and paid only 27 per cent of the land revenue. In this way, the non-Muslims had left behind about 20 lakh acres in excess of what Muslims had left in the East Punjab. The East Punjab shared 44 per cent of the population of the united Punjab with only 38 per cent of its land. Besides, the East Punjab received only three million canal-irrigated acres out of a total of over fourteen million acres, that is, about 21 per cent. In order to promote an equitable distribution, the government adopted the following scheme of graded cuts in such a way that the small landholders were to have a minimum cut:

Area abandoned (acres)	Net allotment (acres)
10	7½
30	21

40	27
50	32 ½
60	37 ½
100	51 ½
150	66 ½
200	79
250	89
500	126
1000	176 ½
3000	281 1/3
4000	326 ½
5000	376 ½

See Kirpal Singh, p. 151.

12. Interview with Jagjit Singh, Malaut Town, Muktsar on 24 October 2008.
13. On the resettlement of agriculturists, the policy executed by MS Randhawa and Tarlock Singh, see Khushwant Singh, *A History of the Sikhs,* vol. II, 2011, pp. 279-85.
14. Poonam Seth, The Municipal Committee of Jullundur, M.Phil, Dissertation, GNDU, Amritsar, 1985, pp. 36-9.
15. A.N. Bali, *Now It Can be Told,* 1944, p. 103.
16. Ibid., pp. 104-7.
17. Gopal Das Khosla, 'Stern Reckoning', 2004, pp. 145-6.
18. Namdhari Sikh Karnail Singh, resident of village Rajinder Nagar, district Fatehgarh Sahib disclosed that half of the Sikh population of village Khanduwala (Chianwali district, Sialkot) became Muslims and stayed back. Although Karnail Singh did not state the reasons of their conversion, can be presumed that these people took communal violence and conversion as temporary phenomena.
19. Interview with Sarpanch Gurcharan Singh on 10 November 2008 at his house.
20. M.S. Randhawa, *Out of Ashes,* 1954 p. 67.
21. Cited by Tarlok Singh (Land Resettlement Manual): Satya Murthy Ray, *Punjab Since Partition,* 1986, p. 160.
22. For detail, see, Arvind Singh Sehgal, Assimilation of an Ethnic Group, 1990.
23. Tara Singh Anjan, *Namdhari Sikhs: A Brief History,* 2007, pp. 78-80.
24. Namdhari claim over this land was contested by the Forest Deptt. of Punjab government in the court. But the verdict went in favour of the Namdhari Guru.
25. '. . . the Congress, perhaps for the first time, officially introduced the notion of land ceiling soon after independence. In November 1947, the A.D.C.E. appointed a committee, which drew up the economic programme of the Congress. The Committee, headed by Jawaharlal Nehru had

recommended, 'The maximum size of holdings should be fixed. The surplus land over such a maximum should be acquired and placed at the disposal of the village cooperatives.' Subsequently, Kumarappa Committee also recommended a ceiling on landholding.' The Nagpur session of the Congress (1959) reiterated that ceilings should be fixed on existing and further holdings and legislation to this effect should be completed in all status by the end of 1959.', *India After Independence 1947-2000* (ed. Bipan Chandra and M. Mukherjee), 2000, pp. 385-6.

26. Suwaran Singh Virk, *Kuka Lehar Da Punjabi Sahit*, 2009, pp. 190-1.
27. See Tables: 2.6, 2.7, 2.8, 2.9.
28. Interview with Dalip Singh, village Fatehwali, Ferozepur, 25 February 2008.
29. Other agriculturists of village Fatehwali are Gurdip Singh, Dhian Singh, Bohar Singh, Jota Singh.
30. Heads of these families of village Sabuana are Sarabjit Singh, Gurjant Singh, Baj Singh, Jagtar Singh and Resham Singh.
31. Heads of these families are Gurmukh Singh, Bohad Singh (village Rajiwal), Hardip Singh (village Rajiwal), Darbara Singh (village Rajiwal), Manjit Singh (village Rajiwal) and Hardev Singh (village Rajiwal).
32. Heads of these families are Bagicha Singh and Gurmit Singh.
33. According to Census of 1931/41 the Muslims and Sikhs population of the following districts comprised

	Muslims (%)	Sikhs (%)
Lahore Sheikhupur	63.62	18.85
Sialkot	62	11.7
Gujranwala	70.4	10.9
Montgomery	69.1	13.9
Lyallpur	62.8	18.8

Kirpal Singh, 1972, p. 65.

34. M.S. Randhawa, 1954, p. 59.
35. Ibid., p. 80.
36. See Tables 2.6, 2.7, 2.8, 2.9.
37. See Table 2.6.
38. See Table 2.7.
39. See Table 2.8.
40. See Table 2.9.
41. M.S. Randhawa, 1954, pp. 68-9.
42. M.S. Randhawa noted that 'in many cases it was seen that it was the pull of good land, than *biradari*, which attracted people. It was often seen that brothers who had been allotted land in different villages usually desired to get consolidation in a village with good land, and when the choice of consolidation was given in an inferior village, they preferred to stay where they were', pp. 116-17.
43. Khushwant Singh, 2011, p. 153.

44. Interview with Tarlock Singh on 19 August 2007.
45. Ibid.
46. 'The exodus of Muslim skilled labour from the East Punjab substantially crippled the industries, like hosiery, metal works and railways in which the Muslims formed about 90 per cent of skilled or semi-skilled labour. The east Punjab, which was already backward in industrial development suffered much on this account. Most of the factories and workshop were closed', Kirpal Singh, 1972, p. 153.
47. *District and State Gazetteers of the Undivided Punjab*, vols. III-IV, 1914, pp. 530-1.

CHAPTER 3

Internal Migration and Occupational Diversification

Next to the partition of Punjab 1947, rural to urban migration of Namdhari Sikhs of all occupational castes was major demographic variable bringing important ramifications for the community. As noted in the first and two chapters, a large section of the Namdhari artisan migrants of West Punjab settled in the urban centres of Amritsar, Gurdaspur, Jalandhar, Goraya, Phagwara, and Ludhiana and thus formed the Namdhari urban concentrations. Table 3.1 shows that 300 Namdhari agriculturist, artisan and business families moved from rural to urban centres after Independence. Consequently, the major concentrations of the Namdhari Ramgarhia families are found in the cities of Ludhiana (48), Amritsar (38), Batala (34), Chandigarh & Mohali (27), Jalandhar (25), and Rupnagar (14). Whereas Namdhari agriculturist families are found in Chandigarh, Mohali, and Batala. This table also shows that 71 per cent of Namdhari Ramgarhia, 19 per cent of Namdhari agriculturist and 5 per cent of Namdhari Arora/ Khatri families were migrants to urban centres. The other migrants of other occupational castes too moved to these centres, but their number was marginal.

This chapter examines general and specific variables responsible for the internal migration of these occupational castes. We shall take account of geo-political conditions which dislocated the native places of the Namdhari agriculturist, artisan and business families.

Since Independence, a large number of families of each Namdhari occupational caste moved from rural to urban centres. However, the pattern of migration was not uniform. The family of each occupational caste left its native village for some specific concerns and reasons and ultimately settled in a place in that *mohalla* of a town where its kin had already been settled. Soon thereafter, more families of that *zat-biradari* of the same village (or another village) came and settled. The underlying reason was social security. Proximty to the workplace and purchasing power were additional variables for resettlement in a particular locality. However, variables for leaving the native villages and resettling in the urban centres differed from one occupational caste to another. The Namdhari artisan and business families moved for employment and better business prospects, whereas the agriculturists moved for entrepreneurship and urban facilities. The success of one family induced a 'practice of chain employment and chain-migration'. However, the common variables behind the rural to urban migration of all occupational castes were the creation of an Indo-Pakistan Border and the Khalistan movement.

Before we proceed with the analysis of these variables it is essential to have a brief note on the social order of Punjabi villages of contemporary Punjab. The Green Revolution which started in 1960s had radically transformed Punjabi rural society, demographically, socially, and economically. Each aspect of this transformation has been studied in depth by the social scientists and demographers.[1] In Punjabi villages live Sikhs, Hindus, Christians, and Muslims. Except for Sikhs, as we shall note, all are minority communities. The major Sikh population comprises peasants and artisans. They are followed by the Hindus who are generally shopkeepers, traders, commission agents, and priests. The number of Hindu zamindars is marginal. Most Christians form a service community. Among all the religious communities, however, are professionals like teachers, doctors, clerks, chemists, and lawyers.

The partition of Punjab in 1947 and subsequently the formation of a Punjabi speaking province in 1966 transformed the demography of Punjab. The undivided Punjab had comprised 1,38,105 sq miles East Punjab was 50,362 sq miles. The formation of the Punjabi speaking province further reduced the territory to 20,254 sq miles. In British Punjab, Muslims constituted 53.2 per cent, Hindus 29.11 per cent and Christians 1.9 per cent in 1941. The formation of the Punjabi-speaking province in 1966 made Sikhs a majority (60 per cent) and Hindus a minority comprising 36 per cent of the total population in 1971. According to the Census 1991, the Sikh population increased to 62.95 per cent whereas the share of the Hindu population declined to 34.56 per cent. The Muslims and Christians constituted only 1.18 and 1.11 per cent respectively. However, the population of the scheduled castes/tribes constituted 28.31 per cent. In the last quarter of the twentieth century, the share of the Sikh population rose in the rural and urban areas whereas, the share of the Hindus declined in both areas.[2]

IMPACT OF INDO-PAKISTAN BORDER AREAS

The partition of Punjab and the communal violence that drove Muslims out of East Punjab and non-Muslims out of West Punjab, radically changed the demography of these two Punjabs in 1947. Demographic changes in Amritsar, Gurdaspur, and Ferozepur districts were more conspicuous in regard to some of their tahsils touching the border. For instance, in 1951, the population of Amritsar District was 1,367,040 (958,533 rural, and 408,507 urban). The proportion was thus 70:30. Partition and communal riots forced the Muslim population of this district to move towards Pakistani Punjab. In 1941, the Muslims numbered 657,695. In 1951, number of displaced persons was 332,260. The gap between the two was of 325,435 persons. This gap further widened to 4,9,093, when the number of Muslims of 186 villages of the Patti subdivision was transferred to Amritsar District in 1947. It was estimated as 1,00,243. The resettlement of non-Muslim refugees in place of Muslim emigrants not only affected the rural areas but also the urban areas, especially Amritsar and Patti. The newcomers resettled in this district were far less in number than the Muslims who had left.

> The district as a whole, has decreased in population in 1951 by 16 per cent over its 1941 population in the rural areas, there was a decrease of 17 per cent only. The 1951 density of the rural areas was 501 persons per square mile. It was in the urban population that the largest decrease of 358,985 which had brought about a fall of 927 persons to the square mile had occurred. There were 214321 in the urban area in 1941 while the displaced persons who had come in their place number 143779.[3]

The impact of forced migration was also visible in the villages and smaller towns situated near the India-Pakistan border in 1947. In Amritsar district, the border towns and villages were Tarn Taran, Khem Karan, Attari, Ramdas and Ajnala. Tarn Taran had lost in population by 263. Its 1941 population was 16,607 as against 16,344 of 1951. Patti's population was 14,297 as against 17,595 of 1941. Ramdas had 5,397 population in 1941 but it was reduced to 3,946 in 1951. A loss of 2,351. Similarly, the 1951 populations of Khem Karan and Sur Singh were found to be 7,069 and 6,506 respectively as against 8,023 and 3,361 of 1941.[4]

Similarly, there was a fall in the density of population in the districts of Ferozepur and Gurdaspur: in Ferozepur from 348 in 1941 to 323 in 1951 and in Gurdaspur tahsil from 662 in 1941 to 632 in 1951.

In Ferozepur, the Muslim population of 641,448 in 1941 which was reduced to 4,875 in 1951, the number of displaced persons was 358,341 in 1951. In Gurdaspur, the Muslim population was 440,323 in 1941 but fell to 10,425 in 1951. The number of displaced persons (migrants from the West Punjab) was 297,581 in 1951. Displaced persons (migrants) did not prefer to settle in these border districts of the state.[5]

The people on the border areas were yet to recover from communal violence, caught up as they were by gangs of criminals and bad characters. These gangs indulged in murdering, dacoities, burglaries, and other crimes. Although they operated in the whole territory of the East Punjab they were more dreaded in the border area where it was easier to operate, in the wake of the collapse of the law and order machinery. Moreover,

> a large number of displaced persons, who had migrated to the East Punjab, had been deprived of means of livelihood. Many of them had exhausted all their savings in the process of migration from the West Punjab to the East Punjab. With limited prospect of employment in the near future and prices of essential commodities soaring high, a number of displaced persons were forced into a life of crime, resulting in the emergence of a new class of 'criminals'.[6]

The princes and landlords and the reactionary communal parties they supported liberally supplied arms and jeeps to rank communalists, which led to the accentuation of crime.[7] Above all, gangs of criminals and 'bad characters' enjoyed the patronage of political leaders involved in the communal killings.

The creation of the Indo-Pakistan border adversely affected the livelihoods of agrarian and non-agrarian castes of the border villages and towns. Among these towns and villages were Attari, Dhanoa (popularly called Pulkanjari), Ajnala, Ramdas, Rajatal, Khem Karan, and Sabroan of Amritsar district.[8] An immediate but quick impact was felt by the non-agrarian castes. Before Partition, the business or traditional occupational callings of non-agriculturists (artisans and traders or shopkeepers) continued as they had access to urban markets and workplaces. After the formation of Pakistan, these people lost access to these markets and work places. The artisans and petty-businessmen/traders of border areas were greater sufferers as they could not commute to the districts of Sialkot and Lahore. Moreover, they were more insecure in the wake of continuous disturbances on the border area, with hostility between India and Pakistan. The loss of markets of the West Punjab and sense of insecurity were felt by the agriculturists too but they could not move to places other than their own villages as they were tied up with their own landholdings. They could depend upon agriculture for their livelihood. The non-agrarian castes have had no such advantage. The situation became serious for the people when the Indo-Pakistan war in 1965 exposed them to Pakistan's air and land attacks. The attack on Chheharta caused terrible loss of life and property. A whole row of houses stood roofless. Seventy-seven houses and shops were razed, and 150 more heavily damaged. Fifty-five people were killed.[9] The picture in rural aleas was also grim. Before the war broke out, the Indian army evacuated villages on the border. The villagers had to move with their livestock and valuables. They took shelter with relatives in towns, cities and villages away from the borders. Production came to a halt and trade and industry were temporarily disturbed. In the subsequent years, growth of commerce and trade and industry in the towns of Attari, Khem Karan, Ajnala and Ramdas stagnated due to the tension created by another Indo-Pakistan war in 1971 and a massive terrorist movement in the last quarter of the twentieth century. In fact, the latter movement forced much of the rural society to move to the cities of Punjab. Amritsar, the epicentre of terrorism, several industrialists and traders/businessmen closed down their manufacturing units and trade centres and moved out of Punjab. The terrorist movement partly changed demography of the towns and cities of Punjab including Amritsar. In the initial stage, rural to urban migrants were Hindus; subsequently, the rich Sikh peasantry including artisans started migrating to the towns and cities of Punjab. It is not suggested that terrorism was only factor driving Hindu population out of rural and urban centres of Punjab. The Hindus, largely industrialists, traders, merchants, shopkeepers, commission agents, and professionals have been more mobile as compared to land-based communities.[10] However, they were in a minority in the rural areas and more scared of the Sikh militants than of Sikhs in general. Moreover, the intensity of terrorism was more perceptible in the border areas of Ferozepur, Amritsar, and Gurdaspur. Peasants, shopkeepers, traders, and artisans left their native villages and towns (especially of border area) for big cities in which they were less vulnerable to extortion, kidnapping, and communal terrorism.

As a result of these developments, our data show only nine out of a hundred Amritsar Namdhari families came from Sialkot and Lahore.

Among these families three were of Ramgarhias, two Jats, 1 Sawarankar and 2 Ghumars. In the process of interviewing the Namdhari Sikhs of the West Punjab (Pakistan) I was amazed at the ignorance expressed by the Namdhari-Sikhs in the age-groups of 50 to 60 and 60 to 70 about the sufferings borne by their grandparents or parents when they were uprooted from their native places in the West Punjab. They could not recall the life stories of their grandparents. There was only a small number of Namdhari Sikhs still nostalgic for the golden days, such as those who had huge landed property and houses and flourishing businesses. They regretted that the lands and houses allotted to them in East Punjab were small in comparison to what they had last. The cases of two families can be cited. Amrik Singh, a retired head cashier, State Bank of India, told the author that his father belonged to village Datewal, district Sialkot. There were 14 to 15 families of Khatris/Aroras and Jat Sikhs in the village. His father owned six large shops of for clothing and departmental shops and a big *haveli* and house. At the time of Partition, the property and other assets amounted to Rs. 10 lakh approximately. In lieu of that, his father got compensation of only Rs. 12,000. He also remembered a fraud committed by his uncle, a well-connected man who, with the help of *patwaris* (village accountants) and judges, appropriated a large share of the property. He also remembered Partition as violence in which his father was killed and his mother was badly wounded. Amrik Singh narrated a story of mass violence in which three to four hundred Sikhs were killed by the Pathans in Bahawalpur. Luckily, his elder brother worked in a bank and was posted at Amritsar. He himself got a job in the State Bank of India. With his salary and share of the property claim, he could begin his life again after Independence. Amrik Singh was posted in this bank in Abohar town. Then he was transferred to Gorakhpur. After a while, he was again transferred to Phagwara, Punjab. Since his brother and several relatives were living in Amritsar, Amrik Singh decided to settle in Azad Nagar, Sultanwind Road, Amritsar. While narrating the story of loss of property and father, Amrik Singh's voice still had a subdued pain and regret.[11]

Gian Singh's family did not suffer any loss of life or property. He is an artisan of the Jhans gotra, and came from village Narwar near Wagha village, Lahore. The people of this village did not know for quite some time whether it was to belong to Pakistan or to India. Gian Singh informed the author that the Sikhs and Hindus of this village were the last to move towards tehsils of Amritsar and Tarn Taran. Proximity to the border meant miner hardship of journey, and fewer risks of communal violence. His family first moved to Ibban Jhabbal near the Khem Karan sector and stayed there for a month, and then moved to Amritsar. Gian Singh's father opted to stay around Chawk Lachhmansar because there was a large number of families of his own biradari (Ramgarhia) living here. After a while Gian Singh's father was allotted land in compensation in Fazilka tahsil, but he disposed it of for Rs.6,000. Gian Singh did not get a share. Since 1953, he has been working either as mason or carpenter on daily wages. His two sons are still living in a house which was donated by a Namdhari devotee to Satguru Jagjit Singh.

There was a large number of the Namdhari families in the East Punjab whose members had gone to the towns/cities of the West Punjab for earning a livelihood; others owned businesses in those towns and cities. However, a typical case was of those Namdhari Sikhs whose native villages were equidistant from Lahore and Amritsar, Sialkot and Gurdaspur. The artisans and traders of these villages had usually commuted between their villages and these towns before Partition. One of such families belonged to Dera Baba Nanak. The head of this family was Natha Singh who manufactured wooden photo frames and his shop was in Lahore. Like other people, Natha Singh did not leave his shop when incidents of violence took place in Lahore. He thought that the communal violence was a temporary phenomenon. However, he was soon trapped in the violence and managed to reach Amritsar by train. He decided to resettle in the area inside Khazana Gate. Natha Singh had a special reason for selecting this area. His son Amrik Singh told me that his father had acquaintance with the timber merchants/traders of this area of Amritsar. They used to go to his father's shop in Lahore. Before Partition there were Muslim artisans and traders who lived around Khazana Gate. They went to Pakistan leaving their houses vacant. Like other migrants, Natha Singh too occupied one such a house. Perhaps more important reason of settling down here was that Natha Singh's relatives had been living in this area. Living among the people of his own biradari gave him a sense of social security. This sense further strengthened when some of the timber merchants of Lahore too came to stay here (Khazana Gate). Personal acquaintance with artisans and merchants and facility of the timber market (*lakkar mandi*) helped Natha Singh and his sons to restart his old occupation of manufacturing wooden frames. Amrik Singh informed me that in the wake of financial constraints, he used to take timber on loan from a former M.P., Kirpal Singh, himself a timber merchant and owner of mechanical saws. Natha Singh occupied a small house of 100 square yards. The real owner of this house was husband of Natha Singh's sister. Subsequently, Natha Singh bought the house.[12]

Like their counterparts, the Namdhari artisans, traders, merchants and shopkeepers left their native villages and towns for Amritsar city and its towns like Chheharta and Verka. Most of these Namdhari Sikhs belonged to the villages Pulkanjari, Chaugawan and Khiyala. Three Namdhari families of the Kharbanda sub-caste (of Arora caste) were forced to leave their native village, Pulkanjari during the communal disturbances of 1947. Ancestors of these families were moneylenders, *sarafas* (bullion dealers), and cloth merchants. The actual name of village Pulkanjari is Dhanoe. It was a *kasba* known for its mercantile centre and huge shops of *banias* during Maharaja Ranjit Singh's time. The Maharaja used to stay here on his way from Lahore to Amritsar. The village became a resort comprising *barandari* (having twelve gates). From far and wide, artists displayed their skills here. Among them was Muslim nautch girl named Moran. The Maharaja enjoyed her dance performances. Such occasions turned into annual fairs which attracted trading merchants who sold their goods.[13] Gradually, this village became a commercial centre. When Maharaja Ranjit Singh built a bridge over a canal for easy access, it came to be known as Pulkanjari.

At present, three families of this village are represented by Namdhari Patwinder Singh, Namdhari Jit Singh Pardhan, and Namdhari Sangat Chheharta. They informed the author that before the communal violence engulfed their area in 1947, they shifted their women and children to Mandi Town of Himachal Pradesh, where Namdhari Guru Partap Singh had made arrangements for the stay of Namdhari refugees. As soon as communal violence flared up the Namdhari men too left for Mandi. However, even when communal violence subsided, the Namdhari Kharbanda families decided to leave. They took this decision in the wake of continuous disturbances on the Indo-Pakistan border. They chose to settle at Chheharta—a urban centre on the Amritsar-Attari Road. Two factors prompted them to take this decision. First was that by the Punjab Government's Notification No. 6541-G.G. BDS 38/34758 dated 19 October 1938, Chheharta area comprising revenue estates of Wadali Guru and Kala Ghanupur had been put under the Municipal Committee. Its status was raised to that of a second-class municipality in 1952.[14] By this time, Chheharta had emerged an industrial hub of Amritsar city. Moreover, in subsequent years, the main market in Partap Bazar had come into being on the road connecting GT Road and Wadali. It had prospects for running retail-shops and a business centre. It began to attract artisans and petty traders and shopkeepers of the rural area. The Kharbanda families availed this opportunity. Besides, these families had relatives in the Guru Ki Wadali—a nearby village. Before settling down here, the Kharbanda families had explored means of livelihood in other places too, had not succeeded. For instance, Pardhan Jit Singh told the author that his father sold cloth pieces on a handcart in Sunder Nagar, Himachal Pradesh but found it hard to meet his day-to-day requirements. He went to Patti town in the then tahsil Tarn Taran of Amritsar. Ultimately he too came back to Chheharta. In terms of volume of business, Patwinder Singh is at the top. He is followed by Jit Singh, and Gurbax Singh. All of them are income tax payees.[15]

There are several Namdhari Arora families who have settled in the towns of Mohali, Moga, Nawan Shahr, and Tarn Taran. Among them six families of Mohali and Chandigarh are cloth merchants and estate agents. They came from district Sialkot, Pakistan. There is one family each in Moga, Nawan Shahr and Tarn Taran cities. They are petty shopkeepers.[16]

THE IMPACT OF THE TERRORIST YEARS

The terrorist movement in the last quarter of the twentieth century, as noted earlier, affected the lives of Punjabis irrespective of caste and religion. However, the Sikhs belonging to particular sects like the Nirankari and Namdhari became special targets of the terrorist groups. The clash between the followers of Damdami Taksal and Akhand Kirtani Jatha on the one hand and the Nirankaris on the other on 13 April 1978 at Amritsar is widely believed to be the origin of Sikh militancy. In the course of the terrorist movement, the Namdhari Sikhs became targets for their belief in the continuity of deh-dhari-guru and their supplication in the name of the twelfth Guru, Ram Singh. Nevertheless, before we take up a few such cases, it is necessary to mention that threats, violence, and extortion. were common features of the terrorist movement. We came across several Namdhari respondents who mentioned threats and violence perpetrated by terrorists on respective families. During the heyday of Sant Jarnail Singh Bhindranwale, several complaints were written by fundamentalist Sikhs against Namdhari families for their beliefs and practices. The fundamentalist Sikhs tried to convince Sant Bhindranwale that the Namdharis must be punished for their *manmat* (self-orientation). However, local Sikhs, including Nihangs came to the support of the Namdharis and told Sant Bhindranwale that the latter were *Gur-Sikhs* (true Sikhs of Guru).[17] In Kalanaur, district Gurdaspur, the Mahant of Namdhari Dharamsala was forced to surrender the keys of this establishment so that the Namdhari Sikhs could be checked. A similar but tragic incident took place in Amritsar. Mahant Kunan Singh, popularly known as Baba Rabb Ji, was threatened by some unidentified terrorists on the pretext that he indulged in exorcism. Under pressure, Mahant's son joined a terrorist outfit. After sometime, he was killed. His second son was picked up by the police and was also killed. Trapped by the terrorists and targeted by the police, the whole family of this Mahant was destroyed. Similarly, Mahant Santokh Singh of The Namdhari Dharamsala, Amritsar was threatened by the terrorists and was forced to seek refuge at Bhaini Sahib.

The family of President of Namdhari youth of Tarn Taran, Gurbhez Singh too suffered harassment at the hands of the terrorists like Avtar Singh Brahma and Sukhwinder Singh Sangha who were active in the tahsils of Patti and Tarn Taran.

> Leaders of these multiple outfits vied with one another to glorify their so-called achievements. The quick way of self-adulation was sought through the infliction of punishment to *mukhbars* (informers) and the *dokhis* (enemies) of the Panth and Khalistan. It was called *Sodha Launa* literal meaning reformation but actually the killing of the enemies. The news that each leader was ahead of his counterpart in killing more number of enemies was projected through those newspapers which were read keenly by the rural-people. These were Punjabi newspapers published from Jalandhar city. The militants got their names published for taking responsibility for their actions. Similarly, these militants got published their press-statements paying homage to their departed comrades. The game of self-adulation proved both curse as well as blessings for the journalists and the trustees of the Punjabi newspapers.[18]

Gurbhez Singh informed the author (5 January 2010) that terrorists in groups descended on his *dera* (farm household) and forced his parents to serve them food. Then the terrorists also asked his father to lead them to safe-places. His family lived under the constant dread of the terrorists but was lucky to survive unharmed. The basic factor which saved his family was that Sukhwinder Singh Sangha was a distant relative. After Sangha's elimination, his family faced hardships. Once the terrorists even forced Gurbhez Singh's grandmother to poison the family dog who used to raise the alarm (barking loudly) whenever strangers passed by the farm-house. Being a devout Namdhari, his grandmother did not want to kill an animal. But the terrorists gave her an ultimatum: either kill the dog or get killed.

The terrorist movement forced many to move to the cities. This section comprised rich zamindars, sahukars, and shopkeepers. The non-Sikhs were also forced to move. In fact, all these people were victims of assaults of terrorists who indulged in extortion and immoral practices. However, there are only four Namdhari families of artisan castes who shifted their households to Amritsar city for security. Two of these families came from the villages of District Gurdaspur and other two from the villages of district Amritsar. Ram Singh, now resident of New Azad Nagar, Sultanwind, told the author that his house was located outside his native village, Roranvalli, Kahnuwal tahsil, district Gurdaspur and was exposed to anti-social elements who were drug addicts too. Moreover, they always felt threatened. To avoid any eventuality, his sister who was already living in Amritsar city, advised him to shift to Amritsar in 1987-8. Ram Singh regretted that his family had to sell its land (3 acres) and house cheaply as demand was low in those times.[19] Harbhajan Singh belonged to the village Dayalghar of district Gurdaspur. His father went to Bombay in 1973 where his uncle was working. He himself went to Bombay and started a car-repairs workshop. His successful work enabled him to own a house in Bombay. But as luck would have it, anti-Sikh riots destroyed his business there. He came to Amritsar where his in-laws were living and set up another workshop. Unfortunately again, a burglary in his workshop gave him severe financial set back. As a result, he had to close down his workshop. He is struggling to revive his business but success is now eluding him.[20]

Balbir Singh, resident of Kapur Nagar, Sultanwind Road, was also a victim of terrorism. He was a teacher in Sur Singh Jhabal Amritsar. He disclosed that the employees working in different government/ private institutions got threats from terrorists. They began to feel insecure when some students also joined the terrorist organizations. Several incidents took place in the area he belonged and the atmosphere was quite tense. Although he did not have any particular political or communal affiliation, he felt insecure, most probably due to his Namdhari affiliations. There was a section of Khalistani terrorists who were opposed to the socio-religious deviations of the deras. Living in constant fear was quite taxing. He decided to move to Amritsar city in 1990. It is interesting note that in this year terrorism was losing its grip over the mind of the people.[21]

The experience of Balwinder Singh Nagi was different from the three cases cited above. Balwinder Singh Nagi belonged to the village Santu Nangal, tahsil Ajnala, Amritsar. He trained as an electrician and motor-cycle and scooter mechanic. Then he started his own workshop of repairs of electrical gadgets of scooters and motor cycles. Till 1987, he used to commute between his village and workshop. When, terrorism took over, it became unsafe to commute in the evenings. Several incidents of loot and killing took place. For some years, he rented a house in Amritsar and then raised some money to purchase a plot, and he built his own house. Several friends and relatives came to his support.[22] A similar case has been reported by a Namdhari family of Jalandhar city. At present, this family is running a small business. The respondent of this family told the author that his family lived in the village Ahmedpur–Kohali in Kapurthala District. While working as carpenter-cum-sepidar, he was able to purchase a plot in Jalandhar for starting a new project. During the terrorist movement, his shops were looted. Scared by this incident, he decided to quit the village as early as possible. On one night, the family packed up its luggage into a truck and moved to Jalandhar city. After living in a rented house for some time, he built up shop-cum-residence on the above-mentioned plot.[23]

There were several families which suffered physically due to the terrorist movement. Ms Gurdip Kaur's father late Mohinder Singh was killed in March 1992. She informed the author that her father was a political leader and contested elections of the Municipal Corporation of Jalandhar on the Congress ticket. It was during the election campaign that he was shot dead. It seems that it was a political murder. Her family has been old Congress supporter. She herself was General Secretary, National Students Union, India (NSUI).[24] There was a similar case of killing of Joginder Singh son of Sant Atma Singh Sankhatarvi of town Ahyiapur, district Hoshiarpur in 1988. Joginder Singh was Mahant of local unit of Namdhari congregation. His father Mahant Atma Singh took his son's killing as God's will and performed

TABLE 3.1: RURAL TO URBAN MIGRATION OF NAMDHARI FAMILIES*

Districts	Jat/ Rajput	Ramgarhia	Arora/ Khatri	Swarankar	Parjapat	Mehra	Mazhabi	Cheemba	Saini	Brahmin	Total
Amritsar	5	38	7	2	1	1					54
Chandigarh & Mohali	16	27	1		1		1	1			47
Ferozepur	2	1						1			4
Jalandhar	3	25									28
Ludhiana	1	48									49
Moga		3	1			1					5
Muktsar				1				1			2
Nawan Shahr		3	1						3		7
Patiala	6	5							1	1	13
Rupnagar		14									14
Tarn Taran	6	2	1								9
Phagwara (Kapurthala)	10	10	–	–	–	–	–	–	–	–	20
Batala (Gurdaspur)	9	34	–	1	2	1	1	–	–	–	48
Total	58	210	11	4	4	3	2	3	4	1	300
%age	19	70	5	0.92	0.86	0.86	0.43	1.29	2	0.43	

Notes: *Data provided by Namdhari respondents.
This table does not include the Namdhari migrant families of Pakistan.

the last rites according to the Namdhari maryada. Gurmukh Singh, son of late Joginder Singh, told the author on the telephone on 26 December 2009 that his father was one of twelve or thirteen victims (Hindus) of bazaar of Ahyiapur town. This incident took place on the occasion of Diwali, 1988.[25]

From the proceeding narrative the following inferences can be drawn: there are basic similarities of the patterns of migration and rehabilitation of the Hindus and Sikhs and of the Namdhari Sikhs. Like other Hindus and Sikhs, the Namdhari Sikhs too suffered in terms of loss of life and property. However, in case of the Namdhari Sikhs, the volume of loss of life is far less as compared to the others. Secondly, like the other Hindus and Sikhs, the Namdhari Sikhs did not want to resettle in Amritsar city essentially because they felt insecure. Therefore, the number of migrant Namdhari families resettling in Amritsar city is insignificant (4 out of 100). Third, the creation of the international frontier not only created a sense of insecurity (due to the tension and conflict between India and Pakistan) but also stagnation in commerce and industries. As a result, the Namdhari businessmen and artisans preferred to move out of their native villages and towns to Amritsar city. Fourth, the terrorist movement too forced a migration to urban centres. The migration of the Namdhari families substantiates this type of migration. Fifth, the location of resettlement of Namdhari families was determined by biradari affiliations and the availability of job and business avenues.

MIGRATION OF AGRICULTURISTS AND OCCUPATIONAL CHANGES

Several categories of agriculturists too migrated from rural to urban centres due to the new avenues opened by the Green and Industrial Revolutions and by political exigencies. The capitalist development of agriculture has had a differential effect on the different categories of the peasantry. Big farmers have been the largest beneficiaries in terms of appropriating a large chunk of state grants and network of marketing. They are producing surpluses which are being invested in expanding their landholdings and in other income generation activities. Some of them are investing in transport and entertainment and catering industries like cinema houses, hotels, and marriage halls. Others have invested in 'estates' and agencies of different vehicles, etc. As required by the new professions, many of them have constructed their residences in the towns and cities of Punjab. Table 3.2 shows the occupational diversification of the Namdhari agriculturists (of all categories). It also shows that these are the medium and the big farmers who have become transporters and estate agents and commission agents in Malwa region. Their counterparts in Doaba and Majha regions are shopkeepers and small manufacturers. However, the percentage of occupational change is low: out of 849 agriculturists, Saini, Rajput, and Kamboj, only 37 families showed the spirit of occupational entrepreneurship.

The low percentage of occupational diversification can be explained in terms of conservatism. Social scientists argue that the agrarian communities are conservative and believe in maintaining *status quo*.[26] The Namdhari agriculturists are not exceptions in this regard. The Table 3.3 shows the low level of professional diversification: 843 families of Namdhari agriculturists could produce 40 professionals only. So professionals form just 4.75 per cent of these families.

This observation is more appropriate in the behaviour pattern of the Namdhari agriculturists of those rural areas where the level of urbanization is low. To quote the example of the Namdhari agriculturists of Barnala District, we find that they are a highly differentiated class. Out of 48 families, only twenty own 1 to 4.99 acres of land. The number of families having 5 to 9.99 acres of land is five. Whereas the number of medium farming families owning 10 to 24.99 acres of land is 20. There is only one family of big zamindar which owns 33 acres of land. These agriculturist families could produce only 5 teachers, 2 employees, 4 shopkeepers, 5 drivers, 1 soldier, and 1 dairy farmer (Table 3.4).

It is important to note here that it is only in this district that a large number of Namdhari Jat families are in debt: 20 per cent. Nevertheless, if we look into the nature of loan-taking by these agriculturists, we find that the problem is serious only in certain cases.

TABLE 3.2: OCCUPATIONAL DIVERSIFICATION OF AGRICULTURISTS

Number of transporters of Ferozepur, Jalandhar, Sangrur	9
Number engaged in estate business in Patiala, Ferozepur, Tarn Taran, Jalandhar, Nawan Shahr, Sangrur	13
Number of industrialists/ manufacturers of Jalandhar, Nawan Shahr, Kapurthala	7
Number of traders including commission agents of Ferozepur, Sangrur, Muktsar	8
Total	37

TABLE 3.3: PROFESSIONAL CLASSES OF NAMDHARI AGRICULTURISTS*

Districts	Doctors	Lawyers	Teachers	Engineers	Officers	Govt. Job	Rtd. Persons	Employees
Nawan Shahr	–	–	–	–	–	–	–	1 (Jat)
Hoshiarpur	1 (Jat)	–	–	–	–	–	–	1 (Jat)
Sangrur	–	–	–	–	–	–	1 (Jat)	–
Muktsar	–	–	–	–	–	–	–	–
Ludhiana City	–	–	–	–	–	–	–	–
Ludhiana rural	–	–	–	–	–	–	–	1 (Rajput)
Rupnagar	–	–	–	–	–	–	–	–
Tarn Taran	–	–	–	–	–	–	–	2 (Jat)
Moga	–	–	–	–	–	–	–	–
Barnala	–	–	1 (Jat)	–	–	–	–	1 (Jat)
Ferozepur	–	–	–	–	–	2 (Jat)	1 (Rajput)	–
Patiala	–	–	–	–	–	2 (Jat)	1 (Jat)	2 (Jat)
Bathinda	–	–	–	–	–	–	1 (Jat)	
Jalandhar	–	–	1 (Jat)	–	–	–	1 (Jat)	–
Amritsar	–	–	–	–	–	1 (Jat)	1 (Jat)	–
Chandigarh & Mohalr	1 (Jat)	–	5 (Jat)	–	–	6 (Jat)	3 (Jat)	3 (Jat)
Fatehgarh Sahib	–	–	–	–	–	–	–	–
Total Namdhari population of these districts 1099	2	–	7	–	–	11	9	11
%age								

Notes: *Data provided by Namdhari respondents.
Average percentage of professionals = 120 out of 1099 (11 per cent)

TABLE 3.4: OCCUPATIONAL CHANGES AMONG THE NAMDHARI SIKHS OF BARNAŁA DISTRICT*

	Jat	Ramgarhia	Chhemba
Doctors	–	1 RMP (4.76%)	–
Lawyers	–	–	–
Teachers	5 (27.77%)	–	–
Engineers	–	–	–
Officers	–	–	–
Govt. Employment	–	–	–
Retired	–	–	–
Employees	2 (11.11%)	2 (9.52%)	–
Business/ Estate Business	–	–	–
Industrialists	–	–	–
Traditional Occupation		2 (9.52%)	
Shopkeepers	4 (22.22%)	1 (4.76%)	1 (100%)
Journalists			
Drivers	5 (27.77%)		
Defence Services	1 army (5.55%)		
Workshops		1 (4.76%)	
Transporters			
Government. Contractors			
Contractors		1 (4.76%)	
Skilled labourer		3 (14.28%)	
Labourers		10 (47.61%)	
Dairy farming	1 (5.55%)		
Musicians			
Religious Functionaries			
Total			

Notes: *Data provided by Namdhari respondents.
Total number of families = 83

The table shows that these are the Namdhari marginal farmers who have taken loans ranging from Rs. 40,000 to 1 lakh. They may face the problem of returning these loans. Medium farmers have taken loans from the registered banks and have the capacity to return the loans. Commenting upon the nature of indebtedness among the Namdhari agriculturists, Satwant Singh, teacher-cum-agriculturist of village Gehal, tahsil Barnala, says they are relatively prosperous, free from vices and may not be richer but lead a happy life. The respondents of marginal families themselves said: with Satguru's blessings we are managing our needs.

Nevertheless, contentment has dampened entrepreneurship. There is only one family out of 62 whose member is a teacher. Similarly, there is only one family running a shop. Occupational diversification is almost nil. The level of higher and technical education among them is very low. In the 62 families, there are only two males who are B.A./B.Sc. There is no post graduate. Only three males have had professional training. Of course, females of these families are better qualified but are not working outside the home.[27]

Similarly, the low level of occupational diversification is perceptible in the case of Namdhari agriculturists of tahsils Dasua and Mukerian. The area of these two tahsils, particularly along with the bed of river Beas, is backward educationally and industrially. Therefore, it is not surprising that the Namdhari agriculturists of this area are backward.[28] Forty-six out of 54 Namdhari families are primarily engaged in agriculture (Table 3.5).

The small and marginal farmers experienced some gains in the initial period which they were unable to consolidate. The landholdings of several of them have become non-viable. Due to the crisis of stagnation in productivity, the small and marginal farmers are finding it difficult to survive. Consequently, they have pulled out of the agriculture sector.[29] They have started small and petty business or income generation activities allied to their landholdings which often force them to partially migrate to the towns. This type of migration is noted in the case of a family of Jat Purewal, Model Town, Jalandhar. The then head of the family found that his meagre holding would not sustain his family and he decided to migrate to Jalandhar city. Another factor which prompted the family to move to the city was the village factional politics. He was afraid of this politics lest it could entangle his family in criminal cases. Consequently, he left the village and settled in the city. He started a moderate business of transport and expanded it gradually.[30]

TABLE 3.5: OCCUPATIONAL CHANGES AMONG THE NAMDHARI SIKHS OF HOSHIARPUR DISTRICT*

	Jat	Parjapat	Total
Doctors	1 RMP (2.85%)	–	
Lawyers	–	–	
Teachers	2 (5.71%)	–	
Engineers	–	–	
Officers	–	–	
Govt. Employment	3 (8.57%)	–	
Retired	4 (11.42%)	–	
Salaried Employment	5 (14.28%)	–	
Business/ Estate Business	1 (2.85%)	1 (50%)	
Industrialists	–	–	
Traditional Occupation	–	–	
Shopkeepers	9 (25.71%)	1 (50%)	
Journalists	–	–	
Drivers	–	–	
Defence Services	3 PP 2 ARMY (14.28%)	–	
Workshops	–	–	
Transporters	–	–	
Government. Contractors	–	–	
Contractors	–	–	
Skilled labourers	1 (2.85%)	–	
Labourers	–	–	
Dairy farming	1 (2.85%)	–	
Musicians	–	–	
Religious Functionaries	3 (8.57%)	–	
Total	35	2	

Notes: *Data provided by Namdhari respondents.
Total number of families = 57

At the same time, the behaviour pattern of the urbanized Namdhari agriculturists is more progressive. They have responded to the modern educational, technological, and cultural changes. The progressive behaviour of the Namdhari agriculturists of Mohali and Chandigarh is perceptible in their lifestyle.

There are 22 families of Namdhari Jats in Mohali and Chandigarh. Eight families were natives of the villages and *kasbas* of the West Punjab, whereas 16 families came from different villages/towns of East Punjab and a few from Ambala, Sirsa and Delhi. Fifteen, out of twenty two, either are doing jobs or have retired from the public/private departments. Four to five families are engaged in business, largely estate-business. However, all of them own land in their respective villages, which they have given on contract. There are a few families whose members are staying back in the villages and farming. Seen in this background, the pattern of settlement of the Namdhari Jats is different than the patterns of the Ramgarhias and other occupational castes. Many Namdhari Jats have settled in Chandigarh and Mohali to enjoy the facilities of a developed urban centre. They had the money to buy plots, and constructed houses. They came here from the business-point of view and it still remains their primary concern. Their performance in the higher and technical education is good but they are not ahead of their counterpart Ramgarhia families. The level of higher/technical education among the Ramgarhia women is especially better than the level of Namdhari Jat women (Table 3.6).

The general prosperity ushered by the Green Revolution has enabled all sections of agrarian society to impart higher and professional education to their children. There is a large number of qualified rural youth but few of them get jobs in the service sector. They have shifted to the towns and cities and have constructed houses in a phased manner. Some of them have gone aboard to seek green pastures, and have remitted money to their families. Like their counterparts, they too have built their houses in urban centres. Another section of rural society comprises retired civil and military personnel who have built kothis in towns. All these sections operate their landholdings from urban households.[31]

As noted, the Namdhari marginal and small agriculturists constitute 54 per cent of the total Namdhari agriculturist community. Like their counterparts, they too find that their holdings are increasingly becoming non-viable economically. Several have been forced to start

TABLE 3.6: OCCUPATIONAL CHANGES AMONG THE NAMDHARI SIKHS OF CHANDIGARH & MOHALI DISTRICT*

	Jat	Ramgarhia	Arora	Kamboj	Parjapat	Suniara	Chhemba	Mazhabhi
Doctors	1 (2.04%)	–	–	–	–	–	–	–
Lawyers		1 (2%)	–	–	–	–	–	–
Teachers	10 (23%)	3 (5%)	–	–	–	–	–	–
Engineers	–	1 (2%)	–	–	–	–	–	–
Officers	–	2 (3%)	–	–	–	–	–	–
Govrnment Employment	7 (14%)	6 (10%)	–	–	–	–	1 (50%)	1 (100%)
Retired	4 (8%)	6 (10%)	–	–	1 (33%)	–	–	–
Salaried Employment	5 (10%)	18 (31%)	1 (14%)	–	1 (33%)	–	1 (50%)	–
Business/ Estate Business	9 (18%)	5 (9%)	2 (29%)	–	–	–	–	–
Industrialists	1 (2%)	–	–	–	–	–	–	–
Traditional Occupation	–	–	–	–	–	–	–	–
Shopkeepers	2 (4%)	3 (5%)	4 (57%)	–	–	1 (100%)	–	–

Journalists								
Drivers								
Defence Services	2 PP 4 CP (12%)	1 PP 1 CP (3%)			1 home guard (33%)			
Workshops		1 (2%)						
Transporters								
Government Contractors								
Contractors		3 (5%)						
Skilled Workers	1 (2%)	7 (12%)						
Labourers	1 (2%)							
Dairy farming								
Musicians								
Religious Functionaries				2 (100%)				
Writers/Scholars/ Intellectuals	2 (4%)							
Total	49	58	7	2	3	1	2	1

Notes: * Data provided by Namdhari respondents.
Total number of families = 74

subsidiary occupations and to move to the towns for work. Details about the migration of Suba Mohkam Singh, Narinder Singh, and Prem Singh Randhawa of Amritsar city can be mentioned here. The story of Narinder Singh's success in business is a story of rags to riches. Narinder Singh told the author that he and his family experienced very hard days. He was the eldest of three brothers. His entire family depended upon agriculture, but owned only 7 *kanals* (less then an acre). He narrated a story of his school-going days, when he did't have adequate clothes to wear to school. One day he was humiliated by a teacher and told to pull off the *chadar* (cotton sheet) by which they had covered themselves. When he didn't obey teacher's order, he was abused but later when the teacher found that he was without a shirt, he sympathized. The school headmaster and class-teacher tried to give money to him to buy clothes but Narinder Singh said that he refused, because his dignity was hurt.

Narinder Singh started his career as a milk vendor collecting milk from villages and ferrying and selling it in the city. In the beginning, he had a bicycle and then he bought a motor cycle and a three-wheeler pick-up. Since his brothers were now grown up, he decided to hand over fieldwork to his second and third brothers. He himself switched on to the job of *arhtia* (commission agent). This business was successful. At present, he has three shops in different *mandis,* (Chaugawan, Rajasansi and Bhagtanwala Chowk). Besides, he owns a kothi on the Ajnala Road and 20 acres of land.

There are two more Namdhari Jat families who have migrated to Amritsar city. One of them is Ranjit Singh who belongs to village Lohar Kalan, tahsil Amritsar. One of the primary reasons for his migration was that the landholding of his father was small (5 acres) and to be equally divided among his brothers. One of his relatives suggested to Ranjit Singh that educational and economic prospects were better in the city. The relative also suggested that he should acquire training in a technical course, which he did. He got a job in ESSMA Mills, Putlighar for a year. After that, he joined another firm on Sultanwind Road on Rs. 800 per annum for four years. In 1980, he started his own work dealing with textile designing. He was able to raise surplus earning for his sister's marriage. He also purchased a house, worth Rs. 24,000. In subsequent years, he faced an economic depression, but after some time, his own small factory started yielding a profit which he used for imparting good education to his children.

The case study of Prem Singh Randhawa is different. He is a retired Military Subedar but now working for in the Indian Railways. He belongs to village Gorenangal, tahsil Ajnala, where his grandfather owned 25 acres of land. Being in military service, he was able to save money to buy 4 acres. However, his share of the ancestral property was not sufficient to sustain him and his family. His father disposed of his share and bought a larger tract in UP. This again was disposed of for a better deal in village Rania, district Sirsa (Haryana). At present, the landed property of his family is worth a crore. After retirement from the Railways, Prem Singh proposes to resume his ancestral occupation.

Sardool Singh Chohan comes from village Jagdev Kalan, tahsil Ajnala. His father was a *sahukar* (banker) and owned a brick-kiln. His father also served in the Indian Army for some years, during which he came to realize the relevance of modern education, and so decided to move to Amritsar city. After acquiring college education, he and his father started a factory for textile processing. From 1978 to 2000, there were 50 workers in the factory. Afterwards, they had to close it down for reasons he did not wish to disclose. At present he is manufacturing chess boards. The annual returns of the production vary from six to seven lakh.

There were several Namdhari agriculturist families who faced crises when holdings fragmented. In this context, the cases of two Namdhari Jats of Tarn Taran district can be cited here. Sham Singh of village Sohawa belonged to a marginal family which owned only two *kanals* of land and a kacha house. After doing his +2, he got himself attached to a doctor and started his own practice as RMP. As per custom, when he and his brothers were married, a division of ancestral landed property took place. The portion of the house which he got was not worth it and bickering over petty issues made life hard. So he moved to Tarn Taran city in 2001. He purchased a plot for Rs. 127,000 and disposed of it for 550,000. This transaction gave him an initial start and he started an estate and moneylending business. Sham Singh stated that it was due to the blessings of his Satguru that he succeeded.

Gurbhej Singh, President, Namdhari Youth Wing, narrated a different story of migration. He comes from an agriculturist family which owned ten acres in the village Varian. Namdhari Guru Jagjit Singh deputed his father to look after the Namdhari Bunga (near Darbar Sahib Tarn Taran) and his father had to stay in Tarn Taran. Meanwhile, he constructed his own house at this town. He opened a steel furniture and repair shop at Naushehra which is not far from his ancestral village.

MIGRATION OF ARTISANS AND OCCUPATIONAL CHANGES

Ramgarhias

During the Partition of Punjab in 1947, Muslim artisans were forced to leave East Punjab and this left a void for Hindu and Sikh artisans of West Punjab to fill. In the process, most of the Namdhari artisans came and settled in the cities of Amritsar, Jalandhar, Ludhiana and towns of Batala, Phagwara, and Goraya. As noted elsewhere, the majority of them were from Sialkot and Lahore.[32] Another major variable of migration of artisans was the disintegration of the *sep* system in the pre- and post-Independence periods, which made artisans redundant in the traditional agrarian economy. Major factors for disintegration were the commercialization of agriculture, the development of modern means of transportation such as approach-roads linking villages to towns, and the founding of manufacturing units around the towns. Such developments encouraged those artisan families to leave their villages who found that their nominal share of agricultural produce was inadequate. In fact, due to increased agricultural production and higher prices peasants of all categories preferred to get the skilled artisan labour on contract. Consequently, the artisans were released from the bondage of customary-relationship between the zamindars and menial castes. Moreover, the artisans demanded higher wages when the demand for their skills rose for the construction of canals, railway lines, bridges, roadways, military cantonments, administrative headquarters, and new markets. Such growth and development took place in Punjab before and after Independence. Above all, the mechanization of agriculture made the *jajmani* system redundant. A large number of persons (artisans) engaged in subsidiary services were now forced to take up diverse activities. Some of them opened workshops for repairing tractors, water-pumps, electric motors and other agricultural implements. Others switched to woodwork and masonry. New transport facilities encouraged artisans to go to towns for jobs. According to economists, there has been a large migration of the rural population to urban areas. Between 1951 and 1961, the share of the migration to the total increase in urban population was 27 per cent and in the

TABLE 3.7A: OCCUPATIONAL STATUS OF RAMGARHIAS

Number of daily wagers (carpenters, iron smiths or factory-workers)	32	50.00%
Number of sepidars	12	18.75%
Number of manufacturers of small wooden articles and bullock carts	8	12.5%
Number of agriculturists cum sepidars	6	9.37%
Number of moneylenders, professional/proprietors	6	9.37%
Total	64	

subsequent three decades it was respectively 15.75, 49.13, and 30.32 per cent.[33]

As said in the beginning, the Namdhari artisans especially Ramgarhias of rural areas migrated to Batala, Amritsar, Phagwara, Goraya, and Ludhiana. Namdhari artisans were conscious of the fact that they were largely dependent on the agrarian economy of the Punjab. They were also conscious of the fact that their social status was considered low and underprivileged. Among them the Sunars, Tarkhans, Lohars, Ghumhars, and Julahas were regarded as 'clean' but Chamars and Mochis, 'unclean'. Whether Muslim, Hindu, or Sikh, the 'clean' artisan castes were broadly treated on a par with the Sudra. The castes of goldsmiths, carpenters, blacksmiths, and potters were considered superior to weavers, the lowest among the 'clean' castes. The Chamars and Mochis who worked in leather were considered untouchables.[34] The artisans understood the connection between their social status and the nature of their work. The disintegration of the *jajmani* system freed the artisans from the bonds of hierarchy. Colonial rule also provided new job avenues for artisans. By the turn of the twentieth century, the percentage of artisans who had abandoned their traditional occupations became rather significant: Chamars 67, Ghumhars 48, Tarkhans 42, Lohars 45, Mochis 64, Julahas 36 and Sunars 16 per cent. Like their counterparts, artisans availed of educational opportunities. Moreover, they went abroad where skilled and unskilled labour was required. In that situation, traditional norms were disrupted, social relationships tended to lack consistent and coherent meaning, and the traditional 'universe of meaning' was undermined.

Seen as a part of their *biradari*, the economic condition of the majority of Namdhari Ramgarhias in the early twentieth century was deplorable. There were a few families who were economically well of. This information has been gathered from the respondents of these

TABLE 3.7B: OCCUPATIONAL CHANGES AND ECONOMIC DEVELOPMENT OF NAMDHARI RAMGARHIAS OF LUDHIANA DISTRICT*

P. No.	Ancestral Occupation	New Occupations and Status
1(u)	Small house/labourer	Labourer in Dubai, very small house
2	Carpenter/small house in village	Workshop and house in city
3	Sepidar/small house	Workshop of fabrication in house in city
4	Carpenter/small house	Business of plastic and nylon/manager in Pvt. Firm, owns factory and kothi type house
5	Manufacturer of wooden sleepers and iron vessels/small house in village	Operating lathe machine in house in the city
6	Carpenter, small house	Property dealer & owns house
7	Cart manufacturer/small house in village	Factory of auto parts in house in city and business of property
8	Owned shop (carpentry), good house	Two factories, good house
9	Private job, small house	Pvt. Job (Purchase Manager). Kothi type house
10	Sepidar & small house	Workshop of Steel Furniture, kothi type house
11	Carpenter, house in Lyallpur city	Job and, printing press in home
12	Sepidari, pakka house	Factory, owned house
13	Pvt. Job and small house in village	Workshop of steel furniture, owns house in city
14	Agriculture, good house	Business of Cotton Import Export, kothi
15	Manufacturer of wooden sleepers/ small house	Manufacturer of hosiery machines and owns house
16	Factory of auto parts, pakka house	Factory of cycle parts and owns house
17	Sepidar, kacha house	Pakka house, carpenter, iron work
18	Sepidar, small house	Handloom industry, kothi
19	Agriculture and sepidar (4-5 acres of land) Workshop of cycle parts, plots and kothi	
20	Carpenter/small house	Manufacturing Auto parts in his house
21	Carpenter, small house	Confectionary shop, owns house

22	Carpenter, small house	STD booth at Apollo Hospital, owns house
23	Cart manufacturers, pakka house	Factory, owns house
24	Sepidar, kacha house	Workshop and owns house
25	Carpenter, small house	Karyana shop and house
26	Workshop, pakka house	Workshop, pakka house
27	Cart manufacturers, pakka house	Scooter workshop and owns house
28	Sepidar, small house	Makers of inter-lock machine in his house
29	Carpenter, small house	Operate lathe machine in his house
30	Cart manufactures, pakka house	Iron work and owns house in city
31	Sepidar, kacha house	Workshop, owns house
32	Pvt. Job, pakka house	Business- parts of embroidery machines in house
33	Carpenter, kacha house	Business, owns house and plot
34	Cart manufacturers, small house	Operate lathe machine in the house, three sons settled in England
35	Iron Smithy, small house	Govt. Teacher, kothi
36	Labour in cycle market, small house	Lathe machine operator, small house
37	Carpenter and sepidar, small house	Manufacturer of auto parts in the house
38	Sepidar, small pakka house	Manufacturer of auto parts in the house
41	Carpenter, small house	Good house, job of cable (connections), STD
42	Carpenter and sepidar, kacha house	Shop of auto parts, kothi
43	Carpenter, small house	Karyana shop in the house
44	Carpenter, small house Manufacturer of Auto parts in the house	
45	Carpenter, pakka house	Workshop of combines and shop of auto parts, kothi type house
46	Job in Iraq and good house	Professional, big kothi, son- BAMS
47	Carpenter, small house	Shop of cycle tyers, kothi type house
48	Sepidar, small house	Shopkeeper, kothi type house
49	--	Job in Knitting firm, small house
50	Sepidar, small house	Car repairing workshop, good house
51	Carpenter, small house	Truck repairing workshop, kothi type house

52	Truck repairing Workshop, good house	Truck repairing workshop, good house
53	Mason, small house	Mason, small house
54	Agriculture, good house (35 acres of land)	Senior Manager in Bank of Baroda at Bombay, good kothi
21 (r)	Agriculture, good house	Doing community job in dera, dependent
23	Contractor and shops, good house	Pensioner
24	Moneylander, good house	Community job, Retd. SDO, owned house at Bhaini Sahib
25	Hydraulic Engineer in Nairobi (Kenya)	Community job as a Music Teacher
27	Owned brick kiln, good house	Factory, owns house
28	Carpentry/smithy, small house	Land, house, factories
29	Carpenter	Two brothers in Govt. Job, factory, good house
30	Smithy	Community job
31	Agriculture, good house	13 acres land, Govt. Job as a Teacher
32	Community job	Community job

Note: *Data provided by Namdhari respondents.

families of each district. A sample of Namdhari Ramgarhias of districts of Ludhiana, Amritsar, Jalandhar and Gurdaspur shows that among the migrants, the Ramgarhias alone constitute 70 per cent. The parents of these Ramgarhias had worked as carpenters, iron-smiths, and daily wage-labourers. They earned their livelihood by manufacturing wooden-sleepers, furniture, and bullock carts. More than 18 per cent were sepidars who got a nominal share of the agriculture produce. In fact, our data suggests that most of them were in a deplorable condition. This is reflected in their kacha and small houses in their native villages. However, the economic condition of less than 20 per cent was slightly better. Some of them had small landholdings which generated supplementary produce along with the sep system. They were a few sahukars, professionals and agriculturists.[35]

It was not merely economic deprivation but social discrimination and humiliation which forced them to join that social order which could ensure egalitarian and humanitarian behaviour. Recent work on the artisan classes cites a number of cases of humiliation suffered by the village-artisans in their respective villages.

They could be beaten over trivial issues; and they were not allowed to share the same platform on social and religious gatherings. The artisans could not enter even the shrines of *pirs* (Muslim saints) and *babas* (holy men) on particular festivals let alone other religious establishments because the dominant agriculturist castes would not allow that. In larger villages the artisans of different castes were expected to live within their separate residential enclosures or *galis* (streets). The Chamars, however, were supposed to live away from the main residential site. The situation was not much different in urban areas.[36]

Most of the Namdhari artisans came from the West Punjab and first settled in the villages of East Punjab. Like the native artisans, they then migrated to the towns for work. However, the number of the native artisans is larger than the migrant artisans of West Punjab. In Batala itself, the number of migrant Namdhari families from Pakistan is not more than half a dozen: 6 out of 44. The number of rural to urban migrations in the post-Independence period is larger. Thirty-eight out of 44 Namdhari-Ramgarhias came to this town. In Kapurthala district, there are 56 Namdhari Ramgarhia families in the urban centres. Most of them were engaged in the ancestral callings of carpentry and iron-smithy. Some of them owned one or two acres of land which they themselves cultivated. With the passage of time, their strips of land were fragmented and the income generated by hard work was not sufficient to sustain them in the ancestral villages. In the initial stage, elders of the Namdhari Ramgarhia families got jobs in workshops and shuttled between their native villages and towns. Then they made arrangements for their families to stay in the town. Either they disposed the small pieces of land in the villages or gave them on rent. However, they maintained social relations with their relatives in the villages. There are only a few families who left their villages for reasons other than livelihood. It was narrated by one person that when his family became Namdhari-Sikh, their brothers and neighbours turned against them. To buy peace and a normal life, he shifted to Batala.[37]

As noted in the previous chapter, the majority of the Namdhari Ramgarhias of Jalandhar came from West Punjab, Besides, 25 families migrated from the villages and settled either in Jalandhar city or Goraya. However, those who came from West Punjab were engaged in woodwork and the manufactue of iron implements. Some of them were daily wagers working as carpenters, masons and black-smiths in their own villages and nearby towns. Some were also sepidars and provided skilled labour to the agriculturists and got nominal wages both in kind and cash. A few of them owned small tracts that they cultivated themselves. They also installed *kharas,* bullock driven flour mills, and generated additional income. Only two families claimed that their grandparents owned 10 to 25 acres of land and were *sahukars* who built *havelis.* Similarly, one Namdhari stated that his great grand father was a big business man in Lahore. Another migrant Namdhari stated that his grandfather was a *granthi,* a scripture reader, along with his traditional calling of carpentry.[38] It is a paradox that in the industrial town of Goraya, there is only one Namdhari Ramgarhia family which is running a mechanical workshop. The other seven families are either petty shopkeepers or own wood workshops. Two of them still retain small landholdings in their native villages. A member of one of these families disclosed that his father was a sepidar who owned four acres. His family faced a financial crisis when its share of agriculture produce declined and its holdings fragmented. Moreover, he and his brothers experienced that *sep* work was not honourable. To switch over to another occupation, he acquired the skills of wood-craft and worked as carpenter in Goraya. Then he bought a plot here and started a furniture shop. He and his sons themselves manufacture the furniture.[39]

The Namdhari-Sikhs of Phagwara town comprise 14 Ramgarhia and one Jat families. Only two families came from Pakistan, the others from nearby villages. First, they shuttled between their native villages and this town but gradually constructed houses here. Excepting one or two, the rest of them belong to one sub-caste Chana. However, all of them have left their sepidari and now own big and small workshops and manufacturing units. The head of one family is working in a private firm and another is a car dealer.

It was not merely industrial development that pushed the Namdhari Ramgarhia artisans to towns. There were several socio-political factors which forced these artisans to leave their native villages. The migration of Namdhari Ramgarhia families to the city of Rupnagar was due to these factors. Out of 17 of these families, 8 migrated from districts Amritsar, Gurdaspur, Jalandhar, and Ludhiana and 2 came from West Punjab. The respondents of families from the village Jagdev Khurd, Amritsar said that since their village was nearer to the Indo-Pakistan border, there was no scope of getting skilled jobs over there. These respondents are four brothers. When their sister was married in the city of Rupnagar, they came to know that there were jobs for skilled workers. They migrated to this city in 1972. The Indo-Pakistan war 1971 had already created the problem of social security for their families. It seems that in the initial stage, it was a single family. Their father established a flour mill but when they grew up, they started their own businesses. These four brothers have built good houses and seem to be prosperous. The respondents of the other families coming from Batala, Qadian and Gurdaspur also came to Rupnagar. One of respondent's father had government post and was transferred here. He himself got a job in a factory. It seems that families of these respondents migrated to this city in 1980s (Table 3.8).

In socio-economic terms, the Namdhari Ramgarhias of district Mohali and Chandigarh are ahead of their counterparts in Punjab. Out of 26 families, the parents of 22 families carried on their traditional calling of carpentry, masonry, and iron-smithy. Some did farming as they had small land holdings. A few of them still own land in their ancestral villages. However, their parents lived in kacha houses. A few of them claimed that their parents lived in *pacca* houses of brick and cements (Table 3.6). An interesting feature is that a large number of them came to Chandigarh and Mohali as carpenters, masons and skilled labourers but subsequently gave up their tradition calling. More than 40 per cent now work in private or government firms and the rest run their own business. By dint of their hard labour, they raised capital, purchased small plots, borrowed from friends and relatives, took loans from banks, and purchased flats or constructed their own houses. In spite of their limited sources, the Namdhari Ramgarhias performed well in acquiring higher and technical education. They were aware that only higher and technical education can improve their lives.

In sum, after settling in the towns and cities, the Namdhari Ramgarhias made the best use of their traditional skills. It was their experience and technical knowledge which helped them start new occupations. Table 3.9 shows the frequency of occupational diversification among them.

Other Artisans

As noted in the beginning of this chapter there was a marginal response from artisans like Swarankars, Parjapats, Mehras, and Nais. In the towns and cities, their number is as follows: 3 families of Swarankars in Amritsar, 1 family in Mohali and 1 in Malot, 3 Parjapat families

TABLE 3.8: MIGRATION OF RAMGARHIA FAMILIES AND THEIR OCCUPATIONAL CHANGE*

Name	From Native Place	To Rupnagar City	Occupation	
			Ancestral	Present
Shingara Singh	Chak 35, Pakistan	–do–	Saw/Flour Mill	Insurance Surveyor
Mani Singh	Jagdev Khurd, Amritsar	–do–	Carpentry	Timber Merchant
Darshan Singh	–do–	–do–	–do–	Shopkeeping
Harbhajan Singh	–do–	–do–	–do–	Hardware Shop
Gurdev Singh	–do–	–do–	–do–	Electrical Shop
Achhar Singh	Duldi Majra, Rupnagar	–do–	Saw/Flour Mill and Sepidari	Saw/Flour Mill
Hardial Singh	Raigo, Rupnagar	–do–	Iron Smithy	Shopkeeping
Hartej Kaur	Santokhgarh Tapprian, Rupnagar	–do–	Flour Mill	Flour Mill
Jodha Singh	Maduli Kalan, Morinda	–do–	Flour Mill	Flour Mill
Gurmeet Singh	Duldi Majra, Rupnagar	–do–	Match Making	Repair Workshop
Kulwant Singh	Sairon, Jalandhar	–do–	Carpentry	Retd. Teacher
Santokh Singh	Samrala, Ludhiana	–do–	Iron Smithy/ Carpentry	Wood Works
Ujagar Singh	Santokhgarh Tapprian, Rupnagar	–do–	Flour Mill	Flour Mill
Iqbal Singh	Mojalipur, Rupnagar	–do–	Farming/Iron Smithy	Farming
Sucha Singh	Khwaspur, Rupnagar	–do–	Property Dealer	Property Dealer
Varinder Singh	Qadian, Gurdaspur	–do–	Private Job	Govt. Job
Lakhwinder Singh	Batala, Gurdaspur	–do–	Carpentry	Medical Practioner

Note: *Data provided by Namdhari respondents.

in Amritsar, 1 in Mohali, 3 in Dasua and Mukerian and 1 in Patiala; 1 Mehra familie each in Amritsar, Moga, and Sangrur. Fifty per cent of these families came from Pakistan. All of them had started new

TABLE 3.9: OCCUPATIONAL STATUS OF NAMDHARI RAMGARHIAS

	Jalandhar (104)	Amritsar (41)	Ludhiana (66)	Gurdaspur (92)	Kapurthala (114)
Professionals	5	4	13	12	11
Employees	9	1	08	7	07
Traditional occupation	45	13	11	21	29
Workshops	12	17	18	12	20
Industrialists	–	6	02	5	01
Business	20	–	03	1	33
Shop keepers	5	–	11	32	02
Transporters	2	–	–	–	04
Drivers	6	–	–	2	07
Total	104	41	66	92	114
					417

Traditional occupations: masonry, carpentry, iron-smithy and skilled labourer, etc.
Professionals: teachers, lawyers, engineers/technicians, doctors/RMP, etc.
Employees: clerks, security Men, heads of the offices, etc.

but petty occupations like shop-keeping and selling clothes but four Parjapat families engaged in business and two are police personnel.

In summing up, we can say that numerically the migration of the Namdhari Ramgarhias from rural to urban areas was larger than that of the Namdhari Jats. The pattern of migration of Namdhari Ramgarhias was essentially determined by the problems of earning a livelihood on the one hand and of social discrimination on the other. Since they were skilled labourrrs they moved to industrial towns. However, they took time to resettle in the urban centres. In the initial stage, they stayed either in rented-houses or commuted between villages and towns. Gradually they brought their families to live near their places of work. However, they continued their interaction with

TABLE 3.10: OCCUPATIONS/JOBS OF ARTISANS

Families	Shopkeeping	Business	Jobs/ Services	Skilled labourers	
Swarankar	4	–	–	1	
Parjapat	3	1	3	–	
Mehra	–	–	2	1	
Total	7	1	5	2	15

their biradaries in the native villages. There were several variables which determined rural to urban migration including the creation of the Indo-Pakistan border and the terrorist movement. Nevertheless, the pattern of migration of the Namdhari agriculturists was different than that of the artisans. Most Namdhari agriculturists moved to the urban centres for better opportunities. The small and marginal farmers moved to these centres due to fragmented landholdings which could not sustain them. With the passage of time, they acquired technical skills and started small manufacturing units and petty busineses. Nevertheless, the rate of occupational changes was slow: 776 Namdhari Jat families (half the total Namdhari population), could produce only 40 professionals and 37 transporters, industrialists/ manufacturers, traders, and commission agents. In contrast, Namdhari Ramgarhias have shown remarkable occupational changes. Their 566 families (37 per cent of the total Namdhari population) produced 40 professionals and 79 owners of workshops, 14 industrialists, 57 businessmen, 50 shopkeepers, and 15 drivers. Yet 29 per cent of Namdhari families are engaged in their traditional occupation.

NOTES

1. Ethne K. Marenco, *The Transformation of Sikh Society,* 1976; W.H. McLeod, *The Evolution of Sikh Community,* 1975; Gopal Krishen, 'Demography of the Punjab', 2004; Ian Talbot and S. Thandi (eds.), *People on the Move, Punjabi Colonial and Post Colonial Migration,* 2004; Pritam Singh and Shinder Singh Thandi (eds.), *Punjabi Identity in a Global Context,* 1999.
2. I. Area: 58,362 sq km Census 1991

   II. Population: 2,82,81,969; 2.44 per cent of India's total population

Census	Hindus	Sikhs	Muslim	Christians	SC/ST
1951	62.30%	35.00%	–	–	–
1971	36.09%	60.00%	–	–	24.87%
1981	38.09%	60.00%	1.07%	–	26.87%
1991	34.56%	62.95%	1.18%	1.11%	28.31%

Urban Population

Census	1951	1961	1971	1981	1991	2001
	22.3%	23.2%	23.7%	27.7%	29.72%	33.95%

Census	Urban Hindus		Urban Sikhs		Rural Hindus		Rural Sikhs	
	1971	1981	1971	1981	1971	1981	1971	1981
	66.39%	64.16%	30.79%	33.19%	28.56%	26.61%	69.37%	71.39%

Cited in *Punjabi Identity in a Global Context*, 1999, pp. 286-312; Indu Banga (ed.), *Five Punjabi Centuries*, 2000, pp. 358-483.

3. *Census of India 1951*, vol. VIII, pt. 1-A, Simla 1953, p. 157, also see, *Punjab District Gazetteers*: Amritsar, 1976, pp. 119-20.
4. *Census of India 1951*, vol. VIII, pt. I-A, Simla, p. 217.
5. Ibid., pp. 15, 26-7.
6.

Year	Murders	Decoities	Burglaries	All reported crises exclusive of security cases
1947	2,623	585	6,719	33,907
1948	877	214	8,814	45,474
1949	706	199	8,416	49,757
1950	607	93	8,968	37,035

—*Punjab Since Partition*,(Satya Murthy Rai), 1986, p. 126.

7. Ibid., p.125: In Ferozepur and Amritsar districts, cattle lifting was another problem hitting the peasantry. The cattle were often sent across the border.
8. *Punjab District Gazetteers:* Amritsar, 1976, p. 66.
9. Ibid., p. 67.
10. See Appendix 3A.
11. Interview with Amrik Singh, 10 August 2007, in Amritsar.
12. Interview with Amrik Singh 18 August 2007.
13. Joginder Singh Kairon, *Batan-Shere-Punjab Dian*, 2001, pp. 78-9; Hari Ram Gupta, *History of the Sikhs*, vol. V, 1992, p. 567.
14. *Punjab District Gazetteers*: Amritsar 1976, pp. 433-4.
15. Interviews with Patwinder Singh, Jit Singh, Gurbax Singh, Chheharta in August 2007.
16. Occupations of Arora/Khatri Namdhari Sikhs of Amritsar, Mohali & Chandigarh, Moga, Nawan Shahr and Tarn Taran: Shopkeepers 9, Cloth Merchants 6, Commission Agents 1.
17. This information was provided by Namdhari Sikh Ajit Singh, village Feroze Raulia, district Hoshiarpur, 28 December 2009.
18. Joginder Singh, *Myth and Reality of the Sikh Militancy in Punjab*, 2006, pp. 237-8.
19. Interview with Ram Singh on 28 August 2007.
20. Interview with Harbhajan Singh on 8 August 2007.
21. Interview with Balbir Singh on morning of 12 August 2007.
22. Interview with Balwant Singh Nagi on 27 August 2007.
23. Interview with Hazara Singh, Ajit Nagar Road, Damoria Pul, Jalandhar, 14 August 2007.
24. Ms Gurdip Kaur prepared the text of the lectures which her father delivered at the political functions. In compensation for her father's murder, she was nominated as PCS officer by the then chief minister,

Beant Singh. Interview at her house in Preet Nagar, Jalandhar, August 2007.

25. Suwaran Singh Virk, *Kuka Lehar Da Punjabi Sahit,* Sri Bhaini Sahib, 2009, p. 281.
26. For detail, see, Eric Wolf, *Peasant Wars of the 20th Century*, Faber and Faber Co., London, 1973.
27. Table 3.4.
28. It is a coincidence that of the Namdhari families we interviewed, 55 out of 57 are migrants from the villages of district Sialkot. Only two families belonged to district Gurdaspur. The process of migration and resettlement of these migrant families has been discussed elsewhere. In this section, we propose to analyse their land holdings.
29. Sucha Singh Gill, *Economic Development and Structural Changes in Punjab: Some Policy Issues*, 1994, pp. 76-7.
30. Proforma No. 99 (Jalandhar).
31. Gill, op. cit., 1994, p. 79.
32. Ramesh Bhandari, *Industries and Industrial Workers of Batala 1849-1947,* p. 68.
33. Sucha Singh Gill, 1994, p. 15.
34. Harish C. Sharma, *Artisans of the Punjab,* 1996, p. 27.
35. Table 3.7b.
36. Sharma, op. cit., pp. 35-6.
37. Joginder Singh, 'The Namdhari Sikhs of Punjab: A Case Study of Demographic and Occupational Changes in District Gurdaspur', *Indian History Congress Proceedings*, 2005, pp. 730-1.
38. Appendix 3B
39. Interview with Nirmal Singh, village Bara Pind, Goraya (Jalandhar), 3 November 2007.

APPENDIX 3.A

Caste and Religion of Migrant Families (Police District-wise)

Caste	Amritsar		Majitha		Tarn Taran		Batala			Total			Grand Total	
	H	S	H	S	H	S	H	Ch	S	H	Ch	S		
Brahmin	33	–	93	–	67	–	15	–	–	208	–	–	208	
	(15.87)		(44.71)		(32.21)		(7.21)			(100)			(42.12)	(100)
Khatri/ Arora	9	1	22	8	34	4	–	–	–	65	–	13	78	
	(11.54)	(1.28)	(28.21)	(10.26)	(43.59)	(5.13)				(83.33)		(16.67)	(15.80)	(100)
Bania	–	–	5	–	–	–	–	–	–	5	–	–	5	
			(100)							(100)			(1.01)	(100)
Jat	–	9	–	37	–	32	–	–	40	–	–	118	118	
	–	(7.63)		(31.36)		(27.12)			(33.89)			(100)	(23.90)	(100)
Ramgarhia	–	–	–	–	–	6	–	–	2	–	–	8	8	
						(75.00)			(25.00)			(100)	(1.62)	(100)
Kamboj	–	–	–	1	–	–	–	–	–	–	–	1	1	
				(100)								(100)	(0.20)	
Suniara	–	1	7	1	1	4	–	–	–	8	–	6	14	
		(7.14)	(50.00)	(7.14)	(7.14)	(28.58)				(57.14)		(42.86)	(2.83)	(100)
Chhimba	–	–	–	11	–	6	–	–	3	–	–	20	20	
				(55.00)		(30.00)			(15.00)			(100)	(4.05)	(100)

(*Contd.*)

APPENDIX 3A (*Contd.*)

Caste	Amritsar		Majitha		Tarn Taran		Batala			Total			Grand Total	
	H	S	H	S	H	S	H	Ch	S	H	Ch	S		
Kumhar	–	1 (33.33)	–	1 (33.33)	–	1 (33.33)	–	–	–	–	–	3 (100)	3 (0.60)	(100)
Thathiar	–	–	–	–	–	1 (100)	–	–	–	–	–	1 (100)	1 (0.20)	(100)
Nai	–	–	–	3 (75.00)	–	1 (25.00)	–	–	–	–	–	4 (100)	4 (0.81)	(100)
Jheer	–	–	–	1 (50.00)	–	1 (50.00)						2 (100)	2 (0.40)	(100)
Julaha	–	–	–	–	–	–	1 (100)	–	–	1 (100)	–	–	1 (0.20)	(100)
Vairagi	6 (100)	–	–	–	–	–	–			6 (100)	–	–	6 (1.21)	(100)
Chamar			1 (33.33)		1 (33.33)				1 (33.33)	2 (66.67)	–	1 (33.33)	3 (0.60)	(100)
Sansi	–	–	–	2 (50.00)	–	–	–	–	2 (50.00)	–	–	4 (100)	4 (0.81)	(100)
Mazhbi/ Masih	–	–	–	3 (16.67)	–	3 (16.67)	–	1 (5.55)	11 (61.11)	–	1 (5.55)	17 (94.44)	18 (3.64)	(100)
Total	48 (9.72)	12 (2.43)	128 (25.91)	68 (13.77)	103 (20.85)	59 (11.94)	16 (3.24)	1 (0.20)	59 (11.94)	295 (59.72)	1 (0.20)	198 (40.08)	494 (100)	(100)

Note: H: Hindu, S: Sikh, Ch: Christians.

Souce: Harish K. Puri, Paramjit Singh Judge, Jagurp Singh Sekhon, *Terrorism in Punjab: Understanding Grassroots Reality*, 1999, pp. 144-6, 'It shows that 59 per cent of the total migrants in area of our study belonged to the Hindu community. Among the Hindu migrants those of Brahmin caste were the largest in number. It is clear that a considerable proportion of migrant

APPENDIX 3B

Namdhari Ramgarhias of Jalandhar District*

Name	Ancestral Village/Tahsil	Present Village/ Tahsil	Occupation	
			Ancestral	Present
Gurdeep Kaur	Lalasidha/ Lahore	Jalandhar City	Big Farming 60 acres of land	PCS Officer
Davinder Singh	Chak No. 57, Pakistan	–do–	Black Smithy, Bullock driven Flour Mill, 5 acres of land.	Lab Technician
Harbhajan Singh	Balshanda, Sialkot	–do–	Black Smithy and Sepidari	Carpentry
Harbhajan Kaur	Munanwali, Sialkot	–do–	Carpentry	Marble Shop
Gurmukh Singh	Uppal Khalsa, Phillaur	–do–	Carpentry/ Lathe Machine Operator	Workshop
Darshan Singh	Arfwala, Montgomery	–do–	Saw Mill	–do–
Satnam Singh	Lyallpur, Pakistan	–do–	Wood Works	Contractor
Prithavi Singh Likhari	Mandi Aarfwala, Montgomery	–do–	–do–	Workshop, Saw Mill
Jagpreet Singh	Talwandi Kahlon, Sialkot	–do–		Electric Shop, Job
Baldev Singh	Talwandi Kahlon, Sialkot	–do–	Sepidari	Workshop
Jasvir Singh	Tapiala, Sialkot	–do–	Contractor	Contractor, 25 acres of land
Lakhwinder Singh	Channianwal, Pakistan	–do–	Marginal Farmer	Masson/ Newspaper Wendor

Harbhajan Kaur	Dabrianwala, Narowal/ Sialkot	–do–	Carpentry	Carpentry
Surjit Singh	Noorpur, Jalandhar	–do–	–do–	Repair Shop
Mangal Singh	Jalandhar	–do–	Carpentry/ Masonary	Carpentry/ Masonary
Prem Singh	–do–	–do–		Telephone Booth/ Auto Rikshaw
Piara Singh	Pakistan	–do–	Black Smithy	Motor Mechanic
Gopal Singh	Jalandhar city	–do–		Hardware/ Repair Shop
Gurnam Singh	Jalandhar	–do–	Masonary	Mason/ Contractor
Gurcharan Singh	Narowal/ Sailkot	–do–	Marginal Farmer	Civil & Production Engineer
Santokh Singh	Sialkot	–do–	Carpentry	Carpentry
Gurbax Singh	Sangal,Narowal/ Sialkot	–do–	–do–	–do–
Kulwant Singh	–	–do–	Contractor	Mechanic
Pritam Singh	–	–do–	Black Smithy	Carpentry
Balbir Singh	Pannuan, Sialkot	–do–	Carpentry, Farming	Auto Electric Shop
Hazara Singh	Tapiala, Narowal/ Sialkot	–do–	Big Farming (25 Acres), Manufacturer	Contractor
Sukhwinder Singh	Ballowali, Sialkot	–do–	Contractor	Job
Jeet Singh	Bharoke, Sialkot	–do–	Carpentry	Carpentry
Kuldeep Singh	Kala, Sialkot	–do–	–do–	–do–
Harpreet Singh	–	Jalandhar City	–do–	Job-cum-Shopkeeping
Balwant Singh	Uchhi, Sialkot	–do–	Masonary	Asst. Post Master
Hazara Singh	Balshah, Sialkot	–do–	Lathe Machine Operator	Sepidar
Teja Singh	Bharoke, Sialkot	–do–	Lathe Machine Operator, Moneylending	Contractor

Gurvinder Singh	Panawan, Gurdaspur, Pakistan	–do–	Masonary	Scooter Repair Shop
Surinder Singh	Panawan, Gurdaspur, Pakistan	–do–	–do–	Auto Parts Shop
Sukhwant Kaur	Chahal, Narowal/ Sialkot	–do–	Carpentry	Carpentry
Kirpal Kaur	Mumtafpur, Sialkot	–do–	Masonary	Scooter Repair Shop
Gian Singh	Gigewali, Sialkot	–do–	Black Smithy/ Carpentry	Lathe Machine Operator
Bachan Singh	Balsahidawind, Sialkot	–do–	Carpentry	Carpentry
Swaran Singh	Tapiala, Sialkot	–do–	Lathe Machine Operator	Sales man
Lakhbir Singh	–	–do–	Masonary	Contractor
Sardara Singh	Pakistan	–do–		Masonary
Saudagar Singh	Pasrur, Sialkot	–do–	Lathe Machine Operator	Lathe Machine Operator
Tara Singh	Bhureke, Sialkot	–do–	Carpentry/ Black Smithy	Timber Merchant
Surat Singh	Bal, Sialkot	do	Black Smithy	Masonary
Gurmeet Singh	Malikpur/ Mojoke Sialkot	–do–	Carpentry	Govt. Job
Baldev Singh	–	–do–	–do–	Furniture Shop
Davinder Singh	Kandhala, Sialkot	–do–	–do–	Carpentry
Kulwant Singh	Chambabath, Sialkot	–do–	Carpentry/ Black Smithy	Contractor
Palwinder Singh	–do–	–do–	–do–	do
Jaswinder Singh	–do–	–do–	–do–	–do–
Lakhwant Singh	–do–	–do–	–do–	–do–
Gurcharan Singh	–do–	–do–	–do–	–do–
Swaran Singh	–do–	–do–	–do–	–do–
Amarjit Singh	–do–	–do–	–do–	–do–

Tarlochan Singh	Pannwan, Sialkot	–do–	–	Spare Parts Shop
Balbir Singh	–	–do–	Carpentry	Job
Gurbachan Singh	Budheshah, Gurdaspur	–do–	–do–	Contractor
Charan Singh	Vazirpur Khandala, Sialkot	–do–	–do–	Wood Workshop
Harbhajan Singh	–do–	–do–	–	Carpentry, Electrician
Swaran Singh	Narowal/ Sialkot	–do–	Wood Workshop	Wood Workshop
Deep Singh	Abdal, Sialkot	–do–	Small Farmer	Retd. Pensioner
Balbir Kaur	–	–do–	Wood Workshop	Mobile Repair Shop
Mohinder Singh	Bharai Lohian, Sialkot	–do–	–do–	Wood Workshop
Joginder Singh	–	–do–	–do–	Businessman
Chanan Singh	Puhla, Sialkot	–do–	Marginal Farmer	Property Dealer
Amrik Singh	Bhudha Bhindar, Kapurthala	–do–	Carpentry	Industrilist
Harjeet Kaur	Sialkot, Pakistan	–do–	–do–	Sale Purchase
Joginder Singh	Kakkar, Amritsar	Jalandhar City	Wood Workshop	Granthi
Gurvinder Singh	Paddi Khalsa, Phagwara	–do–	Lathe Machine Operator	Wood Workshop
Kamaljit Singh	Jalandhar	–do–	Carpentry	Govt. Job
Jaspal Singh	–do–	–do–	–do–	Contractor
Rupinder Kaur	–	–do–	–do–	Interior Decorator/ Musician
Jagdish Singh Waryam	Theh, Sialkot	–do–	–do–	Journalist/ Writer
Baldev Singh	Loharan Partappura, Jalandhar	Lohar Partappura Jalandhar	Masonary	Workshop, Manufacturing Dyes
Paramjit Singh	Loharan Jalandhar	Lohar Partap Pura/ Jalandhar	Black Smithy	Mechanic and Teaching

Jasvir Singh	Paddi Khalsa, Jalandhar	Paddi Khalsa/ Jalandhar	Carpentry	Engineering
Manjit Singh	Lyallpur, Pakistan	Jalandhar City	Saw Mill, Big Farming	Diesel Machine Workshop
Harjeet Singh	Muthada Kalan, Jalandhar	Muthada Kalan	Carpentry/ Black Smithy	Wood Workshop
Avtar Singh	Paddi Khalsa, Phagwara	Paddi Khalsa	Sepidari	Carpentry
Gian Singh	–do–	N.R.I U.S.A.	Black Smithy	Workshop
Jasbir Singh	Paddi Khalsa, Goraya	Paddi Khalsa, Goraya	–do–	Transporter
Gurmukh Singh	–do–	–do–	Carpentry	Saw Mill, Transporter
Amrik Singh	–do–	–do–	–do–	Truck Driver
Balwinder Singh	–do–	–do–	–do–	–do–
Sucha Singh	–do–	–do–	–do–	–do–
Makhan Singh	–do–	–do–	Saw Mill	Carpentry
Amar Kaur	—	–do–	Black Smithy	Retail Shop
Mohan Singh	Pakistan	–do–	Wood Workshop	–do–
Surinder Singh	–do–	–do–	Black Smithy	Diesel Machine Workshop
Balwinder Kaur	–do–	–do–	Wood Workshop	Retail Shop
Pritam Singh	Pasla, Phillaur/ Jalandhar	–do–	Carpentry	General Store
Gurmeet Singh	Boparai, Phillaur/ Jalandhar	–do–	Sepidari	Repair and Sanitary Shop
Nirmal Singh	Johllan, Jalandhar	Goraya	Carpentry	Marginal Farmer
Sukhjit Kaur	Loharan	Lohar Partappura	–do–	Driver
Amrik Singh	–do–	–do–	–do–	Carpentry
Rajinder Singh	–do–	–do–	–do–	Saw Mill
Ranjit Singh	–do–	–do–	–do–	Driver
Sarabjit Singh	–do–	–do–	–do–	–do–
Gurmeet Singh	–do–	–do–	–do–	Carpentry
Avtar Singh	–do–	–do–	–do–	–do–

Note: *Data provided by Namdhari respondents

CHAPTER 4

Beliefs and Practices

The Namdhari spiritual master, Satguru Jagjit Singh, exhorts his followers to lead their lives according to the *rahitnama* (a manual of principles) of Satguru Ram Singh. This rahitnama is contained in the *Namdhari Nitnem* published by the Namdhari Darbar Sri Bhaini Sahib in 2000. This rahitnama has been written for the benefit of all sangats. This work also mentions the modes of preparing *amrit* (nectar) and its administering to those who seek to become Namdhari Sikhs; the mode of performing havan; and the *banis* (words of God/works of Gurus) to be recited on these occasions. Also it contains the Namdhari *ardas* (supplication). Over the period of 150 years, the Namdhari Gurus and writers evolved the structures of ceremonies of birth, *namkaran* (a ritual for giving name to child), *anand-karaj* (marriage custom), and death. They have also structured the maryada of the *Path* (reading of Granth Sahib), *Akhand Path* (unbroken reading of Granth Sahib), *Jap-Paryog* (recitation of bani/meditation), and *Akhand Varnia* (continuous recitation of bani/meditation). Last, they prescribe the Namdhari mode of dressing and eating.

In the light of the normative Namdhari *maryada*, we now analyse some of the beliefs and practices of the Namdhari community, gleaned from 925 Namdhari families of 18 districts. Before we begin with the analysis, it is necessary to repeat a word of caution about the reliability of this data. In the introduction to this volume. We stated that on the basis of a questionnaire, we conducted interviews of the senior members (both men and women) of the Namdhari families and noted their oral information. We tried our best to verify the authenticity of data by cross-examining Namdhari respondents. Since interviews were conducted at their residentce, we were careful to observe Namdhari symbols such as the mode of dressing and eating; display of calendars of the Sikh Gurus along with their spiritual masters; the use of ornaments and cosmetics, the means of recreation; and the comforts of the home. Nevertheless, reliability of information on the frequency of practice of *nam-simran*, recitation of *banis*, observation of *anand-karaj* and last rites, paying homage to Satguru at Bhaini Sahib and *daswand*, all depend upon the integrity of the Namdhari respondents. One is conscious of the possibility of errors in the statistical information. For instance, a tendency to exaggerate is common among the Namdhari elite. At the same time, hundreds of Namdhari artisans and agriculturists were not shy of sharing their limitations while practising the Namdhari maryada.

THE STATUS OF THE GURU

Namdhari beliefs and practices revolve around the concepts of the embodied Guru and the Sikh scriptures (primarily the *Adi-Granth* and *Dasam Granth*). The Namdhari Sikhs have unflinching faith in the living Guru, and address him as *Satguru* or *Sache-Patshah* (true spiritual preceptor) reverently. For them he is a spiritual master who banishes ignorance and darkness. He enlightens them and reveals God's words. He is God's voice and divine self revelation. He liberates them from the sins of *kam* (sexuality), *krodh* (anger), *moh* (infatuation) and *lobh* (greed) and from suffering. He is *bakshanhar* (forgiver) and saviour. A substantial number of Namdharis perceive Satguru Jagjit Singh in these terms and narrate stories of his miraculous powers. Some of them proudly told us that he healed them from incurable diseases. Others informed us that he protected them from calamities. Still others attribute their success in the temporal world to the grace of Sache Patshah. Some of the Namdhari couples disclosed that *Satguru* blessed them with children.

For the Namdhari Sikhs, Bhaini Sahib is Satguru's abode. Here arrive followers, in groups or families, to pay homage. They receive *gurmantar* (mystical or holy word whispered in their ears) and often listen to his discourses. Some of them submit *arz* (requests) about problems which could be family disputes or personal grievances. They believe that their Satguru is non-partisan and his verdict is fair. His *hukam* (order) is infallible, unquestionable, and they receive it with grace. A few of them seek financial assistance for their personal needs such as clearing medical bills and debts and generating a livelihood. Satguru Jagjit Singh and his predecessors are known for their generosity. It is a rare occasion when an arz is ignored. It is against this backdrop that the Namdhari followers make periodic visits to Bhaini Sahib headquaters. According to our survey 99 per cent Namdhari families perform their religious obligations and reiterate their faith in the supremacy of Satguru Jagjit Singh (Table 4.1).

TABLE 4.1: STATUS OF EXTANT RELIGIOUS BELIEFS AND PRACTICES OF THE NAMDHARI SIKHS OF PUNJAB*

Number of Namdhari families observing Maryada (Birth, Namkaran & Death)			
Fully observing	Partially	Indifferent	Total
206 22%	617 67%	102 11%	925
Number of Namdhari families not observing Sodh			
Chhoti Sodh	Vadi Sodh	No	
162 17.51%	62 6.70%	701 75.78%	925
Number of Namdhari families believing in Scripture			
Adi-Granth/Dasam Granth	Guru-Granth		
456 49%	469 51%		925
Number of Namdhari families performing nam-simran			
Yes	No		
896 97%	29 3%		925
Number of Namdhari families reciting Banis			
Yes	No		
554 60%	371 40%		925
Number of Namdhari families visiting Bhaini Sahib			
Yes	No		
920 99%	5 1%		925
Number of Namdhari families visiting Sikh historical places and gurdwaras			
Yes	No		
841 91%	84 9%		925
Number of Namdhari families wearing prescribed dress			
Full	Partial	Khule	
409 44%	203 22%	313 34%	925

Number of vegetarian Namdhari families

Yes	No	
902	23	925
98%	2%	

Note: *Data provided by Namdhari respondents.

The *Adi-Granth* and *Dasam Granth* are sacred texts of the Namdhari Sikhs. In his discourses, Satguru Jagjit Singh persistently emphasizes the religious relevance of these scriptures. He says that Satguru Ram Singh had several *dharamsalas* repaired and placed in them these scriptures; he revived Sikh maryada of performing path, akhand path and *katha-kirtan* (religious discourse). He further tells them that Satguru Ram Singh also revived and revitalized the Sikh maryada of performing *nit-nem* (daily recitation of gurbani). It may be mentioned here that performing *nit-nem* had become an established practice in the early seventeenth century. Bhai Gurdas d. 1636) records the maryada of the daily singing of *Japuji* in the morning, *Rehiras* in the evening, and *Kirtan Sohila* in the late evening.[1] Subsequently, the number of texts increased from three to five: *Japuji, Japu, Savaiyye, Sodaru Rehiras* and *Kirtan Sohila*.[2] The Namdhari *nit-nem* includes more than five banis. The Namdhari rahitnama exhorts both men and women to memorize *Japuji, Japu, Shabad Hazaire, Rehiras* and *Arti-Sohila* and recite them daily.[3]

Emphasis on the *gurbani* (Guru's works) and its continuous recitation has enabled the all Namdhari followers to memorize, at least, the correct titles of the Sikh scriptures the *Adi-Granth* or *Guru Granth* and *Dasam Granth*. Similarly, emphasis on the concept of the living Guru has yielded the desired result: 49 per cent Namdhari respondents address *Guru Granth Sahib* as the *Adi-Granth* whereas the rest still share the popular Sikh tradition of addressing their scripture as *Guru Granth* (Table 4.1). However, this statistic does not imply that their faith in Satguru Jagjit Singh is weaker than that of those who address it as the *Adi-Granth*. They too believe and worship Satguru Jagjit Singh. Moreover, the Namdhari Sikhs revere the *Dasam Granth*. Namdhari scholars believe that the *granth* of the Tenth Guru Gobind Singh was an integral part of the *Sri Adi-Granth* and make no distinction between the bani of Guru Gobind Singh and his predecessors– from Guru Nanak Dev to Guru Tegh Bahadur. The Namdhari scholars contend that the title *Dasam Granth* denoting a separate text became common by about 1900.[4] For the Namdhari

Sikhs, there is no doctrinal crisis. Their faith in *deh-dhari* guru is strengthened by compositions like *Chaubis Avtar* in the *Dasam Granth*. The *Chaubis Avtar* narrates the twenty-four incarnations of Vishnu, including lengthy narratives on Rama and Krishna. Recently, on Satguru Jagjit Singh's command, the Namdhari Sant Darshan Singh prepared a CD with an authentic recitation (*Shudh Path*) of the *Adi-Granth* and *Dasam Granth*. It may be pointed out here that the common Sikhs including the Sant Samaj too revere the Dasam Granth 'as it contains the bani of Guru Gobind Singh including the Jaap Sahib, the Savaiyyas and the Chaupai which are integral part of the Sikhs' daily regimen of the devotional recitation'.[5] For Sikh scholars and the SGPC, the installation of the *Dasam Granth* alongside of *Sri Guru Granth Sahib* and 'worship' of the former is sacrilegious and most undesirable.[6]

The Namdhari maryada comprises rituals and ceremonies which are related to birth, nam karan, marriage, death, nam-simran, eating, and dressing. The Namdhari Gurus and scholars have evolved these beliefs and practices on the basis of Sikh scriptures, and traditions. Nevertheless, the impact of Sikh rituals, of Punjabi customs, and of both older traditions and modern lifestyle, are perceptible. Namdharis are unable to practise the normative Namdhari maryada in its true spirit. For their own convenience they have made two categories of *Sodh: Vadi* and *Chhoti*. The Vadi Sodh is a ritual when a Namdhari Sikh cooks his own food and uses utensils as per maryada. He also performs nam-simran for the stipulated time whereas Chhoti Sodh obliges one to observe some norms of nam-simran and mode of eating. Table 4.1 shows that only a marginal section of the Namdhari Sikhs observe Vadi Sodh. Similar is the status of Namdhari dress. In routine life, more than 44 per cent Namdhari Sikhs wear the Namdhari dress. Yet, the Namdhari leadership has made a tremendous success in persuading 98 per cent the Namdhari followers to be vegetarians (Table 4.1). The remaining 2 per cent are those Sikhs who have received *bhajan* from Satguru but are not practising Namdharis, even if they claim otherwise. Similarly, there are several former Namdhari families who have given up Namdhari eating taboos.

DRESS

Following precedents, the present spiritual leader Satguru Jagjit Singh makes every possible effort to teach his followers the importance of white clothes comprising *kurta* and *churidar pajama* and *sidhi pag*. He tells his followers that it was Satguru Ram Singh who chose this dress with specific meaning. For understanding the relevance of the colours, Satguru Jagjit Singh quotes scriptures. He says that *bani* (*gurbani*) mentions four ages in regard to the colours: 'ਬੱਗਾ ਰੱਤਾ ਪੀਲਾ ਕਾਲਾ ਵੇਦਾਂ ਕਰੀਂ ਪੁਕਾਰ॥' Dark is the metaphor of *Kalyuga* whereas white is of Satjug. In the Vedic scriptures, there are references to seven colours. Hindu gods and goddesses and mythological characters appear in dresses of different colours. For instance, mother goddesses are shown in black, *rishis* (saints) in white. Satguru Ram Singh chose a dress of white colour and *sidha dastara* (straight turban) as the uniform of his soldiers. Moreover, since it was introduced by Satguru Ram Singh, this dress also serves as a reminder of the master's message.[7] Namdhari Guru Jagjit Singh exhorts Namdhari Sikhs not to compromise with their dress and turban. It prepares them mentally and physically to face any odd situation. He asks them to be ready to face any challenge in regard to the Namdhari turban. He quotes examples of some Namdhari professionals whose determination prevailed upon their employers to allow them to wear turbans. The Namdhari Guru tells the Namdhari parents to send their children in white dress and turban. He also tells them that the childhood is the right time for orientation in the Namdhari maryada. He wishes that the children should not be self-conscious about Namdhari dress. Instead, they should feel proud of their cultural heritage.[8]

The Namdhari Guru reminds his followers that the pants and shirts were the clothes of alien rulers who bled Hindustan and tortured Indians and Namdhari Sikhs.[9] Western dress is thus a symbol of slavery and repression. Why should we carry on this legacy, he asks his followers.

Thousands of Namdhari Sikhs, both men and women, pay their obeisance to their spiritual master on several occasions at Bhaini Sahib headquarters. They dress in Namdhari *bana* (dress) to honour their Satguru's wishes. Similar scenes are seen at the district headquarters where periodical (especially Sunday) congregations are held. Wherever their Satguru visits thousands of them clad in the Namdhari dress throng. Amidst such a gathering, any non-Namdhari person would carry the impression that the Namdhari Sikhs always wear the prescribed dress.

However, the external images of these followers begin to fade when they are seen in their houses, place of work, or on the street.

Random survey of Amritsar city shows that the Namdhari males are more conspicuous by their ***kurta pajama*** and ***dastars*** of white colour than women. The majority of women in the age group of 30 to 50 are seen in ***salwar/kamiz*** of light colours. The girls and married young wives wear coloured clothes including ***dupatta*** or ***chunni***. A dress of light colours is a subtle compromise with the dress code. The women do not want to show disrespect to the Namdhari custom, yet they have grown up in the Punjabi culture. Like other Punjabi women they are fond of fashion. The wearing of white ***dupatta*** or ***chunnis***, is in Punjabi custom for occasions of sorrow and death.

Importantly, with a few exceptions, the majority of Namdhari women do not wear ornaments or use cosmetics. Simplicity is the virtue of the Namdhari women. Aged/retired women are dressed in the Namdhari style and carry a white woollen rosary. A majority of urban Namdharis in the age group of 20-30 administrative personnel, businessmen, and factory workers, wear shirts and pants but with white dastars. However, a small section of the Namdhari Sikhs, both in rural and urban areas, has emerged with a tendency to compromise on dress. They wear neither the proper white dress nor keep external symbols like an untrimmed beards. This tendency is more conspicuous among the rural youngsters. The fashion of trimmed beard and Western dress is so pervasive that some of the Namdhari Jathedars have not succeeded in keeping their sons and daughters in the Namdhari dress. Our survey shows that 34 per cent Namdhari Sikhs have given up their customary dress. Similarly, 22 per cent do not wear full Namdhari dress. Among them are Namdhari men who wear ***sidha-dastara*** only (Table 4.1).

The Namdhari youth of cities like Mohali and Chandigarh yearn to give up the Namdhari traditional lifestyle. They come from middle and upper middle classes and use electronic gadgets, cosmetics, modern dresses and modern means of transportation and communication. They often enjoy the theatre, cinema, and eating out in restaurants. There are several families whose daughters wear Western dress and hair-styles and use the latest cosmetics. The photographs of the Namdhari Gurus and woollen rosaries hung in their drawing rooms and cars alone tell us that they belong to the Namdhari community.

Like their Satguru, Namdhari parents express their concern over this tendency among the Namdhari youth to deviate. They ascribe several factors responsible for this deviation. As hinted above, the

Namdhari Satguru perceives this crisis in terms of the impact of the TV and cinema culture. He thinks that if parents could orient their children in the Namdhari maryada and keep them away from this bad impact, the crisis could be resolved. Some of the parents showed their helplessness in the face of teenage defrance. In the schools and colleges, the Namdhari boys complain that they became objects of ridicule/taunts. Similarly, the managements of public schools have introduced school unniforms. There are, however, a few Namdhari parents who could refuse to compromise on Namdhari dress.

Likewise, a considerable number of the Namdhari parents have not succeeded in keeping themselves and their children away from the impact of TV and media culture. Ninety-nine per cent Namdhari houses have television sets. I was amused to hear the Namdhari elders to say that they only viewed news bulletins. Other said they watched only religious programmes. Still others said that they did not find time to watch television. Several parents pointed out to the social ground realities and expressed their inability to check their children from using electronic media. They underlined the relevance of TV media in terms of its exposure of youth to the technological and scientific discoveries and advancements, and to social and cultural issues of the day. Such exposure broadens the vision of people. Some parents also pointed out that if they removed TV sets from their houses, the children would sneak into neighbours' houses or shops. We cannot isolate ourselves from the rest of the world; the world has been overtaken by the consumer-culture.

EATING TABOOS

Eating taboos, as sociologists point out, 'serve as a social marker, creating and maintaining social classifications'.[10] The Namdhari Sikhs are Sikhs but distinct in terms of food taboos. Right from the beginning of the Namdhari movement around 1850 its founders Satgurus Balak Singh and Ram Singh laid strict injunctions with regard to what food they should eat in the wake of conflicting Sikh traditions about taboos. By that time, a section of the Khalsa (baptized Sikhs), like common Sikhs, ate meat. One of the literal meanings of *prasad* is food offered to gods. In Sikh history, this implied the meat of an animal slaughtered with a single stroke.[11] However, the Nihangs of the eighteenth and the nineteenth century also used this word for *Jhatka-meat*. In fact, according to *Mehma Prakash*, cooked meat was also served in the *langar* occasionally. At the same time, the tradition of vegetarian food was equally strong. The Udasis and Nirmalas, *sants* and *babas* opposed the killing of animals, perceiving it as a sin.[12]

A survey of 925 Namdhari families shows that 98 per cent Namdhari men and women are vegetarians. Non-veg food in any form (bakery products) and intoxicants are taboo in the Namdhari house. This taboo is observed even outside home. When I asked the Namdhari respondents whether they ate food on the occasions of marriages and akhand paths/bhogs performed by the non-Namdhari Sikhs, the majority of them (80 per cent) said that they attended these occasions but did not eat. Twenty per cent said that they eat on these functions if vegetarian food is served. Only a marginal number of the Namdhari Sikhs said that they eat vegetarian food only on all such functions. Eating vegetarian food outside home is becoming acceptable among the Namdhari Sikhs. Such acceptability is also seen in regard to tea/coffee and soft drinks in Namdhari houses. A substantial number of Namdhari Sikhs take and serve tea/coffee and soft drinks with snacks bought from the market, but many still serve milk to visitors/guests. Those who are well off also serve dry-fruit.

There are several families who accept food (sweets or cooked vegetarian food) from neighbours or friends/relatives on occasions like *lohri, divali,* and cultural fairs. But the majority of Namdhari Sikhs, especially in the urban areas, do not eat them. Either they distribute such eatables to 'others' or throw them away. When I pointed out to some Namdhari Sikhs of Amritsar city that in Punjabi society, this practice was not approved, perceived discourteous, they replied that after some time our neighbours, friends and relatives respond to our sensibility and take it as normal. However, limited interaction of Namdhari Sikhs with others has tended to build-up a social exclusiveness and eventually may isolate them from the community of other Sikhs.

SOCIAL CUSTOMS: STATUS OF WOMEN

The report of the National Commission for Religious and Linguistic Minorities (2007) shows a serious concern to ascertain the status of women. It names some variables in the status of women, economic, educational, social, and political.[13] At the same time, the report considers factors which undermine the status of women: the patriarchal family, its customs, traditions, and beliefs. Women are victims of foeticide and various crime. However, the report argues that.

> religion acts as an important cultural factor, which reinforces the traditional perception of women as subordinate to males and under male control. The unequal position of women in the family is determined and reinforced by the dictates of organized religion. None of the major religions—Hinduism, Buddhism, Islam and Christianity ever conceded complete equality to women and have in fact institutionalized the secondary position of women versus men through written and oral interpretation by the male clergy. The ideal of womanhood is still modeled on the Brahmanical tradition and linked to a strongly patriarchal culture assigning a secondary position to women. Also within each of the religious groups, there is no homogeneity as regards women's status. Women belonging to the same religion might yet have very different conditions of life, which are influenced by their earning capacity, employment, rural-urban setup, educational level, and so on.[14]

In the context of prevailing expensive social customs, how far do the social hierarchy of the Namdhari community and its maryada accord status to its women?

Expensive Social Customs: A variety of rituals have had been integral part of birth, marriage and death ceremonies. They are very expensive and beyond the means of the common Sikhs. To begin with the birth, the parents of the mother visit their daughter's home taking clothes and gifts for her and the mother-in-law and a turban for the father-in-law and son-in-law. Apart from a feast, gifts are given to the baby and to relatives of the bridegroom. On this occasion, the family's friends are also honoured.

Weddings are attended by a variety of expensive social customs. Ceremonies begin with the betrothal which is arranged either with the help of mediator called *vichola* or parents of bride and bridegroom themselves. In any case, they perform ceremonies of *shagun* or *roka* or *mangni* which involves exchange of gifts. The volume and quality of these gifts depend on social status. The spirit behind the exchange of gifts is the acceptance of premarital contacts and relationship. However, this spirit has been supplanted by demands by parents of the bridegroom for motorcycles, cars, domestic appliances, clothing and ornaments (golden *kara*—bangle, *mundari*—ring and watches, etc.). The preparations for the wedding ceremony are preceded by *maiyan* and *vatna*. On these occasions, the bride and the bridegroom discard their old clothes and wear traditional dress and ornaments.

The cost of these articles run into thousands of rupees. A night prior to the departure of *barat* (marriage procession), a procession called *jago* (awakening) is taken out. The women of the groom's family and relatives wear gaudy dresses, hold lamps on their heads and are lead by professional dancers who perform *gidha* and *bhangra*. The procession goes around the streets of the village or *mohalla*. The charges of professional dancers again run into thousands of rupees (depending upon the prominence of the dance troupes and their charges). Besides, there are several ceremonies which conclude the wedding. Important among these are the final departure of the bride from her paternal home. This ceremony is known as *vidai*. When she reaches her in-law's parents, some more ceremonies are performed.

Perhaps the most expensive items are hosting of the *barat* and relatives. In Punjab, it is common practice to host grand-parties for the *baratis* and relatives in marriage halls. The rent for these places itself may vary from Rs. 20,000 to 2,00,000. In addition, the expenses on the drinks, snacks, lunch and dinners run into lakhs of rupees. 'Today, rural Punjab is dotted with swanky marriage palaces while government schools and hospitals are in an abysmally poor state.' Commenting upon the outrageously ostentatious marriage celebrations, the Resident Editor of the *Hindustan Times* says 'the big, fat Punjabi weddings' represent a 'socially disconcerting trend of vulgar display of wealth. The political class of the poor-rich state has not only been in the forefront of this splurge-and-show-off trend, it has actually perfected that art of turning weddings into mammoth political soirees.' [15] Dowry has lost its original sanctity and become a social evil. In northern India, a bride's family offered a voluntary gift to the groom's family in order to establish a good relationship. In the Punjab, there was a special custom of giving bedding past of the dowry.[16] In fact, dowry was 'intimately interlinked with the institutions of hypergamous marriage and the inheritance of property.' Unfortunately, the dowry has ceased to be the status of the bride's family in terms of compensation for a daughter's full inheritance. [17]

A large number of the people perceive dowry as means of becoming rich overnight. Their demands comprise cars, motorcycles, tractors, electric gadgets, and jewellery. The rural and urban elites have set a practice of organizing ostentatious marriage celebrations in addition to the exchange of dowry. Thus dowry demand has become one of the major factors behind indebtedness. It is a major factor responsible for the peasantry going under debt, and pushing some farmers to commit suicide.[18] A Delhi-based social activist and Kisan Unions found that it was dowry, not low returns, which forced farmers to commit suicide. The minimum dowry expected from Jat Sikhs is Rs. 2 lakh and Rs. 60,000 among landless peasants. The women of the affected families frankly admitted that the girls were a liability. In a survey of 125 suicide-affected families in villages in Ferozepur, Muktsar, Bathinda, Moga, Mansa, Sangrur, Patiala, Ludhiana, Barnala, and Faridkot districts, a study titled 'Impact of Agrarian Crisis on Peasant Women' has found that the majority of small and marginal farmers took loans for agricultural or other purposes, but used the money to pay for dowry or medical expenses.

While 46 per cent of the widows acknowledged using loan amounts for dowry or weddings of daughters, 36 per cent said the money was used for treatment of family members ailing from diseases like gallbladder stones, hysterectomies, eye surgeries, hernia or cancer.

'The majority of suicides in the Malwa—a region most affected by the agrarian crisis—were 'directly or indirectly' linked to social obligations.'[19]

Over a period of 150 years, the Namdhari Gurus evolved a distinct pattern of marriage. The Namdhari maryada allows the *anand karaj* of adult bridge and groom irrespective of caste. They are administered *amrit* and should know the five *banis* by heart. On the day early in the morning after performing kirtan of *Asa-di-War*, havan is started under Vedi and *banis* of *Jap*, *Jaap*, *Chandi Charitar* and *Akal Ustat* are recited. Four lavan from the *Adi-Granth* are read, the couple circumambulates a sacred fire. There is no circling the *Adi-Granth* in the manner of modern Khalsa. The bride does not cover her face.

Besides, the customs like *thaka/roka*, *kurmai*, bride/bridegroom or parents visiting houses of in-laws are not allowed. Similarly, marriage-parties, feasts, and the exchange of gifts and dowry are strictly prohibited.

The pattern of *anand karaj* of the Namdhari Sikhs comprise four inter-related features. The first is the mode of *anand* ceremony (Namdhari or non-Namdhari *maryada*), second is the place where the *anand-karaj* is performed; third whether marriage is endogamous, and fourth, whether dowry is exchanged. A substantial section of the Namdhari Sikhs of all occupational castes are helpless to consummate the marriage of their sons and daughters according to the Namdhari *maryada*. They follow the *anand karaj* of mainstream Sikhs.

According to the Table 4.2, almost half the Namdhari families perform this ritual according to popular Sikh maryada. (However, this percentage differs from caste to caste of these Sikhs.) Some reasons of endogamous marriages were disclosed by the Namdhari respondents themselves. They argued that they were microscopic minority of their respective big *zat-biradaries* and live with their relatives. Moreover, they also argued that a great majority of them were engaged in the same occupation and lived in same localities both in villages and towns. Above all, they and their counterparts (non-Namdhari Sikhs) shared a common cultural heritage, caste ethos, work experience. It was due to these reasons that the majority of the Namdhari Sikhs preferred endogamous marriages according to the *anand-karaj* of Sikhs of mainstream.

Till 1955 only endogamous marriages were legal and the customary law did not permit inter-caste marriages. Yet these marriages were common among some tribes and low castes. Similarly, marriages within the same *got* were considered invalid, but only *sagotra* (exogamous caste within the *zat*) marriages were valid among some tribes. The Hindu Marriage Act 1955, removed the prohibitions of inter-caste, inter-sub-caste, inter-tribe and *sagotra* marriages.[20] Namdhari guru was the first social reformer to defy the customary laws and conducted inter-caste marriages in village Khote, Ferozepur in 1863. Satguru Jagjit Singh himself conducted four inter-caste marriages.[21] It is said that several hundred inter-caste marriages have been conducted at the Bhaini Sahib headquarters but my sample survey does not corroborate. this. More than 98 per cent Namdhari parents, especially Jats, still prefer endogamous marriage even though Namdhari Guru Jagjit Singh allows his followers to accept wives from non-Namdhari families. Our survey also shows that the percentage of inter-caste marriages among the business and artisan classes is higher than among agriculturists. A young Namdhari husband of Amritsar disclosed the fact that his wife came from a Brahmin family and she also took *amrit*. He disclosed that Satguru Jagjit Singh himself fixed the match.

In the post-Independence period, dowry became a widespread evil and as 'Cases came to the public notice where brides, on account of their failure to bring the promised dowry were beaten up, kept without food for days together, locked up in dingy rooms, tortured physically and mentally, strangulated or burnt alive or let to commit suicide.'[22] Thus the Namdhari guru directed Namdhari Sikhs to

TABLE 4.2: PATTERN OF *ANAND KARAJ* OF NAMDHARI SIKHS OF PUNJAB*

	Mode of Ceremony		Ceremony performed at				Dowry	
	Mode of Ceremony	Non-Namdhari Maryada	Bhaini Sahib/ Dharamsala	Home/ other places	Within caste	Inter caste	Accepted	Not-accepted
Amritsar	61	42	54	49	98	5	54	49
Barnala	30 NA** = 4	49	29 NA = 5	49	78 NA = 5		51 NA = 3	29
Bathinda	16 NA = 1	9	16 NA = 1	9	25 NA = 1		9 NA = 1	16
Chandigarh & Mohali	44	21	38	27	65		25	40
Fatehgarh Sahib	43	10	43	10	53		13	40
Ferozepur	17	49	15 NA = 1	50	65 NA = 1		55	11
Gurdaspur	156 NA = 11	81	128 NA = 18	102	30 NA = 218		3 NA = 222	23
Hoshiarpur	31	26	27	30	56	1	46	11
Ludhiana	77 N = 1	26	73 N = 2	29	99 N = 1	4	32 N = 4	68
Moga	16 N = 2	86	11 N = 3	90	100 N = 4		88 N = 3	13
Muktsar	6 NA = 1	10	5 NA = 2	10	16 NA = 1		8 NA = 1	8

(*Contd.*)

TABLE 4.2 (*Contd.*)

	Mode of Ceremony		Ceremony performed at				Dowry	
	Mode of Ceremony	Non-Namdhari Maryada	Bhaini Sahib/ Dharamsala	Home/ other places	Within caste	Inter caste	Accepted	Not-accepted
Nawan Shahr	22	27	21	28	49		36	10
							3	
Patiala	13	12	10	15	28	1	7	19
	NA = 12		NA =12		NA = 8		NA = 11	
Rupnagar	14	7	14	6	19	2	15	5
	NA = 1		NA = 2		NA = 1		NA = 2	
Sangrur	25	47	24	48	72	--	49	23
Tarn Taran	24	50	22	52	73	1	64	10
Total	595	552	530	604	926	14	555	375
	NA = 33		NA = 46		NA = 240		NA = 250	
	1180		1180		1180		1180	

Note: *Data provided by Namdhari respondents.**NA = No Answer by Namdhari respondents.

solemnize marriages at Bhaini Sahib headquarters only. This was a mechanism to save the Namdhari Sikhs from indulgences. It is heartening to note that more than 45 per cent of his followers have begun to honour this commandment. It is also heartening to note that 40 per cent of his followers do not accept dowry.[23]

A large segment of Namdhari respondents admitted the prevalence of dowry. However, form and volume of dowry practised by the Namdhari Sikhs is substantially different than the practice among the Punjabis. First, there has not been a single case of breakdown of marriage on account of dowry. Rather there are one or two cases of the Namdhari Sikhs being punished by Satguru Jagjit Singh for giving some articles. An old Namdhari Sikh of Chheharta told the author that after settling the proposal, parents of the boy came to his house just for a courtesy call as they knew each other earlier. When they left, he gave a gift packet of some clothes as a token of honour (following a Punjabi custom). However, his son's father-in-law placed the same gift at Satguru's feet, and Satguru imposed a huge fine of Rs. 1 lakh on him.[24]

The meagre volume of dowry is also reflected in the homes of Namdhari Sikhs in Sultanwind area, Amritsar district. As noted earlier, these localities house artisan families, in one or two rooms of 60 to 150 sq yards. In such houses all things (clothes, beddings, skeleton furniture and trunks) are stored up. The women and children dress simply. Women wearing golden ornaments is rare. In the evening of 22 August 2007 an old carpenter (but physically fit) ushered the author into the bed room of his son who had not come back from the workshop. When the author asked him about the exchange of dowry, he made a gesture of acceptance and said that the chair you occupy and the double-bed and few pairs of shirts and salwars you see comprise the dowry of my daughter-in-law which she brought. The practice of dowry being perceived as means of becoming rich overnight is an exception.

Inspite of dowry being a taboo, there are specific reasons for its continuity. The studies carried on by the symbolist, structuralist and functionalist researchers show the meaning of the ritual activities on the one hand and their social utility on the other.

> In many cultures weddings often employ symbols representing royalty, fertility and prosperity, as it is an exclusive event establishing socially and culturally approved relations for reproduction. In Punjabi weddings there are several items, such as different food, clothes, ornaments, colors and seeds, which

could point to these meanings if we are acquainted with the symbolic universes of people in the Punjab. In the context of an agrarian society, grains, which a newly wed bride throws over her shoulder, may signify the prosperity she wishes for her family and native home. On a structural level, there are sets of symbolic acts within the ceremonies that may signify the transformational processes of the bridal couple when these acts are compared.[25]

These ceremonies assume social relevance in the functioning of patriarchal society of Punjab. For instance, the bride is uprooted and separated from her natal home and she requires social and psychological support. 'Many ceremonies include the giving of gifts and counter gifts' to confirm closeness and 'facilitate new relations between two families'.[26] Besides, sending a daughter empty-handed is perceived as inauspicious. The consummation of marriage lays the foundation of a new family which requires a house and household articles and an income for running the kitchen, for which parents feel an obligation to help their daughters. The consciousness of this obligation becomes a compulsion. Note that more than 98 per cent Namdhari girls are not given proper education enabling them to earn and contribute to run their respective households. A local leader of Chheharta, raised a fundamental question: When daughters are not given dowry or some financial help on the occasion of marriage, are we not depriving our daughters of their due share in parents' property? Where are the laws which oblige fathers-in-law and sons-in-law to acknowledge property-rights of their daughters-in-law?[27] To mend his question we can say that the Indian Penal Code stands for share of daughters in the parental property. Like other daughters, the Namdhari daughters too are helpless to assert their rights.[28]

Lastly, there is another reason for the prevalence of dowry among the Namdhari Sikhs. Several Namdhari respondents argued that they were not inspired by the top of the Namdhari leadership since some of the Subas, Pardhans and Secretaries had ceased to honour the rules. This leadership practised dowry but under the table. Lavish dowry sent the wrong signals to the daughters and sons of poor Namdhari Sikhs who also hoped to get something from their parents.

There is yet another reason for a larger number of reported cases of the dowry exchange. The major sections of the (interviewed) Namdhari Sikhs belong to 40-50 and 60+ age group. We can make two categories of these groups. One group comprises those Namdharis

Sikhs who took *bhajan* after their marriages. Very obliviously, they exchanged dowries as Punjabis generally do. Among the second group, Namdhari Sikhs by birth, several heads of families informed us that when their marriages were solemnized dowry had not assumed evil proportions. The people were simple and accepted whatever was given. The people gave dowry according to their means, and in fact, it was never requested. Majority of heads of the Namdhari artisan families told the author that lohars and tarkhans were poor and struggled hard to earn their livelihood through the sep system. There were a few families in the *ilaka* whose sons worked in towns and cities, fewer operated lathe machines in some factories. Savings sent back to their homes were meagre. The economic condition of the agriculturists was better, but they too had no surplus funds. If we contextualize, we can say that before the Green and Industrial Revolutions in Punjab, a majority of the agriculturists and artisans remained hand to mouth. It was the Green Revolution followed by industrialization that generated the money for constructing houses fitted with modern equipment and taking care of comforts. One of side effects of the Green Revolution was the growth of the consumer culture. Dowry-demand was but a component of the vulgar display of wealth.[29] There was a shift from solemnization to commercialization of marriages. As noted above, the people began to arrange and conclude customs in the marriage-halls that had sprouted up in towns and suburban areas. The Namdhari Sikhs too, particularly the well off, became victims of the consumer-culture.

According to the elderly Namdhari Sikhs, 'dowry' given according to one's financial condition or capacity was once acceptable. These Namdhari Sikhs quoted Satguru Partap Singh's statements in this context. According to them, Satguru Partap Singh objected to people borrowing money for dowry: parents should help their daughters according to their means.[30] However, the religious discourses of Satguru Partap Singh, clearly show that knowing the evil outcome of the practice of dowry, he rejected it in principle. Yet his discourses made a space for the individual to think and act according to his or her wisdom to decide what was good or bad.[31] Nevertheless, through persuasion and punishment, the Namdhari guru exhorts his followers to give up the practice of dowry.

Namdhari baptism, rituals, and customs are not retrogressive in terms of gender-equality. Namdhari women are free to take baptism and participate in religious activities. Namdhari Guru Jagjit Singh upholds the belief in the administrative and intellectual capacity of women. He has appointed a number of women as *subas*, *pardhans*, and secretaries. Women control and manage the Istri Vidhyak Jathas. Although taboos about dress and food shield Namdhari women from the impact of vulgarity, these taboos compromise their liberty and freedom too.

In recent times, demographers have evolved several indices for measuring the status of women: the sex-ratio, earning capacity, the employment of women, work participation and health status. Our profile of the Namdhari family too covered some of the indices. Table 4.3 shows aspects of social status of modern Namdhari women. The rate of literacy as compared with the average rate of literacy rate (63.09 per cent) of the Sikh women is the highest (88.27 per cent). Excepting the rate of elementary education, the rate (49.38 per cent) of school and secondary education among Namdhari women is for better than the Sikh average (26.13 per cent). Similarly, the rate of higher education (BA, MA, BSc.) of Namdhari women is 9.53 per cent only a few had technical/professional qualifications 2.82 per cent and among the 2,938 Namdhari women less than 2.21 per cent are engaged in the various jobs. This rate of work participation is very poor when we compare work participation rate of the Sikh women of India, at 20.2 per cent. This projection indicates that the major segment of the Namdhari females is confined to the household. It implies that the Namdhari community discourages its women to go out to work. This is true when we notice the higher rate of higher and professional education among them. This latter varies from district to district: the Namdhari women of Amritsar, Chandigarh, and Mohali, Jalandhar and Kapurthala are ahead of their counterparts in other districts. Similarly, the percentage of working Namdhari women is far higher in Chandigarh and Mohali than eleshwhere.

One of the primary indices of the social status of women is the sex-ratio. Our random survey shows that on average there are 906 Namdhari women to every 1,000 males. On the other hand, the ratio among Sikhs at the all India level is 893, and in the Punjab it is just 880. Yet the younger generation of the Namdhari community has started compromising with the ideal of gender equality, and couples in the age group of 20 to 30 indulge in foeticide. This social evil is reflected in the ratio of 770 girls to 1,000 boys in the age group of 0-6 years. The average ratio of the Punjab is 798.[32]

TABLE 4.3: FEMALE LITERACY (PERCENTAGE)*

District	Illiterate	Number of Children in Age group 1-3 yr	Elementary education Upto 5th	School education Upto +12	Higher education B.A./M.A.	Technical/ Professional Education	Jobs	Number of females
Amritsar	14	8	71	146	38	5	6	291
	4.81	2.74	24.39	50.17	13	1.71	2.05	
Bathinda	13	2	18	43	5	5		86
	15.11	2.32	20.93	50	5.81	5.81		
Chandigarh	3	7	25	61	40	14	21	157
and Mohali	1.91	4.45	15.92	38.85	25.47	8.91	13.37	
Fatehgarh	35	10	44	69	10	--	2	168
Sahib	20.83	5.95	26.19	41.07	5.95		1.19	
Ferozepur	40	7	51	84	13	3	3	197
	20.30	3.55	25.88	42.63	6.59	1.57	1.52	
Hoshiarpur	19	11	37	91	13	7	4	169
	11.24	6.50	21.89	53.84	7.69	4.14	2.35	
Jalandhar	6	6	34	88	25	7	5	172
	3.48	3.48	19.76	51.62	14.53	4.06	2.90	
Kapurthala	28	21	93	205	58	18	8	421
	6.65	4.98	22.09	48.69	13.76	4.27	1.90	
Ludhiana	39	12	53	170	33	5	2	317
	12.30	3.78	16.71	53.62	10.41	1.57	0.63	
Moga	67	15	74	164	18	5	3	343
	19.53	4.37	21.57	48.81	5.24	1.45	0.82	

(*Contd.*)

TABLE 4.3 (*Contd.*)

District	Illiterate	Number of Children in Age group 1-3 yr	Elementary education Upto 5th	School education Upto +12	Higher education B.A./M.A.	Technical/ Professional Education	Jobs	Number of females
Nawan Shahr	17	8	39	71	14	1	2	150
	11.33	5.33	26	47.33	9.33	0.66	1.33	
Sangrur	31	7	57	133	12	9	6	240
	12.91	2.91	23.75	55.41	5	3.75	2.5	
Tarn Taran	32	16	45	126	1	4	3	227
	14.09	7.04	19.82	55.50	0.44	1.76	1.32	
Total	344	130	641	1451	280	83	65	2938
%age	11.70	4.42	21.81	49.38	9.53	2.82	2.21	

Note: *Data provided by Namdhari respondents.

THE CONCEPT OF *NAM-SIMRAN* AND ITS PRACTICE

Since the origin of the Namdhari movement, the concept of *nam-simran* and its practice has been integral to the Namdhari *maryada*. The tradition of nam-simran practised by the Sikh Gurus was revived by Namdhari Gurus Balak Singh and Ram Singh in the nineteenth century. The constant remembrance of God, the Sikh tradition of *nirguna bhakti*, liberates a man from his mundane attachments and lifts him to the spiritual plane. Guru Arjan Dev explains the attributes of *simran* and its fruit in his *Sukhmani*. Similarly, in his *Sidh-Ghost*, Guru Nanak lays emphasis on *simran* through the remembrance of *shabad* and at the end of his Japuji says that not only does *nam-simran* liberate its meditator, it also liberates those who accompany him. According to bani, without simran a man degenerates and spreads poison.[33]

The Namdhari Gurus too evolved a practice of meditation on the name of God and made Bhaini Sahib a *tap-asthan* (a centre of meditation). The Namdhari *Rahitnama* enjoins the Namdhari followers,

> Rise during the last watch of the night and taking a pot of water [for cleansing] go into the fields to relieve yourself. When you return scour the pot twice, remove the clothes that you were wearing in the field, clean your teeth, bathe, and recite [the prescribed portions of] sacred scripture. If you do not already know these by heart you should learn them. Everyone should do this, including women both old and young. Commit both Japuji and Jap to memory, and also Shabad Hazare. You must also learn Rahiras and Arati Sohila by heart. All should lead a life of restraint and contentment. Offer praise to the Guru, [the Lord] of Truth, throughout the day and night.[34]

Those followers who come to Bhaini Sahib and stay over (permanently or for the time being) join the morning meditation. The meditation on the name of God and recitation of Asa-di-Var, Japuji and other compositions of the *Adi-Granth* are regular features of maryada at Bhaini Sahib headquarters. Similarly, Varni and Jap-Prayog have been going on since 1937. Both rituals operate at the local levels, rural and urban. Only *Sodhi Singhs* perform these rituals. Moreover, the Namdhari Gurus have also established a practice of holding discourses to reiterate the relevance of *nam-simran*. The structure of these discourses shows that the Namdhari Guru Jagjit Singh exhorts his followers to meditate on the name of God as follows. First, for highlighting the relevance of nam-simran, he extensively quotes the Sikh scriptures, principally the *Adi-Granth* and *Dasam*

TABLE 4.4: SEX RATIO OF NAMDHARI SIKHS OF PUNJAB

	Male	Female	Percentage
Amritsar	473	424	89.64
Barnala	313	277	88.49
Bathinda	99	99	100
Chandigarh & Mohali	185	165	89.18
Fatehgarh Sahib	191	166	86.91
Ferozepur	240	220	91.66
Gurdaspur	493	466	94.52
Hoshiarpur	204	185	90.68
Jalandhar	372	349	93.81
Kapurthala	557	474	85.09
Ludhiana	333	283	84.98
Moga	525	504	96.00
Muktsar	60	58	96.66
Nawan Shahr	214	183	85.51
Patiala	119	121	101.68
Ropar	76	67	88.15
Sangrur	263	238	90.49
Tarn Taran	266	238	89.47
Total	4,983	4,517	90.64

TABLE 4.5: SEX RATIO OF NAMDHARI CHILDREN IN THE AGE-GROUP OF 0-6 YEARS*

District	Male	Female	Total	Percentage
Amrtisar	22	13	35	59.09
Barnala	17	11	28	64.70
Bathinda	6	8	14	133.33
Chandigarh & Mohali	18	10	28	55.55
Fatehgarh Sahib	11	13	24	118.18
Ferozepur	18	12	30	66.66
Hoshiarpur	9	18	27	200
Jalandhar	23	23	46	100
Kapurthala	52	40	92	76.92
Ludhiana	39	24	63	61.53
Moga	39	29	68	74.35
Mukatsar	7	2	9	28.57
Nawan Shahr	13	10	23	76.92
Patiala	11	9	20	81.81
Ropar	9	3	12	33.33
Sangrur	24	19	43	79.16
Tarn Taran	24	22	46	91.66
Total	342	266	608	77.77

Note: *Data provided by Namdhari respondents.

Granth. He begins his discourse reminding his followers that since they are known as Namdhari, they carry an obligation to meditate on the name of God whenever and wherever they are engaged.[35]

Namdhari Guru's second approach to reiterate the relevance of nam-simran is to quote it with reference to the attainments of his predecessors. In the religious discourses, Namdhari Guru Ram Singh occupies a premier position. Namdhari Guru Jagjit Singh has made obligatory for the Namdhari Sikhs to devote one hour for *nam-simran* and perform a path of *Sri Adi-Granth* or *Sri Dasam Granth* each month to remembe Satguru Ram Singh.[36]

Moreover, in the religious discourse, successors of Namdhari Guru Ram Singh have elevated his spiritual status. The observance of his edicts can alone attain salvation.[37] The reason for elevating the spiritual status of his predecessor is that the Namdhari Guru Jagjit Singh firmly believes that Satguru Ram Singh was the incarnation of God. He will appear again and bless his successors and Sikhs.[38] However, the Namdhari Guru exhorts his followers to liberate themselves from ego and jealousy. For this liberation, they will have to perform a series of *paths* (one lac and quarter of it) dedicating them to Satguru Ram Singh.

The institutionalization of *nam-simran* by the Namdhari guru has made a deep impact on the Namdhari psyche. When we asked respondents how much time they devoted to *nam-simran*, 97 per cent of them said they devoted one to two hours daily in the morning. Rest of them said that they could not find time for *nam-simran* Nevertheless, those who said that they practised more than two hours, need to be applauded because 97 per cent families devoting one or two hours to meditation is a rare feature of any religious community in the modern age with its urbanization, cultural pluralism, and spread of scientific understanding.[39] Namdhari Sikhs have transformed their life-style but this has not undermined their religion! Routinization of *nam-simran* has transmitted the charisma of the Satgurus (from Ram Singh to Jagjit Singh) to the present generation of Namdharis. For them, their Satguru is relevant in both spiritual and temporal affairs. Excepting the physically handicapped those unable to move, 99 per cent Namdhari families have total faith in the Satguru. They perceive him in the images of *Sache Patshah*, Protector, *Bakhshanhar*, and liberator. It is he who controls and guides their destiny. It is for this reason that before starting any work or journey, or performing a ceremony, they remember him and seek his blessings. In fact, they perform *ardas* in his name in a short or long form-depending upon the occasion.[40] Performing ardas is an act of the Namdhari Sikhs to reiterate their faith in Satguru. At the same time, performing ardas inculcates in them the consciousness of a distinct Namdhari identity.

> Remember Guru Balak Singh, he who has shown us the way to truth. Remember Satguru Ram Singh, Master of our faith, and he who directs our worldly actions, he who knows our inmost thoughts, Sri Akal Purakh who sets us free from the grip of death. Remember Guru Hari Singh, light incarnate, he who heals and restores; and Satguru Partap Singh who in this present Age of Darkness has preached perfect piety, purity, the practice of repeating the divine Name and recitation of the scriptures. May they grant us help and strength in every place. . . . May the name of Satguru Ram Singh be magnified and by your grace may all be blessed.[41]

The Namdhari *rahitnama* enjoins Namdhari Sikhs to recite the following *banis*: Japuji, Jap, Shabad Hazare, Rahiras and Arati-Sohila. But this is not done as regularly as performing the *nam-simran*. Even so, more than half of the Namdhari population reciting *banis* is a unique feature of a religious community. This recitation, along with *nam-simran*, requires a discipline of rising very early, memorization of banis, and a calm atmosphere in the home. Such requisites are hard to find in the competitive world today. Forty per cent of the toiling Namdhari artisans and agriculturists humbly admitted that they were unable to devote adequate time for the recitation of banis.

Their stay at Bhaini Sahib headquarters being temporary, Namdhari followers practise *nam-simran* in the home or attend weekly congregations at local *dharamsalas*. At the *dharamsala*, after performing Asa-di-Var, *kirtan* is held for some hours. Similarly, on certain days and occasions, Varni and Jap-Prayogs are organized. However, attendance, as stated by one of the local leaders of Amritsar city, varies from week to week. It is reported that recent factionalism among the local leaders has discouraged many from participation in weekly congregations. They prefer to carry on their daily routine of nam-simran in the morning at home.

The practice of *nam-simran* varies according to age group and family. Those who are well off reserve a space (separate room or part of it) for *nam-simran*. Several heads of the families took special care to show the author this worship-place. The author had to take off his shoes and wash his hands to step into that room which was neat and clean. On the walls were photographs of the Namdhari Gurus and some texts of scriptures were wrapped and placed in the room. There are a few families who perform *nam-simran* collectively, but the rest have their own times. Seniors in the age groups of 50 to 60 onwards are more regular and devote more time for *nam-simran*. The physically unfit among them expressed their regret or inability to keep up maryada as a whole.[42] There are Namdhari Sikhs who either are indifferent or do not go for *simran*. Incidentally, their number is marginal: 29 out of 925, or 3 per cent. In each district, there are one or two such families. But in urban centres of Mohali and Chandigarh their number is 7 out of 26.

In some urban centres, it was reported that the women of business-families and of professionals are more religious and devote more time to *simran*. In the Sunday congregations, attendance of women is larger than that of men. In Partap Bazar of Chheharta a man told the author that he did not have that much religious temperament which his wife possessed. His wife regularly held *satsang* (devotional singing in congregation) and performed devotional music in which the women of neighbouring houses participated.[43] He further told the author that his daughters-in-law participated in devotional *satsang* and like their mother-in-law were regular in performing *nam-simran*. Namdhari mothers play an important role in orienting their children in maryada in terms of eating and dressing. One of the distinct features of devout Namdhari families is that their children are taught to greet visitors with folded hands and they bow to touch the feet of visitors. (The author met a number of families of Amritsar city whose children greeted him in this manner.)

Namdhari functionaries who attend religious functions, particularly when Satguru Jagjit Singh delivers discourses, confirm the observation that the participation of the Namdhari women is larger than that of the men. A sociological analysis of beliefs and practices of the Sikhs of district Gurdaspur was the first study that underlined the fact that the participation of Sikh women in the religious congregations was larger than that of Sikh males.[44] Sociologists explain women's larger participation in terms of emotional relief from domestic chores, or of being victims of patriarchal domination. In the Punjabi folk culture and literature women are unfaithful and cunning. They are ridiculed and tortured by husbands and in-laws for not producing offspring. Such factors add to stress and strain, economic dependence further multiplies a woman's woes.[45] She seeks solace in the religious congregation. Such a perspective is negative in the sense that it minimizes women's religious commitment. Some of the Namdhari female respondents explained their commitment in terms of their being housewives. Being housewives, they had little interaction with the outside world. On the other hand, a respondent stated, men were out of the house from morning to evening, and interacted with the non-Namdharis and non-Sikhs for their business, and could not confirm to the Namdhari religious obligations.

The Namdhari Sikhs recite *banis* Asa-di-Var, Japuji Sahib, Shabad Hazare, Jap Sahib, Rehiras, Kirtan Sohila, Sukhmani Sahib and Chandi-di-Var. The Sikh tradition emphasizes the recitation of five *banis*. The Namdhari practice of recitation varies from individual to individual and from time to time. Only a few Namdhari Sikhs expressed their inability to recite all *banis*. The routine of modern life doesn't allow them to carry on this maryada. The work of the professionals, skilled and unskilled labourers and businessmen are time-consuming as well as tiresome leaving these Namdhari Sikhs exhausted. Social obligations including household chorus and looking after children and elders are an additional burden, leaving little time for *nam-simran* and recitation of banis.

OTHER BELIEFS AND PRACTICES

The Namdhari Sikhs hold Sikh scriptures and historical gurdwaras in high esteem. Ninety one per cent Namdhari Sikhs of Punjab pay their homage to the Sikh historical places and gurdwaras (Table 4.1). Our survey shows that all Namdhari Sikhs have faith in the *Ad Sri-Granth* or *Guru Granth*. Several referred to *Dasam Granth* along with *Ad Sri-Granth*. A few (relatively more literate) also added that they respect all scriptures including Hindu scriptures. Moreover, there is a large number of the Namdhari Sikhs of Amritsar who often pay their obeisance to Darbar Sahib and Shahidan-da-Gurdwara. This is more true of the Namdhari families of Sultanwind Chowk and Tarn Taran Road, Amritsar. Some of these families strongly believe in the spiritual and supernatural powers generally associated with these religious places. A Namdhari woman narrated the following story. Her young daughter had a mole on a toe, which was ugly. The woman purchased a *jharu* (broom) and some other articles for offering to Gurdwara Dukh-Bhanjani-Beri in the precinct of Darbar Sahib. Here a jujube tree is 'associated with the legend of Bibi Rajani whose leper husband is said to have been cured of his malady by having a dip in the old pond which has existed here since ancient times'.[46] The people 'have a strong faith that water in this portion of the tank will heal their ailments'. Both mother and her daughter went to Dukh Bhanjani Beri and prayed for healing. The prayer bore fruit.[47] Similarly, there are several Namdhari youngsters who regularly participate in the *kar-seva* (community service) at these two gurdwaras. There is a Namdhari family of Tarn Taran Road, Amritsar, who has been cleaning and washing the interior of Shahindan-da-Gurdwara for the last several years.[48]

Among several Namdhari Sikhs who listen to the *path* and *kirtan* in Darbar Sahib[49] are those who have recently been brought into the Namdhari fold. Their religious bonds with historical gurdwaras are relatively strong. On the other hand, there are several families who are alienated from the Namdhari community and have shifted their religious affiliation to the mainstream of Sikhism.[50]

The survey of the Namdhari Sikhs of other Sikh historical towns and cities confirms this pattern. Several Namdhari families of district Tarn Taran informed us that they paid their homage to Darbar Sahib, particularly on the occasion of *massia* (*amavas*), and took a dip in the *sarovar*. They also gave donations to local gurdwaras. Moreover, appropriating the concept of miraculous powers of the Sikh martyrs, the Namdhari Sikhs too have constructed their own mythology. For instance, a Namdhari agriculturist of Tarn Taran district told us that he and his family worshipped Shaheed Behila Singh. The *maata* of a nearby village told them that the financial crisis of their family was due to Shaheed Behila Singh's curse. Another Namdhari agriculturist raised a mound in the name of his great grand ancestor (*jathera*) under a peepal tree. His family paid their obeisance and sought his blessings.

INCOMPATIBILITY BETWEEN MODERN LIFE STYLE AND NAMDHARI *MARYADA*

As hinted above many Namdhari families live their lives not fully according to the Namdhari *maryada*. For them the Namdhari *maryada* is too conservative and rigid. Those who are engaged in business, transportation, and civil/military jobs face difficulties when their work hours and the space change periodically. Among those required to work in the night shifts, it becomes impossible to observe *maryada* related to nam-simran and recitation of *gurbani* on the stipulated time. Similarly, those who are working as skilled as well as unskilled labourers in industrial units cannot operate machines and tools wearing Namdhari dress of *kurta-pajama*. It is in the wake of these practical problems several Namdhari professionals, technicians and skilled/unskilled labourers admit their inability to observe Namdhari *maryada* in day-to-day life. Many now argue for liberalizing the Namdhari *maryada* and making it compatible with modern life style.[51] It is relevant to point out here that the Namdhari Sikhs are no exception to face this problem.

Briefly speaking, since the Namdhari gurus and scholars have evolved Namdhari maryada on the basis of the Sikh scriptures and traditions, it is no surprise that the actual beliefs and practices of the Namdhari Sikhs are similar to the popular Sikh maryada in terms of *nam-simran*, recitation of *banis*, performing paths, observing rituals on the occasion of birth, marriage and death, and paying obeisance to historical gurdwaras and places. They also share the beliefs and practices of their respective *biradaris*. Although the majority of the Namdhari families practise endogamy, they are flexible and accept brides of different castes or religions under certain situations. But they do not give their daughters to the families of lower castes. However, majority of them solemnize anand-karaj according to the Namdhari *maryada* and avoid futile social customs including dowry. A major distinction between Sikhs and Namdhari Sikhs is that the latter believe in the concept of a living guru and address their spiritual master as Satguru. Another distinction which the Namdhari Sikhs can claim is that 97 per cent of them meditate on the divine name daily. In addition, 60 per cent of them recite *banis*. This transmits the charisma of their Satgurus. Still another 'distinction' which they can claim is that 98 per cent of them are vegetarians and free from any addiction.[52] Nevertheless, incompatibility between the modern lifestyle of the Namdhari Sikhs and their maryada is perceptible on several accounts.

NOTES

1. Rattan Singh Jaggi, *Guru Granth Vishavkosh*, vol. 2, 2002, p. 189.
2. Harbans Singh (ed.), *Encyclopaedia of Sikhim*, vol. III, 1996, p. 241.
3. *Namdhari Nitnem*, 2000.
4. Amar Bharti, *Satguru Tiska Noor*, 1979, pp. 128-33.
5. Jasbir Singh Ahluwalia, *Understanding the Dasam Granth*, 2009, p. 38.

6. Ibid., pp. 38-9: In the post-diaspora period, the efforts of Bhai Mani Singh in salvaging whatever could be gathered from different sources resulted in the first recension of the *Dasam Granth*, followed by another by Baba Deep Singh—most of the contents being common to the two recensions. The first Sikh reformation, spearheaded by the Singh Sabha movement in the last quarter of the nineteenth century, yielded another recension—the current one—published in 1902.
7. Harvendra Singh (comp), *Pravachan: His Holiness Sri Satguru Jagjit Singh Ji*, 2001, pp. 99.
8. Ibid., p. 100.
9. Ibid., p. 169.
10. Gordon Marshal (ed.), *Oxford Dictionary of Sociology*, 2006 (reprint), p. 661.
11. For other connotations, see Bhai Kahn Singh Nabha, *Mahan Kosh,* 1981 (rpt.), pp. 794, 935; Rattan Singh Jaggi, *Guru Granth Vishavkosh,* vol.II, 2002, p. 235.
12. Gursharan Jeet Singh, *Gurmat Nirnay Kosh,* 2004, pp. 151-2.
13. *Report of the National Commission for Religious and Linguistic Minorities*, Ministry of Minority Affairs, New Delhi, 2007, p. 41.
14. Ibid., p. 42.
15. *Hindustan Times,* Chandigarh, 19 November 2009, p. 13.
16. Kristina Myrvold, *Wedding Ceremonies in Punjab*, 2004, p. 159.
17. Ibid.
18. In case of farmers, the study shows that the average expenses on social ceremonies was 27.28 per cent in the different regions of Punjab 2001-02: *Forced Fall: A Case of Punjab Farmers* (T.S. Chahal), 2005, p. 58.
19. Cited in *Hindustan Times*, Chandigarh, October 2009, pp. 1-2: The Principal Investigator of this Survey is Ranjana Padhi, who has extensively published her work on issues of urban workers and displaced families. She undertook the study in Punjab in association with farm unions, including the BKU Ekta (Ugrahan), Punjab Kisan Union and the BKU Ekta (Dakonda). The study sample comprised 40 per cent Dalits and rest of the small and marginal farm families.
20. Paras Diwan, *Customary Law*, 1978, p. 71.
21. Surinder Kaur Kharal, *Parkash Punj,* vol. II, 1997, pp. 300-1.
22. Paras Diwan, *Modern Hindu Law,* 1999, p. 69.
23. Balwinder Arora, *female foeticide in punjab,* 2009, p. 110.
24. Interview with Shavinder Singh (name changed), Partap Bazar, Chheharta in August 2007.
25. Kristina Myrvold, 2004, p. 166.
26. Ibid.
27. Interview with General Secretary (name withheld), Namdhari Sangat, Amritsar in August 2007..
28. Paras Diwan, *Customary Law*, 1978, pp. 213-18.

29. T.S. Chahal, *Forced Fall: A Case of Punjab Farmers*, 2005, p. 4.
30. Harvendra Singh Hanspal (comp), *Pravachan- His Holiness Sri Satguru Jagjit Singh Ji*, 2001, p. 230.
31. Ibid., "ਇਕ ਬੀਬੀ ਦੀ ਸਕੀ ਭੈਣ, ਉਹਦੇ ਦੱਸਣ ਅਨੁਸਾਰ, ਦਾਜ ਦੀ ਬਲੀ ਚੜ੍ਹ ਗਈ ਹੋਵੇ ਤੇ ਦੂਸਰੀ ਬੀਬੀ ਦਾਜ ਵਾਸਤੇ ਬੜੀ ਇੱਛਕ ਹੋਵੇ, ਦੇਣ ਜਾ ਲੈਣ ਦੀ, ਫੇਰ ਉਹਨਾਂ ਨੂੰ ਇਹ ਵਿਚਾਰਨਾ ਚਾਹੀਦਾ ਹੈ ਕਿ ਅਸੀਂ ਠੀਕ ਕਰ ਰਹੀਆਂ ਜਾਂ ਨਹੀਂ"।
32. For at All India level, *The Report of National Commission for Religious and Linguistic Minorities*, pp. 46-8; *Basic Statistics of punjab, 2009-2010;* also see Tables 4.4 and 4.5.
33. Rattan Singh Jaggi, *Guru Granth Vishvakosh*, vol. I, 2002, pp. 194-5.
34. W.H. McLeod, *Sikhs of the Khalsa*, 2003, p. 345.
35. Harvendra Singh (comp), *Pravachan- His Holiness Sri Satguru Jagjit Singh Ji*, p.74 : '. . . ਇਕ-ਇਕ ਘੰਟਾ ਨਾਮ ਸਿਮਰਨ ਹਰ ਜੀਅ ਪ੍ਰਤੀ ਪੱਕਾ ਕਰੋ ਸਾਰੇ ਜਣੇ। ਜਿਸ ਵੇਲੇ ਤੁਸੀਂ ਖਰਾਦ ਦਾ ਕੰਮ ਕਰਦੇ ਹੋ, ਦੁਕਾਨ ਵਿਚ ਵਿਹਲੇ ਬੈਠੇ ਹੁੰਦੇ ਹੋ, ਕਾਰ ਵਿੱਚ ਜਾਂਦੇ ਹੋ, ਸਾਈਕਲ ਤੇ ਜਾਂਦੇ ਹੋ, ਉਸ ਵੇਲੇ ਵੀ ਨਾਮ ਜਪਿਆ ਕਰੋ, ਰਸਨਾ ਹਿਲਾ ਕੇ, ਰਸਨਾ ਕਿਸੇ ਵੇਲੇ ਵੀ ਵਿਹਲੀ ਨਾ ਰਵੇ'।
    ਕਣ ਬਿਨਾ ਜੈਸੇ ਥੋਥਰ ਤੁਖਾ॥
    ਨਾਮ ਬਿਹੂਨ ਸੂਨੇ ਸੇ ਮੁਖਾ॥
36. Ibid., p. 160 : ਸਾਰੇ ਇਕ ਇਕ ਘੰਟਾ ਨਾਮ ਸਿਮਰਨ ਕਰਿਆ ਕਰੋ। ਸਤਿਗੁਰੂ ਰਾਮ ਸਿੰਘ ਜੀ ਦੇ ਦਰਸ਼ਨ ਨਮਿਤ ਮਹੀਨੇ ਦਾ ਪਰਵਾਰ ਇੱਕ ਸ੍ਰੀ ਆਦਿ ਗ੍ਰੰਥ ਸਾਹਿਬ ਜਾਂ ਸ੍ਰੀ ਦਸਮ ਗ੍ਰੰਥ ਸਾਹਿਬ ਪਾਠ ਕਰਿਆ ਕਰੋ।
37. Ibid., p. 163; ਜਿੰਨਾ ਚਿਰ ਸਤਿਗੁਰੂ ਰਾਮ ਸਿੰਘ ਜੀ ਦਾ ਹੁਕਮ ਨਹੀਂ ਮੰਨਦੇ ਸਾਡੀ ਗਤੀ ਨਹੀਂ ਹੁੰਦੀ
38. Op. cit., p. 182.
39. Gorden Marshal (ed.), *Oxford Dictionary of Sociology*, 2006, pp. 563-4
40. Performing *ardas* is a Sikh tradition. The Namdhari Sikhs have adapted it in their own way. In the ordinary general sense '*ardas* means a deferential request. In Sikh tradition the term *ardas karana* is used to express the act of laying a petition before the Guru, and the Gurus themselves used it as a form of address to Akal Purakh (*GM*, pp. 36-7). At some stage, however, *ardas* acquired a more specific meaning in Sikh usage. There developed the convention of prefacing requests for divine assistance with the invocation to *Var Sri Bhagauti ji ki* (see pp. 276, 379), an introduction that calls to mind the virtues and grace of the first nine Gurus. To this was added a similar reference to the tenth Guru and the supplemented invocation came to be known as Ardas', W.H. Mcleod, *Sikhs of the Khalsa*, 2005, pp. 194, 346-7.
41. Ibid.
42. Sant Pritam Singh is one of senior Namdhari Sikhs who leads a retired life and remains preoccupied with *nam-simran*. For his saintly behaviour, his employer allowed him to perform *nam-simran* and hold prayers for the progress of business and contentment in the family in Amritsar.
43. Interview with Shavinder Singh (name changed), Chheharta in August 2007.

44. Clarence O. McMullen, *Religious Beliefs and Practices of the Sikhs in Rural Punjab,* 1989, p.90.
45. Kamlesh Mohan, *Clamping Shutters and Valorizing Women: Tensions in Sculpting Gender-Identities in the Colonial Punjab*, 1999, pp. 163-200.
46. Harbans Singh (ed.), *The Encyclopaedia of Sikhism*, vol. I, 1994, p. 112.
47. Interview with Harleen Kaur (name changed), Azad Nagar, Amritsar, 5 September 2007.
48. Interview with Harleen Kaur (name changed), Azad Nagar, Amritsar, 5 September 2007.
49. A Namdhari Sikh of East Mohan Nagar, told me that his father performed *kirtan* in Darbar Sahib once a week. He is carrying on this tradition.
50. Interview with Namdhari Sikhs of Sultanwind Road and Guru Arjan Dev Nagar, Tarn Taran Road on 16 August 2007.
51. These views were expressed by a Namdhari Sikh of a village in Jalandhar who is settled abroad and working as Charted Accountant in USA. Surprisingly, some of the ordinary Namdhari Sikhs of the villages too express similar ideas but in the context of their practical experience. In an interview Namdhari Sikhs of a village in Jalandhar district frankly admitted that being truck drivers they can not perform *nam-simran* when they are on the duty. They stated that at times they are suppose to drive the vehicles throughout night and day because they have to transport goods in time.
52. Table 4.1.

CHAPTER 5

Conclusion

Right from the inception of the Kuka movement in late nineteenth century, the Namdhari Sikhs come mainly from agriculturist, artisan and menial castes of the Punjab. At present, more than half of the Namdhari followers belong to the agriculturist castes: Jats, Sainis, Rajputs and Kambojs. The artisans comprise Ramgarhias, Parjapats, Chhembas, Suniaras, Nais, Julahas, Mehras and Ramdasias/Mazhabis. There is marginal number of Aroras and Khatris whereas the Brahmins and Banias are exceptions. Our analysis shows that the Namdhari Jats and Ramgarhias constitute 88 per cent of the total Namdhari population of the contemporary Punjab. In the wake of this occupational background of the Namdhari Sikhs, it can certainly be claimed that the Namdhari movement was the movement of the agrarian castes. A substantial number of Namdhari Khatris and Aroras can partly be put into the agrarian castes since most of them lived in the rural areas of the undivided Punjab and carried on their traditional occupations. Some of them had owned landholdings too.[1]

Over a period of 150 years, the response of the Namdhari Sikhs of these occupational castes varied from time to time. In the late nineteenth century, the Jat Sikhs responded to the mission of Namdhari Guru Ram Singh in a big way and their rate of conversion was 32 per cent but in due course of time, this rate declined to 14 per cent whereas the rate of conversion of the Ramgarhia Sikhs doubled, i.e. from 12 to 22 per cent. Nevertheless, throughout the period, the Jat and Ramgarhia castes maintained their numerical hegemony. In the late nineteenth century, the Namdhari agriculturists and artisans, by and large, belonged to the deprived section of the agrarian society of Punjab. The police list of influential Kukas highlight the fact that the Kuka converts came from the 'Jat cultivators, Tarkhans, Chamars and Mazhabis'. 'Later police analysis of Kuka membership showed that of these four groups by far the strongest was that of the Jats, and that this element was drawn largely from the poorer Jats.'[2] The police report does not enumerate the converts from Arora, Khatri and Bania castes. Similarly, this report does not mention the Kuka converts from 'minor' agriculturist castes like Saini, Rajput and Kamboj. However, in the Census Report of 1881 and *District Gazetteers of Rawalpindi and Ludhiana*, we find references to the prominent Kukas of mercantile as well as minor agriculturist castes. For instance, the founder of Namdhari mission was Baba Balak Singh, who was an Arora by caste. His followers too were Aroras and Khatris. Prominent were Gurcharan Singh (Arora) who 'travelled all over Afghanistan, visiting Kandhar, Ghazni, Bokhara and Kabul, and met with considerable proselytizing success amongst Aroras and Suniars'. He was a prominent suba of Namdhari Guru Ram Singh. Bhai Kahn Singh was nephew of Namdhari Guru Balak Singh and was acknowledged as the head of the Hazro Kukas. Baba Jagat Singh and Baba Kanhiya Singh were 'descendents' of Guru Nanak Dev and incharge of Namdhari Dharamsala of Haripur (Rawalpindi). Similarly, there were several converts of Namdhari Guru Ram Singh who were Khatris by caste. Prominent among them were Suba Kartar Singh Bedi (one of the descendants of Dera Baba Nanak) and Sodhi Hira Singh, a jagirdar of village Chogawan, district Moga. Sardar Lehna Singh was son-in-law of the famous Sardar Hari Singh Nalwa and *Rais* of Garjakh, Gurjranwala.[3] Most of the well-off sections of the Namdhari followers irrespective of their caste-affiliations either disassociated themselves from the Kuka movement or remained in the background when the British government started persecuting the Kukas. It was most probably for this reason that the police report did not mention the names of well-off Kukas. The Sikh landed aristocracy and traditional religious leaders (Bedis, Sodhis, Mahants and Pujaris) became allies of the colonial rule.

Majority of the agriculturists under the colonial rule suffered in terms of mortgaging their landholdings to the *sahukars* for paying land revenue in cash and meeting their social requirements. Consequently, the Namdhari agriculturists too (like their counterparts) went under debt. Namdhari Guru Ram Singh assured a kingdom which was to be free from socio-economic sufferings and exploitation of the colonial rulers and their allies. He launched a tirade against the priestly classes for their ungodly behaviour and social acts of exploitation. He evolved *maryada* which liberated his followers from social evils (like *sati* female infanticide and dowry). He initiated the concept of mass-marriages rejecting endogamy. He exhorted his followers to settle their disputes including clearing of debts in the panchayats and shun courts. The hallmark of his teaching was to lead a simple life wearing traditional dress of *kurta-pajama* and *sidhi dastar* (turban)—all made of home-spun cotton. Namdhari Guru Partap Singh carried on the traditions of his predecessors, showed serious concern for the cause of *kirti-kisan* followers and criticized the agrarian legislation enacted by the Unionist Government which amended the Land Alienation Act of 1901 to protect and promote the vested interests of the zamindars and *sahukars* on the one hand and deprive the non-agriculturist castes of owning landholdings on the other. Some of his followers like Goda Singh Jat and Pritam Singh Kavi became formal activists of the Kirti-Kisan Sabha movement. It were for these reasons that the thousands of Jat and artisan Sikhs responded to the Namdhari mission under colonial rule.

The partition of Punjab in 1947 radically transformed the demography of the Namdhari community. Thousands of Namdhari agriculturists and artisans were forced to quit their native villages and towns of the West Punjab and migrate and resettle in the villages and towns of the East Punjab. More than 80 per cent of the Namdhari migrants came from district Sialkot. The pattern of their migration was not different from their counterparts—Hindus and Sikhs. They were victims of communal violence, financial and physical hardships. However, the loss of human life was considerably low, essentially because most of them left their native places in time on the advice of their *satguru* before the communal violence broke out. Respondents of several Namdhari families also highlighted the fact that they were given shelter by the Muslims and who helped them to cross the border safely. Nevertheless, the pattern of their resettlement in the villages and towns of the east Punjab shows distinct features. First and foremost is that Namdhari guru Partap Singh played an important role in the processes of resettlement. He purchased thousands of acres of land in the present district of Sirsa (Haryana), developed a headquarters known as Jiwan Nagar, got special permission from the then rehabilitation commissioner to allow Namdhari migrants to settle there and distributed landholdings to the agriculturists as well as artisans. Similarly, he distributed landholdings to his followers in Bir Bhamarsi, district Patiala. He also prevailed upon the then ruler of Mandi town (Himachal Pradesh) to allow his followers, mostly Khatri and Aroras, to stay in this town permanently. Similarly, he prevailed upon the deputy commissioner of Kapurthala to assign small plots in Bhulath for his migrant followers who had settled in the village Meranpur but their crops were damaged by the floods.

Second feature was that the resettlement of the Namdhari agriculturists in the districts of Hoshiarpur, Gurdaspur, Kapurthala, Fatehgarh Sahib and Ferozepur was motivated by the spirit of *bhaichara* and availability of agricultural land. This fact has been corroborated by the common *gotras* of these agriculturists. The clusters of the Namdhari agriculturist families of the common *gotras* are found in the villages of the above-mentioned districts. Thus these families could retain the bonds of *bhaichara* to a greater extent. The official policy of group-settlement was too complimentary to this pattern of rehabilitation. In addition, some of these migrant agriculturists came back to their parental villages where the people of their own *bhaichara* lived.

The pattern of resettlement of migrant artisan families was too marked by the spirit of *bhaichara* as well as religious brotherhood. Because majority of the artisan families wanted to live in the towns and cities of the East Punjab so that they could get jobs as skilled labourers. They were helped by their relatives who lived in the urban centres. These relatives helped their *gurbhais* to take shelter in the houses vacated by the Muslims. Moreover, the official policy of building camps and towns for these migrant families helped the migrant Namdhari families to come together and live in the same localities. Preet Nagar in Jalandhar city is an example of this pattern of re-settlement. There was another pattern of re-settlement. Several families of the Namdhari artisans preferred to settle with those agriculturist families who belonged to their own villages in West Punjab (Pakistan). The bond of the village *biradari* can still be seen in the migrant families of Bholath. However, it is also a fact that due to the internal migration (from rural to urban centres) and occupational changes, the religious and caste-bonds among the Namdhari families were weakening gradually and being supplanted by the 'class-interests' and 'class-culture'. The Namdhari professionals, traders and businessmen, for instance, interact with their counterparts and try to build up social relations with them. However, this process is very slow but sure to happen.

The creation of Indo-Pakistan border, the Terrorist movement and rural to urban migration for better urban facilities and job avenues were some of the variables which formed Namdhari nucleus in the cities of Amritsar, Gurdaspur, Jalandhar and Ludhiana. To begin with the first variable, the creation of the Indo-Pakistan border created two-types of problems for the artisans. First was the problem of insecurity. The anti-social elements like thieves and smugglers frequently crossed the border for transporting goods including intoxicants and live-stock. They also created communal violence. Moreover, two Indo-Pakistan Wars (1965 and 1971) further created a sense of insecurity and killed initiatives for the trade and industrial developments. Secondly, the Indo-Pakistan border destroyed prospectus of development of the towns located nearby. Furthermore, it stopped the access of the businessmen and artisans to the towns and cities of the West Punjab. Consequently, like their counterparts, the Namdhari businessmen and artisans too left their native places and resettled in the cities of Amritsar, Jalandhar and Ludhiana. Some of the Namdhari business families of village Pul Kanjari left their native place for Mandi town in Himachal Pradesh immediately after the partition of Punjab. For earning a livelihood, they had to undertake odd jobs. After some years' stay over there, they thought it advisable to come back to Chheharta and resume family occupation. At present, some of them are successful businessmen.

The terrorist movement in the last quarter of the twentieth century created a hostile atmosphere for Namdhari families. The Namdhari Sikhs lived in the dread of terrorists because of theological differences. In addition to this they also feared the hedonistic behaviour of terrorists. The ideologues of the terrorist movement took serious note of the belief of the Namdhari Sikhs in the continuity of guruship and supplication in the name of the twelfth Guru. The terrorists assaulted some of the *mahants* of the Namdhari dharamsalas in the districts of Gurdaspur, Amritsar and Hoshiarpur. One of these *mahants* was so terrified that he left priesthood as well as Namdhari *maryada*. One of his sons became an Amritdhari Sikh, while the other one remained Namdhari. Similarly, when the terrorists were given to hedonism and indulged in stray-killing to instill fear in the minds of the people, some of the Namdhari Sikhs too became victims. One of these victims was a suba of Ahyiapur town of Hoshiarpur district. Similarly, several Namdhari families left their homes in the villages and re-settled in the cities for security reasons. The Namdhari families of district Gurdaspur became more vulnerable. However, these families suffered minimum loss of life.

The Namdhari agriculturists constitute 55 per cent of the total Namdhari following. In terms of size of landholdings, these agriculturists include 28 per cent marginal farmers, 26 per cent small farmers, 32 per cent medium and 14 per cent big farmers.[4] Since percentage of marginal and small Namdhari agriculturists is less than the percentage of agriculturists of these two categories of Punjab, we can argue that the general condition of the Namdhari agriculturists is better than their counterparts. This is also substantiated by the fact that the percentage of the medium Namdhari agriculturists is bigger than their counterparts of Punjab. Nevertheless, in terms of indebtedness, the condition of the Namdhari agriculturists is no way better than their counterparts. All categories of Namdhari agriculturists irrespective of the size of their land holdings are in debt. In terms of volume of debt of each category, the percentage of the small farmer is bigger: 10.49 per cent of them are under debt. Next to them are 8.42 per cent marginal, 8.03 per cent medium and only 3 per cent big farmers. It is matter of relief to state here that only 30 per cent of the Namdhari agriculturists were in debt; the figure for Punjab is 60 per cent. The Namdhari Sikhs of marginal and small landholdings are beset by financial troubles to meet expenses on the health services and rising price of eatables. The number of marginal category of the Namdhari families under debt is bigger in the districts of Moga, Amritsar and Barnala. Nevertheless, none of the Namdhari agriculturist families expressed its inability to pay back the debt.

The Namdhari agriculturists and artisans have migrated to the urban centres for availing civic facilities and job avenues. Among the artisans, the percentage of migration of the Namdhari Ramgarhias has been higher than the agriculturists. They moved to the nearby urban centres particularly where industrial growth had taken place. Being skilled labourers, they worked on the daily wages and some of them established their manufacturing units and opened show-rooms. They availed educational and technical facilities and imparted higher and technical education to their children. Similarly, all categories of the Namdhari agriculturists (mainly Jats) too moved to the urban centres. Some of the medium and big zamindars showed a spirit of entrepreneurship and started their own business of transportation, manufacturing units and commission agents. They too imparted higher and technical educational to their children. The small and marginal farmers whose landholding became economically unviable started subsidiary occupations mainly dairy-farming. Some of them, after acquiring higher and technical education, opted for the professional jobs or opened manufacturing units of small scale production.

Comparing with the Namdhari Ramgarhias, the rate of occupational changes among the Namdhari agriculturists is very poor. 776 Namdhari Jat families (50 per cent), of the total Namdhari population could produce only 40 professionals teachers, lawyers, engineers/ technicians, doctors/RMPs and retired administrative personnel and 37 transporters, industrialists/manufacturers, traders and commission agents. On the other hands, the Namdhari Ramgarhias have shown a remarkable occupational change. Their 566 families (37 per cent of the total Namdhari population) produced 40 professionals and 79 owners of workshops, 14 industrialists, 57 businessmen, 50 shopkeepers and 15 drivers. But still 29 per cent of the Namdhari Ramgarhia families are engaged in their traditional occupation. The Namdhari Sikhs of other artisan background have given up their traditional occupations. These are Parjapats, Suniaras and Chhembas. The Namdhari Khatri and Arora families still prefer to carry on the family occupation of shopkeeping and business.

As a result of occupational changes, several new classes have come into being. The number of Ramgarhia professionals, industrialists (including small manufacturers), businessmen and administrative personnel is larger than that of Jats. The Namdhari Sikhs of other occupational castes too have produced new classes but they are marginal. The Namdhari professionals, industrialists and businessmen and administrative personnel, if inducted in the administration hierarchy of the Namdhari community, can play a role of modernization and expansion of the Namdhari mission. Analysis of the social background of the contemporary Namdhari leadership and administrative personnel of the headquarters Sri Bhaini Sahib highlight the fact that the role of the Namdhari professionals, industrialists and businessmen is over due.[5]

In terms of observing humanitarian and ethical values, the Namdhari Sikhs of Punjab can take credit for being better human beings. Our statistical analysis shows that 98 per cent Namdhari Sikhs are vegetarians and teetotalers. Rest of them are not practicing Namdhari Sikhs. On the other hand, the Punjabis are notorious for their alcoholic consumption. It is reported that the consumption of alcohol has shown a marked increase in the past three years. 'In 2008-9, over 5.2 lakh bottles of liquor and 1.5 lakh bottles of beer were consumed in the state every day'. Besides, there is a big menace of use of a variety of intoxicants and drugs. The primary factors attributed by the psychologists and social activists to alcoholism and drug-addiction are as follow: net-work of smugglers and their connivance with law-enforcing agencies making for the Punjabi youth to have an easier access to these substances; increasing volume of unemployment pushing youth to frustration which further leads them to alcoholism and drug-addiction and Punjabi tradition of serving sumptuous food and liquor on all social occasions. Similarly, there is a radical change in the food-habits of the Punjabis. The Green Revolution has made tremendous increase in the production of non-vegetarian food: chicken, mutton and fish. Moreover, social and natural scientists, dieticians and multi-national companies engaged in the fast-food production have successfully promoted a myth of non-vegetarian food (as compared to vegetarian) as better food for health purposes. The consumption of non-vegetarian food has exposed the human beings to the several diseases which are transmitted through the use of animal diet. Similarly, the use of alcohol has adversely affected the vital human organs like liver and heart.[6]

The Namdhari Sikhs are free from suicidal tendencies. Our random survey shows that neither a Namdhari farmer nor a tenant nor even a labourer has committed suicide in recent years. On the other hand, thousands of Punjabi farmers, tenants and labourers have committed suicides. The social scientists and economists subscribe to the indebtedness, constant harassment and dejection as major factors which have forced these people to commit suicides. They spend more than 27 per cent of total income on performing social rituals and customs, particularly dowry. Consequently, they take loan from unregistered agencies for non-productive works.[7] The Namdhari Sikhs are relatively free from these vices. Moreover, their spiritual orientation saves them from being frustrated and dejected essentially because the Namdhari Sikhs take the financial and physical hardships as the will of God. They believe that their *satguru* will take care of their problems and troubles. In the context of Punjab, it is rightly argued by the psychoanalysists that frustration and dejection often leads to alcoholism and drug-addiction. Working on the alcohol syndrome, the experts inform us that 'alcoholism is a family condition. But this could be due to environmental factors also apart form genetic predisposition'. If the Namdhari Sikhs are free from alcoholic effects, it is essentially due to their 'family condition'. How far are the Namdhari families genetically free from the alcohol syndrome is a matter to be clinically established. However, the Namdhari community, at least, has been able to maintain respectability of teetotalism which is rare among the Punjabis.

The Namdhari food taboos have, to a larger extant, saved the Namdhari community from the above mentioned adverse effects of the food culture. There is a specific Namdhari tradition of eating and drinking taboos. The non-veg food in any form including bakery products and intoxicants (liquor, opium and other substances) are taboos for the Namdharis. Moreover, majority of them (80 per cent) do not take food even cooked by the non-Namdhari Sikhs. Rest of them are flexible and eat in those hotels, houses and *dhabas* where only vegetarian food is served. In fact, the role of Namdhari *maryada* in the daily life of the Namdhari youth, men and women is more important in this context. The Namdhari guru has made obligatory for the members of each Namdhari family to rise in the early morning and take full bath and meditate on the name of God, at least for one hour. In addition, the Namdhari families are expected to perform *paths* and *akhand-paths* and participate in the collective congregations and perform *jap-prayog* and *varnias.* The Namdhari youth, men and women are thus oriented in the Namdhari spiritual tradition. Moreover, the Namdhari families periodically pay obeisance to their spiritual master—*satguru* at Bhaini Sahib where there is a rich tradition of meditation and religious discourses. The continuous process of spiritual orientation makes the Namdhari Sikhs conscious of their latent powers and Sikh ethics of *kirat karna, vand chhakna* (earning livelihood by honest means and sharing the fruits of labour) and *sarbat da bhala* (well being of all brotherhoods).

It is a paradox that the Namdhari Sikhs under the spiritual leadership of Satguru Partap Singh became the protagonists of Gandhian principle of *ahinsa* (non-violence) and 'abstained from doing haram in thought, word and deed'. Their actions' were 'suffused with love without attachment to personal gain'.[8] The Namdhari woollen rosary symbolized their peaceful disposition and communal harmony. Neither under the colonial rule nor in the post-independence era, the Namdhari Sikhs had been involved in the communal violence. Even during the heyday of communal violence in 1947, they were not swayed by the anti-Muslim sentiment. The Namdhari oral history tells us that Namdhari guru Partap Singh and his followers gave shelter to the Muslims. They felt agony when they listened the stories of assault on the Sikh and Hindu women and their kidnappings. In independent India, Namdhari gurus Partap Singh and Jagjit Singh were honoured with the epitaphs of *gau-palaks* and *gau-rakshaks,* the symbols of peace-loving disposition.[9]

The simplicity of the Namdhari Sikhs also reflects in their social and cultural behaviour. On all the important social occasions: birth and *namkaran*, *anand-karaj* and *saskar* (cremation); or occasions of opening ceremonies, or occasions of success (acquiring jobs and promotions), the Namdhari Sikhs perform only religious ceremonies. The customs on the occasion of the birth of a child, conservative Namdhari Sikhs do not give gifts (dresses and turbans, ornaments and cash) to their daughters, their husbands and parents. The ceremony of *namkaran* is performed by a local *sant* who simply recites composition of the *Adi-Granth* and supplication (*ardas*) and *karah-prasad* is distributed. Some parents accompanied by the mother and father of the child, pay obeisance at Sri Bhaini Sahib and the name is pronounced there and then. No feasts are thrown to the friends and relatives. Similarly, *anand-karaj* is the only marriage ceremony which is performed by the Namdhari parents that too either at a Namdhari dharamsala or Sri Bhaini Sahib. No ceremonies called *thaka* or *roka*, *kurmai*, *mayian*, *chunni-charhauni* are performed and there is no exchange of gifts and dowry. At the occasion of *anand-karaj* at Bhaini Sahib, no relatives or friends are allowed to attend. After her *anand-karaj*, the bride straightway goes to the house of her in-laws. She is supposed to stay for fifteen days there. On the contrary, the Punjabis spend lakhs (even crores) of rupees on social customs and such occasions in the hotels and marriage palaces.

One of the best social attributes of the Namdhari community is that it is relatively free from the social evil of killing daughters. Our random survey shows that the average sex-ratio of this community is more than 90 per cent, i.e. there are 906 females against 1,000 males. On the other hand, the average sex-ratio of the Punjab is just 880 females against 1,000 males. Several variables can be attributed to the healthy sex-ratio of the Namdhari community. First and foremost is that the Namdhari tradition upholds the social status of the women which has been bequeathed by the Sikh religion and history to them. Namdhari Guru Ram Singh attacked widely prevalent practices of female infanticide and selling and exchanging females. He introduced marriage ceremony of *anand* which brought down wedding costs and rejected dowry practice. Embracing the tradition of Khalsa initiation, he brought women at par with men: twenty five women received Khalsa initiation. Moreover, he also evolved to initiate both boy and girl at the time of their *anand*. Namdhari Guru Ram

Singh extended the role of the women in the administrative jobs and appointed a woman suba.[10] Besides upholding these traditions, present Namdhari guru, Satguru Jagjit Singh ensures that excepting religious ceremony no social custom is performed by his followers which make the daughters a burden on her parents. Because one of the fundamental factors which force the parents to indulge in the evil practice of foeticide is that the marriage of a girl requires a big amount for raising dowry and offering a variety of feasts and parties in the marriage palaces. In several cases, even after the marriages, the in-laws build up pressure on their daughters-in-law for a share in their parental property. Unable to meet such demands, the daughters-in-law are harassed, humiliated and even tortured to death. The tragic breakdown of marriages brings disgrace to the parents of daughters and big financial loss also. To avoid these unpleasant incidents, the parents take recourse to foeticide. The Namdhari parents are fortunate to have mechanism of simple and dowry free marriages. According to our survey, 40 per cent of the Namdhari parents did not exchange dowry.

There are some districts where the sex-ratio of the Namdhari Sikhs is below their average sex-ratio. These districts are Kapurthala, Tarn Taran, Mohali and Chandigarh. It is still better than the average sex-ratio of other Punjabis of these districts. However, the healthy sex-ratio of the Namdhari community is not being sustained by its younger generation. In the age-group of 0-6 years of the Namdhari children, there are only 770 girls against 1,000 boys. This sex-ratio is less than the average sex-ratio of this age group of Punjab which is 798 against 1,000. Another negative indice of social status of Namdhari women is their educational backwardness. The level of literacy among the Namdhari women is, no doubt, higher than the average literacy of Punjab but the level of professional education among them is far below the average of Punjab. It indicates that young generation of the Namdhari women is not availing the facilities of modern education.

Inspite of the social relevance of its *maryada*, the numerical graph of the Namdhari community is going down since mid-twentieth century. The Namdhari leadership is aware of this crisis. It often explains this crisis in terms of the rigidity of Namdhari *maryada*. Our statistical analysis too corroborates their perception. Only 22 per cent of these families practise Namdhari *maryada* in its full form; 67 per cent partly and 11 per cent are not concerned about it. No religious community can claim that its people observe code of religious or ethical practices in their totality particularly in the wake of impact of industrialization and urbanization processes on the one hand and of diaspora on the other. Moreover, the downward graph is also reflected in the following rate of conversion of Namdhari community. In mid-twentieth century, it was 49 per cent whereas at the beginning of the twenty-first century it has come down to 18 per cent (Table 5.1). The following probables can be attributed to this downward graph. First and foremost is that their normative beliefs and practices, dress-code and eating taboos are orthodox. They do not accommodate the role of Punjabi folk or popular culture. The folk songs, dancing, music, films and television are inseparable part of the extant Punjabi culture. The Sikh youth has been exposed to this culture and this cultural life style is not seen as contrary to Sikhism and its ethics. On the other hand, the protagonists of the Namdhari *maryada* perceive

TABLE 5.1: CONVERSION OF NAMDHARI FAMILIES OF PUNJAB*

District	Namdhari Gurus				
	Ram Singh	Hari Singh	Partap Singh	Jagjit Singh	Total
Amritsar	5	9	73	29	116
Barnala	16	4	45	15	80
Bathinda	7	8	11	–	26
Chandigarh and Mohali	26	3	30	6	65
Fatehgarh Sahib	6	15	27	5	53
Ferozepur	29	13	20	5	67
Gurdaspur	19	11	77	56	163
Hoshiarpur	23	10	23	1	57
Jalandhar	6	5	66	20	97
Kapurthala	42	17	90	51	200
Ludhiana	22	13	57	12	104
Moga	25	6	57	14	102
Muktsar	10	1	5	1	17
Nawan Shahr	32	5	8	3	48
Patiala	8	7	17	5	37
Rupnagar	2	4	11	5	22
Sangrur	33	–	38	1	72
Taran Tarn	21	4	38	11	74
Total	332 24%	135 10%	693 49.5%	240 17.14%	1400

Note: * Data provided by Namdhari respondents.

it as a deviation. The ground level social reality is that the Namdhari youth yearns for imbibing popular culture. Secondly, the Namdhari perception and practice of embodied guru is viewed by the Sikhs of mainstream as a detraction from popular Sikh tradition of *guru-maneo granth*—belief in the *Adi-Granth* as the embodiment of ten Sikh Gurus. The celebration of this tradition by the state, SGPC and SAD and *sants* and *babas* on a grand scale in recent time has generated a popular psyche among the Sikhs to uphold this Sikh tradition steadfastly. Above all, the phenomenal emergence of Sikh *sants* and *babas* have overtaken the social portal of the rural as well as urban Sikhs away from the Namdhari Sikhs. They have built up big *dera*-complexes and infrastructures on all important places in and out Punjab; appropriated Sikh religion and history for legitimizing their own respective beliefs and practices. Yet they do not confront the main discourse of Sikh religion and history. Lastly, the people of lower castes have responded to the mission of *sants* and *babas* of their own castes which has further shrunk the space for the sanatanist beliefs and practices of the Namdhari community.

NOTES

1. 'The Khatris were pre-eminent among the Hindu mercantile castes of Punjab.' Some of them also held pre-eminent positions in the civil administration of the native rulers. They wielded sword effectively and established themselves good generals of Kingdom of Lahore. The Aroras were shopkeepers, traders and moneylenders. They also pursued agriculture: *Gender, Castes, and Religious Identities* (Anshu Malhotra), 2009, pp. 32-3.
2. W.H. McLeod, 'The Kukas: A Millenarian Sect of the Punjab', 1979, p. 185.
3. Jaswinder Singh, *Kukas of Note in the Punjab*, 1984, pp. 74-5, 92-3, 116-17.
4. In terms of size of land holdings, the Namdhari agriculturists are better off than their counterparts. According to a recent study, 77.20 per cent landowners of Punjab have less than 10 acres whereas the proportion among Namdhari agriculturists (of small and marginal) is 54 per cent. Similarly, the percentage of medium Namdhari agriculturists is 32 per cent as compared to 13.21 per cent of the Punjab agriculturists. The percentage of the big agriculturists in the Namdhari community and in Punjab is almost equal (14 and 13.21 per cent respectively).
5. Babusha Maingi, 'An Analysis of Emergence of Bhaini Sahib Headquarters and Its Administrative Personnel', 2008.

6. P.N. Chhuttani, 'The Alcohol Syndrome', 2008; also Ranvinder Singh Sandhu, *Drug Addiction in Punjab: A Sociological Study*, 2009, pp. 120-5.
7. T.S. Chahal, *Forced Fall: A Case Study of Punjab Farmers*, 2005, p. 58.
8. Surjit Man Singh, *Historical Dictionary of India*, 2003, p. 146.
9. Tara Singh Anjan, *Sankshipt Namdhari Itihas*, 2009, p. 95.
10. Doris R. Jakobsh, *Relocating Gender in Sikh History*, 2003, p. 115.

Questionnaire

1. Name/ ਨਾਮ
   Status (Namdhari Administrative Hierarchy)/ ਰੁੱਤਬਾ
   Address/ ਪਤਾ
2. Name of Father & Mother and Qualification/ ਮਾਤਾ ਪਿਤਾ ਦਾ ਨਾਮ ਅਤੇ ਵਿਦਿਅਕ ਯੋਗਤਾ
3. Date of Birth/ ਉਮਰ ਅਤੇ ਜਨਮ ਤਾਰੀਖ
4. Caste/Sub-Caste/ ਜਾਤ/ਗੋਤ
5. Previous address/ ਜੱਦੀ ਰਿਹਾਇਸ਼ ਦਾ ਪਤਾ
6. Family Background/ ਪ੍ਰਵਾਰਿਕ ਪਿਛੋਕੜ
   (i) When and how family or individual became Namdhari/ ਪਰਿਵਾਰ ਦਾ ਪਹਿਲਾ ਜੀਅ ਕਦੋਂ ਅਤੇ ਕਿਵੇਂ ਨਾਮਧਾਰੀ ਬਣਿਆ?
   (ii) What was family occupation at that time? ਉਦੋਂ ਪ੍ਰਵਾਰਿਕ ਕਿੱਤਾ ਕੀ ਸੀ?
   (iii) What was status of residence and tools of livelihood?/ ਰਿਹਾਇਸ਼ ਅਤੇ ਰੁਜ਼ਗਾਰ ਦੇ ਵਸੀਲੇ ਕਿਹੋ ਜਿਹੇ ਸਨ?
7. Present status of house, occupation, landed-property and business/ ਮੌਜੂਦਾ ਕਾਰੋਬਾਰ, ਘਰ, ਘਰੇਲੂ ਜਾਂ ਜ਼ਮੀਨੀ ਜਾਇਦਾਦ ਦੀ ਸਥਿਤੀ।
8. Volume of debt if any/ ਕਰਜ਼ਾ, ਜੇਕਰ ਹੈ।
9. Involvement in civil or criminal case/ ਦੀਵਾਨੀ ਜਾਂ ਫੌਜਦਾਰੀ ਕੇਸ
10. Family migration/ ਪ੍ਰਵਾਰਿਕ ਹਿਜ਼ਰਤ:
    (a)From Pakistan to India/ ਪਾਕਿਸਤਾਨ ਤੋਂ ਭਾਰਤ ਨੂੰ ਹਿਜ਼ਰਤ
    (i) When did you come to know about Partition/ ਵੰਡ ਬਾਰੇ ਪਹਿਲਾਂ ਕਦੋ ਅਤੇ ਕਿਵੇਂ ਪਤਾ ਲੱਗਾ।
    (ii) When and how did you migrate/ ਕਦੋਂ ਅਤੇ ਕਿਸ ਤਰਾਂ ਆਏ, ਇਕੱਲੇ ਜਾਂ ਕਾਫਲੇ ਨਾਲ
    (iii) Where did you first stay in India/ ਭਾਰਤ ਵਿੱਚ ਸੱਭ ਤੋਂ ਪਹਿਲਾਂ ਕਿਥੇ ਰਹੇ?
    (iv) Loss of property and life/ ਜਾਇਦਾਦ ਅਤੇ ਜਾਨਾਂ ਦਾ ਕਿੰਨਾਂ ਨੁਕਸਾਨ ਹੋਇਆ?
    (v) Property claims submitted or received/ ਜਾਇਦਾਦ ਕਲੇਮ ਕਿਵੇਂ ਮਿਲਿਆ?
    (vi) Rehabilitation: occupations and the help extended by (ਵਸੇਬਾ: ਕਿੱਤੇ ਜਾਂ ਧੰਦਿਆਂ ਦਾ ਵੇਰਵਾ ਅਤੇ ਜਿੰਨਾਂ ਤੋਂ ਮਦਦ ਮਿਲੀ)

11. Rural to Urban migration: reasons circumstances / ਪਿੰਡਾਂ ਤੋਂ ਸ਼ਹਿਰਾਂ ਵੱਲ ਹਿਜ਼ਰਤ ਕਦੋਂ ਅਤੇ ਕਿਉਂ ਕੀਤੀ?
Occupations/ ਕਿਹੜੇ-ਕਿਹੜੇ ਕਿੱਤੇ ਅਪਣਾਏ
Resettlement: its location and help sought/ ਮੁੜ ਵਸੇਬੇ ਲਈ ਸਥਾਨ ਅਤੇ ਪ੍ਰਾਪਤ ਸਹਾਇਤਾ
Relations with village biradari/ community/ ਪੇਂਡੂ ਜਾਤ-ਬਿਰਾਦਰੀ ਤੇ ਭਾਈਚਾਰੇ ਨਾਲ ਸਬੰਧ
12. Structure of the family/ ਪਰਿਵਾਰਕ ਬਣਤਰ

S.No.	Name	Relation	Male/ Female	Age	Edu. Quali	Work
1.						
2.						

13. Mode of marriage / ਵਿਆਹ ਕਿਹੜੀ ਮਰਿਆਦਾ ਅਨੁਸਾਰ ਹੋਇਆ
(a) Within or outside gotra/ ਗੋਤਰ/ਜਾਤ ਦੇ ਵਿਚ ਜਾਂ ਬਾਹਰ ਕੀਤੇ
(b) Whether marriage arranged by father-mother/others/ self/ ਆਨੰਦ ਕਾਰਜ ਦੇ ਸੰਬੰਧ ਕਿਸ ਤਰ੍ਹਾਂ ਬਣੇ, ਮਾਤਾ-ਪਿਤਾ ਵੱਲੋਂ, ਦੂਸਰਿਆਂ ਵਲੋਂ ਜਾਂ ਖੁਦ
(c) Place and mode of conducting marriage/ ਵਿਆਹ ਕਿਥੇ ਅਤੇ ਕਿਵੇਂ ਹੋਇਆ?
(d) Details of ceremonies and dowry/ ਵਿਆਹ ਸਮੇਂ ਕੀਤੀਆਂ ਗਈਆਂ ਰਸਮਾਂ ਅਤੇ ਦਾਜ਼ ਦਹੇਜ਼ ਦਾ ਵੇਰਵਾ।
(e) Case of breakdown of marriage and remarriage/ ਤਲਾਕ ਜਾਂ ਦੁਬਾਰਾ ਵਿਆਹ ਹੋਇਆ
14. Structure of rituals and customs related to: / ਜਨਮ, ਨਾਮਕਰਣ ਅਤੇ ਸਸਕਾਰ ਸੰਬੰਧੀ ਰੀਤੀ ਰਿਵਾਜ਼?
Birth (ਜਨਮ)
Namkaran (ਨਾਮਕਰਣ)
Death (ਸਸਕਾਰ)
15. Do you participate in the socio-religious ceremonies of non-Namdhari Sikhs/ ਕੀ ਤੁਸੀ ਗੈਰ ਨਾਮਧਾਰੀਆਂ ਦੇ ਧਾਰਮਕ ਅਤੇ ਸਮਾਜਿਕ ਰਸਮਾਂ ਵਿੱਚ ਹਿੱਸਾ ਲੈਂਦੇ ਹੋ?
16. Lifestyle/ ਜੀਵਨ ਸ਼ੈਲੀ।
Dress (ਪਹਿਰਾਵਾ)
Diet (ਖਾਣਾ-ਪੀਣਾ)
Recreation (ਮਨੋਰੰਜਨ)
Work (ਕਾਰ-ਵਿਹਾਰ)
Travel (ਆਵਾਜਾਈ ਦੇ ਸਾਧਨ)

Rate of Mortality: Life-span and causes of mortality/ ਚੜ੍ਹਾਈ ਕਰਨ ਸਮੇਂ ਪਰਿਵਾਰ ਦੇ ਮੈਂਬਰ ਦੀ ਉਮਰ ਕੀ ਸੀ, ਦੇਹਾਂਤ ਕੁਦਰਤੀ/ਦੁਰਘਟਨਾਂ ਜਾਂ ਬਿਮਾਰੀ ਨਾਲ ਹੋਇਆ?

Other information/ ਹੋਰ ਜਾਣਕਾਰੀਆਂ

(i) Do you keep 'Sodh'/ ਕੀ ਤੁਸੀਂ ਸੋਧ ਰੱਖਦੇ ਹੋ?

(ii) Do you have a full bath daily/ ਕੀ ਤੁਸੀਂ ਰੋਜ ਸਣਕੇਸੀ ਇਸ਼ਨਾਨ ਕਰਦੇ ਹੋ?

(iii) How much time you spare for meditation in a day/ ਨਾਮ-ਸਿਮਰਨ ਵਿਚ ਹਰ ਰੋਜ਼ ਕਿੰਨਾ ਸਮਾਂ ਲਗਾਉਂਦੇ ਹੋ?

(iv) What is your scripture?/ ਤੁਹਾਡਾ ਧਾਰਮਿਕ ਗ੍ਰੰਥ ਕਿਹੜਾ ਹੈ?

(v) Which of the banis do you recite daily/ ਰੋਜ਼ ਕਿੰਨੀਆਂ ਅਤੇ ਕਿਹੜੀਆਂ ਬਾਣੀਆਂ ਦਾ ਪਾਠ ਕਰਦੇ ਹੋ?

(vi) ਜਪੁਜੀ ਸਾਹਿਬ ਸ਼ਬਦ ਹਜ਼ਾਰੇ ਆਸਾ ਦੀ ਵਾਰ ਆਨੰਦ ਸਾਹਿਬ
ਜਾਪ ਸਾਹਿਬ ਚੋਪਾਈ ਸਾਹਿਬ ਰਹਿਰਾਸ ਸਾਹਿਬ ਕੀਰਤਨ ਸੋਹਿਲਾ
ਸੁਖਮਨੀ ਸਾਹਿਬ ਚੰਡੀ ਦੀ ਵਾਰ

(vii) How many times do you pay obeisance to religious places including Bhaini Sahib? / ਭੈਣੀ ਸਾਹਿਬ ਤੋਂ ਇਲਾਵਾ ਤੁਸੀਂ ਹੋਰ ਕਿਹੜੇ ਧਾਰਮਿਕ ਅਸਥਾਨਾਂ ਦੇ ਦਰਸ਼ਨ ਕਰਦੇ ਹੋ?

(viii) Donation/Daswand/ਦਸਵੰਦ ਜਾਂ ਦਾਨ

17. Social and political activities/ ਸਮਾਜਕ ਅਤੇ ਰਾਜਨੀਤਕ ਗਤੀਵਿਧੀਆਂ

(i) Member of any social and political party or organization/ ਸਮਾਜਕ ਤੇ ਰਾਜਨੀਤਕ ਪਾਰਟੀ ਜਾਂ ਸੰਸਥਾ ਦੇ ਮੈਂਬਰ

(ii) Participation in any political agitation/movement (ਰਾਜਨੀਤਕ ਅੰਦੋਲਨ ਜਾਂ ਲਹਿਰ 'ਚ ਹਿੱਸਾ)

(iii) Comments/ observations on the functioning of Namdhari leadership and organization/ ਨਾਮਧਾਰੀ ਲੀਡਰ ਅਤੇ ਸੰਸਥਾ ਦੇ ਬਾਰੇ ਰਾਏ।

Signature

Contact Number

Bibliography

PRIMARY SOURCES

Census Reports and Gazetteers

Report on the Census of India, 1881 (Suptd. Denzil Ibbetson), Government Printing, Calcutta, 1883.

Report on the Census of India, 1901, vol. XVII (Supdt. H.A. Rose), Government Central Printing Office, Simla, 1902.

Report on the Census of India, 1911 (Suptd. Pandit Hari Krishan Kaul), vol. XIV, pt. 1, Lahore, 1912.

Report on the Census of India, 1921 L. Middleton, vol. XV, pt. 1, Lahore, 1923.

Report on the Census of India, 1931 (Suptd. Khan Ahmad Hasan Khan), vol. XVII, pt. 1, Lahore, 1933.

Report on the Census of India, 1951 (Suptd. Lakshmi Chandra Vashishtha), vol. VIII, pt. 1-A, Army Press, Simla, 1953.

District and State Gazetteers of the Undivided Punjab, vols. III-IV, Low Price Publications, Delhi, 1993 (rpt. 1914).

Ibbetson, Denzil C.J., *Punjab Castes*, Languages Department, Punjab, 1995 (1st pub. 1883).

Punjab District Gazetteers: Amritsar (Suptd. Barkat Rai Chopra), Revenue Department Punjab, Chandigarh, 1976.

Punjab District Gazetteers: Gurdaspur (Suptd. Barkat Rai Chopra), The Controller of Printing and Stationary, Chandigarh, 1979.

Report of the National Commission for Religious and Linguistic Minorities, Ministry of Minority Affairs, New Delhi, 2007.

SECONDARY SOURCES

English

Ahluwalia, M.M., *Kukas: The Freedom Fighters of the Punjab*, Allied Publishers, New Delhi, 1965.

———, 'Understanding the Dasam Granth', *The Sikh Courier International*, The Sikh Cultural Society of Great Britain, 2009.

Anjan, Tara Singh, *Namdhari Sikhs: A Brief History*, Arsee Publishers, New Delhi, 2007.

Arora, Balwinder, *Female Foeticide in Punjab*, Guru Nanak Dev University, Amritsar, 2009.

Bali, A.N., *Now It Can be Told,* Akashvani Prakashan, Jullundur City, 1944.

Banga, Indu (ed.)., *Five Punjabi Centuries*, Manohar, New Delhi, 2000.

Chahal, T.S., *Forced Fall: A Case of Punjab Farmers,* Institute of Development and Planning, Amritsar, 2005.

Chakrabarty, Bidyut (ed.), *Communal Identity of India*, Oxford University Press, Delhi, 2006.

Chandra, Bipan, *India's Struggle for Independence,* Penguin Books, Delhi, 1989.

Chandra, Bipan and M. Mukherjee (eds.), *India after Independence 1947-2000,* Penguin Books, Delhi, 2000.

Darbara Singh, *The Punjab Tragedy (1947),* Stern House Agency, Amritsar, 1949.

Diwan, Paras, *Customary Law,* Panjab University, Chandigarh, 1978.

———, *Modern Hindu Law,* Allahabad Law Agency, Faridabad, 1999.

Fox, Richard G., *Lions of the Punjab: Culture in Making,* University of California Press, Berkeley, 1985.

Gill, Sucha Singh, *Economic Development and Structural Changes in Punjab: Some Policy Issues,* Principal Iqbal Singh Memorial Trust, Ludhiana, 1994.

Gopal Krishen, 'Demography of the Punjab', *Journal of Punjab Studies,* vol. II, no. 1, University of California, Santa Barbara, 2004.

Gupta, Hari Ram, *History of the Sikhs,* vol. V, Munishiram Manoharlal, New Delhi, 1992.

Hanspal, H.S. (ed.), *Namdhari Sikhs: The Pioneer Freedom Fighters,* Namdhari Darbar, Bhaini Sahib, Punjab, 2006.

Jakobsh, Doris R., *Relocating Gender in Sikh History,* Oxford University Press, Delhi, 2003.

Jones, Kenneth., W., *Arya Dharm Hindu Consciousness in 19th-Century Punjab*, Manohar, Delhi, 1976.

Juergensmayer, Mark, *Religious Rebels in the Punjab,* Ajanta Publications, Delhi, 1988.

———, *Religion as Social Vision,* University of California Press, Berkeley, 1982.

Kaur, Inderjit, 'The Alcohol Syndrome', *Tips on Mental and Physical Health* (booklet), All India Pingalwara Charitable Society, Amritsar, 2008.

Khosla, Gopal Das, *Stern Reckoning,* in Mushirul Hasan (ed.): *The Partition Omnibus,* Oxford Indian Paperbacks, Delhi, 2004.

Maingi, Babusha, 'An Analysis of Emergence of Bhaini Sahib Headquarters and Its Administrative Personnel', *The Panjab Past and Present,* vol. XXXIX- II, Punjabi University, Patiala, 2008.

Malhotra, Anshu, *Gender, Castes and Religious Identities,* Oxford India Paperbacks, Delhi, 2009.

Marenco, Ethne K., *The Transformation of Sikh Society,* Heritage Publishers, New Delhi, 1976.

McLeod, W.H., *Sikhs of the Khalsa,* Oxford University Press, Delhi, 2003.

———, *The Evolution of the Sikh Community,* Clarendon Press, Oxford, 1976.

———, 'The Kukas: A Millenarian Sect of the Punjab', *The Panjab Past and Present,* vol. XIII-I, Punjabi University, Patiala, 1979.

McMullen, Clarence O., *Religious Beliefs and Practices of the Sikhs in Rural Punjab,* Jaya Books, New Delhi, 1989.

Myrvold, Kristina, 'Wedding Ceremonies in Punjab', *Journal of Punjab Studies,* vol. II, no. 2, University of California, Santa Barbara, 2004.

Nahar Singh and Kirpal Singh, *Rebels Against the British Rule,* Atlantic Publishers and Distributors, New Delhi, 1995.

Namdhari Hola Mohala, Satguru Ram Singh Ji (booklet), Nagar Raja Garden, Ring Road, New Delhi, 1985.

Puri, H.K., Paramjit Singh Judge, Jagrup Singh Sekhon, *Terrorism in Punjab: Understanding Grassroots Reality,* Har-Anand Publications, New Delhi, 1999.

Randhawa, M.S., *Out of the Ashes,* New Jack Printing Works, Bombay, 1954.

Rai, Satya Murthy, *Punjab since Partition,* Durga Publications, Delhi, 1986.

Sandhu, Ranvinder Singh., *Drug Addiction in Punjab,* Guru Nanak Dev University, Amritsar, 2009.

Shah, Ghanshyam, *Social Movements in India,* Sage, New Delhi, 2005.

Sharma, Harish C., *Artisans of the Punjab,* Manohar, New Delhi, 1996.

Singh, Fauja, *Kuka Movement: An Important Phase in Punjab's Role in India's Struggle for Freedom,* Motilal Banarsidass, Delhi, 1965.

Singh, Ganda (ed.), *Maharaja Duleep Singh Correspondence,* Punjabi University, Patiala, 1977.

Singh, Gurharpal and Darshan Tatla, *Sikhs in Britain: The Making of Community,* Ajanta Publishing, Delhi, 2008.

Singh, Harbans (ed.), *The Encyclopaedia of Sikhism,* vol. I, Punjabi University, Patiala, 1994.

———, *Encyclopaedia of Sikhism,* vol. III, Punjabi University, Patiala, 1997.

Singh, Jaswinder (comp.), *Kuka Documents,* Atlantic Publishers, New Delhi, 1985.

———, *Kukas of Note in Punjab: Documents 1881,* Namdhari Darbar, Bhaini Sahib, Ludhiana, 1984.

Singh, Joginder, *The Sikh Resurgence,* National Book Organisation, New Delhi, 1997.

———, 'The Namdhari Sikhs of Punjab: A Case Study of Demographic and Occupational Changes in District Gurdaspur,' *Indian History Congress Proceedings,* 66th Session, 2005.

———, *The Sikh Militancy,* Shree Publishers, New Delhi, 2006.

———, *A Short History of the Namdhari Sikhs*, G.N.D. University, Amritsar, 2010.

———, *Namdhari Guru Ram Singh: A Biography*, National Book Trust, New Delhi, 2010.

Singh, Khushwant, *A History of the Sikhs*, vol. II, Oxford University Press, Delhi, 2011.

Singh, Kirpal, *Partition of Punjab*, Punjabi University, Patiala, 1972.

Singh, Mohinder, *The Akali Movement*, National Institute of Panjab Studies, New Delhi, 1997.

Singh, Nahar, *Gooro Ram Singh and the Kuka Sikhs: Documents 1863-1871*, vol. I, Amrit Book, New Delhi, 1965.

Singh, Pritam and Shinder Singh Thandi (eds), *Punjabi Identity in a Global Context*, Oxford University Press, Oxford, 1999.

Singh, Surjit Man, *Historical Dictionary of India*, Vision Books, 2003.

Talbot, Ian, *Punjab and the Raj 1849-1947*, Manohar, New Delhi, 1988.

Talbot Ian and S. Thandi (eds), *People on the Move, Punjabi Colonial and Post Colonial Migration*, Oxford University Press, Oxford, 2004.

Wolf, Eric., *Peasant Wars of the 20th Century*, Faber and Faber, London, 1973.

Punjabi

Anjan, Tara Singh., *Sankshipt Namdhari Ithas*, Arsee Publishers, Delhi, 2009.

Bharti, Amar, *Satguru Tiska Noor*, Navjug Publishers, Delhi, 1979.

Hanspal, Harvendra Singh (comp.), *Pravachan: His Holiness Sri Satguru Jagjit Singh Ji*, Namdhari Darbar, Shri Bhaini Sahib, Ludhiana, 2001.

Jaggi, Rattan Singh., *Guru Granth Vishavkosh*, vols. I & II, Punjabi University, Patiala, 2002.

Josh, Sohan Singh., *Akali Morchian Da Ithias*, Navyug Publishers, Delhi, 1972.

Kairon, Joginder Singh (comp.), *Batan-Shere-Punjab Dian*, Guru Nanak Dev University, Amritsar, 2000.

Kaur Simarjeet, 'Nildhari Sikhan Da Uthaan Ate Sansthawan Da Adhyan', *Proceedings of Punjab History Conference*, 16-18 March 2007, Punjabi University, Patiala.

Kharal, Surinder Kaur, *Parkash Punj*, vol. I, Bhagwant Singh Namdhari, Ropar, 1997.

Nabha, Bhai Kahn Singh, *Mahan Kosh*, Bhasha Vibhagh, Punjab, 1981 (rpt.)

Namdhari Nitnem, Namdhari Darbar Sri Bhaini Sahib, Punjab, 2000.

Namdhari, Sant Jagdish Singh, *Satgur Te Jo Muh Phere*, Mata Bhagwati Dharam Karam Ashram, Amritsar 1998.

Sabhra, Sukhwinder Singh, *Santan De Kautak'*, vols. I - IV, Bhai Sukhwinder Singh Sabhra, Amritsar, 2006.

Sada Virsa Sada Gaurav., Sikh Study Circle, Ludhiana, 2007.

Sant Baba Mohan Singh (booklet), Ankur Press, Samadh Road, Batala, n.d.

Singh, Gursharan Jeet., *Gurmat Nirnay Kosh,* Sikh University Press, Belgium, 2004.

Singh, Harvendra (comp.), *Pravachan- His Holiness Sri Satguru Jagjit Singh Ji*, Namdhari Darbar, Bhaini Sahib, Ludhiana, 2001.

Virk, Suwaran Singh, *Kuka Lehar Da Punjabi Sahit,* Satguru Ram Singh Chintan Adaara, Sri Bhaini Sahib, Ludhiana, 2009.

Waryam, Jagdish Singh, *Khilre Patre* (autobiography), Jalandhar, 2005.

M.Phil. Dissertations/Ph.D Theses

Bhandari, Ramesh, 'Industries and Industrial Workers of Batala 1849-1947', M.Phil dissertation, Guru Nanak Dev University, Amritsar.

Dhillon, Gurdarshan Singh, 'Character and Impact of the Singh Sabha Movement', Ph.D thesis, Punjabi University, Patiala, 1973.

Kumar, Narinder, 'Post-Partition Rehabilitation Problem and State Policies', M.Phil dissertation, Kurukshetra University, Kurukshetra, 2002.

Sehgal, Arvind, 'Assimilation of An Ethnic Group: A Case Study of Namdharis of Mandi Town in Himachal Pradesh', Ph.D thesis, Punjab University, Chandigarh, 1990.

Seth, Poonam, 'The Municipal Committee of Jullundur', M.Phil dissertation, GNDU, Amritsar, 1985.

Singh, Kuldip, 'The Namdhari Movement: Continuity and Change 1857-1959', Ph.D thesis, Guru Nanak Dev University, Amritsar, 2000.

NEWSPAPERS AND PERIODICALS (PUNJABI/ENGLISH)

Hindustan Times, Chandigarh

Khalsa Fatehnama, Amritsar.

Khalsa Khandedhar, Amritsar,

Satjug, New Delhi.

The Tribune, Jalandhar/Chandigarh

Index